ANTITRUST
GOES GLOBAL

ANTITRUST GOES GLOBAL

What Future for Transatlantic Cooperation?

SIMON J. EVENETT
ALEXANDER LEHMANN
BENN STEIL
Editors

ROYAL INSTITUTE OF INTERNATIONAL AFFAIRS
London

BROOKINGS INSTITUTION PRESS
Washington, D.C.

Copyright © 2000
THE BROOKINGS INSTITUTION
1775 Massachusetts Avenue, N.W., Washington, D.C. 20036
www.brookings.edu

Library of Congress Cataloging-in-Publication data

Antitrust goes global : what future for transatlantic cooperation? /
Simon J. Evenett, Alexander Lehmann, and Benn Steil, editors.
 p. cm.
Includes bibliographical references and index.
 ISBN 0-8157-2502-7 (alk. paper)
 ISBN 0-8157-2501-9 (pbk. : alk. paper)
1. Trade regulation. 2. Antitrust law. 3. Trade regulation—United
States. 4. Antitrust law—United States. 5. Trade regulation—European
Union countries. 6. Antitrust law—European Union countries. 7. Globalization.
I. Evenett, Simon J. II. Lehmann, Alexander. III. Steil, Benn.
HD3612 .A56 2000   00-010084
338.8'8–dc21   CIP

         9 8 7 6 5 4 3 2 1

The paper used in this publication meets minimum requirements of the
American National Standard for Information Sciences—Permanence of Paper
for Printed Library Materials: ANSI Z39.48-1984.

Typeset in Minion

Composition by Cynthia Stock
Silver Spring, Maryland

Printed by R. R. Donnelly and Sons
Harrisonburg, Virginia

Foreword

Transatlantic cooperation on competition policy is a study in contrasts. The acrimonious disagreement over the merger of Boeing and McDonnell Douglas, which took the United States and European Union to the brink of a trade war, occurred during a decade of sustained and deepening daily cooperation on competition policy cases. Furthermore, the growing procedural cooperation across the Atlantic contrasted with the unsuccessful attempts to launch negotiations toward a comprehensive multilateral agreement on competition policy at the World Trade Organization. This volume not only attempts to sort out the economic and legal factors that have underpinned the growth of transatlantic cooperation on competition policy over the last ten years, it also anticipates how these policies and international cooperation will alter in the light of the relentless trend toward international market integration, the growing importance of network-based industries, and the changing organizational form of global business.

Antitrust Goes Global draws on the insights of academic economists, legal scholars, and legal practitioners. In addition to analytical chapters on major facets of competition policy, several shorter studies document leading cases of transatlantic cooperation on competition policy throughout the 1990s. Taken together, these studies provide both a conceptual framework and important case-specific detail for thinking through the future course of transatlantic competition policy. To avoid the impression that this project represents the views of one side of the Atlantic, Brookings teamed up with the International Economics Programme of the Royal Institute of International Affairs in London. Contributors to this volume were drawn from both sides of the Atlantic, and the principal chapters were discussed at conferences in Washington, D.C., and in London.

This project would not have been possible without the financial support and guidance of nineteen sponsors: Arnold & Porter; British Airways; British American Tobacco; Clifford Chance; Collier Shannon Scott; Commission of the European Communities, DGI; Coudert Brothers; Economists Inc.; Freshfields & Deringer; Gibson, Dunn & Crutcher; Goldman Sachs International; Hogan & Hartson; King & Spalding; Lovell White Durrant; Skadden & Arps; Sonnenschein, Nath & Rosenthal; White & Case, incorporating Forrester, Norall & Sutton; and Wilmer, Cutler and Pickering. Their generous financial contributions helped finance various aspects of this project, and we gratefully acknowledge their contributions.

Several senior public officials provided much-valued feedback on the direction of the project, and the editors would like to record their thanks to Robert Pitofsky (chairman, Federal Trade Commission), Yves Devellennes, Ignacio Garcia-Bercero, Charles Stark, and Randolph Tritell. In addition, they are especially grateful to James F. Rill and Douglas E. Rosenthal for taking time out of their demanding schedules to provide additional advice from the practitioner's perspective.

Coordinating this project on both sides of the Atlantic required considerable support by a dedicated staff, and the editors would like to thank the tireless efforts of Diana Gourvenec, Linda Gianessi, Eileen Robinson, and Evelyn Taylor. Donna Rzewuski provided excellent support as the drafts were formatted and readied for copy editing, and they are grateful to the Department of Economics at Rutgers University for letting her take on this additional challenge. Diane Hammond smoothly copyedited the entire manuscript, Carlotta Ribar proofread the pages, Susan Fels provided an index, and Janet Walker took the manuscript through its paces at the Brookings Institution Press.

The views expressed in this volume are those of the authors and should not be ascribed to the trustees, officers, or other staff members of the Brookings Institution, the Royal Institute of International Affairs, or any other organizations that have supported the project or with which the authors are associated.

MICHAEL H. ARMACOST
President
The Brookings Institution

October 2000
Washington, D.C.

Contents

Case Studies

Contributors

SARAH E. BAUERS is a research assistant at Howrey, Simon, Arnold, and White.

THOMAS L. BOEDER is a partner in the Seattle office of Perkins Coie and was counsel to the Boeing Company with respect to antitrust clearance of the Boeing–McDonnell Douglas merger in the United States and in Europe.

GARY R. DOERNHOEFER, as senior counsel in the Government Affairs Office of American Airlines, has focused on competition issues and guided efforts to gain regulatory approval of American's former antitrust-immunized alliance with Canadian Airlines, the acquisition of an equity interest in Aerolineas Argentinas, and several other code share arrangements.

SIMON J. EVENETT is an economist in the Development Economics Research Group at the World Bank. He is also the moderator of the Brookings Roundtable on Trade and Investment Policy and a nonresident fellow of the Economic Studies Program, the Brookings Institution. A research affiliate at the Center for Economic Policy Research, he also is an assistant professor of economics at Rutgers University.

EDWARD M. GRAHAM is a senior fellow at the Institute for International Economics. He is the coeditor (with J. David Richardson) of *Global Competition Policy*, published by IIE.

MERIT E. JANOW is a professor in the practice of international trade and director of the International Economic Policy Program, School of International and Public Affairs, Columbia University. An attorney, she also served as the executive director of the International Competition Policy Advisory Committee to the attorney general and the assistant attorney general for antitrust, U.S. Department of Justice, and as deputy assistant U.S. trade representative for Japan and China.

WILLIAM J. KOLASKY is a partner in Wilmer, Cutler, and Pickering and practices in Washington. He is a cochair of the firm's antitrust and competition practice group.

ALEXANDER LEHMANN is an economist at the International Monetary Fund.

MATTHEW LEVITT, of Lovells (the merged firm of Lovell White Durrant and Boesebeck Droste), practices EU and U.K. competition law from the firm's London and Brussels offices. He has acted for a variety of clients in cases before the European Commission and EU courts and has published articles on the procedural aspects of contentious competition proceedings.

ROBERT E. LITAN is vice president and director of the Economic Studies Program at the Brookings Insitution, where he also holds the Cabot Family Chair in Economics. During 1993–95 he served as deputy assistant attorney general in the Antitrust Division of the U.S. Department of Justice.

PHILIP MARSDEN is a solicitor in the competition law group of Linklaters and Alliance, London. He is a member of the Joint Working Party on Competition and International Trade at the International Chamber of Commerce, Paris, and the Working Group on the Future of the World Trade Organization at the Centre for European Policy Studies, Brussels. Marsden is also a frequent contributor to the *European Competition Law Review* and the *World Competition Law and Economics Review*.

JANET L. McDAVID is a partner in the Washington office of Hogan and Hartson, where she specializes in antitrust law. She was chair of the Section on Antitrust Law of the American Bar Association in 1999–2000. She has served as a member of the Clinton administration's Federal Trade Commission's transition team and of two Defense Department task forces on competition policies for the defense industry.

ALEX NOURRY is a partner in the Clifford Chance European Competition and Regulation Groups in London and specializes in European Union and competition law, including control of mergers and joint ventures. He has advised on a number of phase 2 cases under the European Commission's merger regulation, including the WorldCom-MCI case.

JAMES F. RILL is a senior partner at Howrey, Simon, Arnold, and White. He also served as the co-chair of the International Competition Policy Advisory Committee to the attorney general and the assistant attorney general for antitrust, U.S. Department of Justice. During the Bush administration Mr. Rill served as assistant attorney general for antitrust.

BENN STEIL is a senior fellow and holds the Linda J. Wachner Chair in Foreign Economic Policy at the Council on Foreign Relations, New York. He is the former head of the International Economics Program at the Royal Institute of International Affairs, London.

JAMES S. VENIT is a partner in the Brussels office of Skadden, Arps, Slate, Meagher, and Flom. With Barry Hawk he cochairs the firm's international antitrust practice group. Mr. Venit has written and lectured frequently on European Commission competition law.

SPENCER WEBER WALLER is professor of law and director of the Institute for Consumer Antitrust Studies at Loyola University Chicago School of Law. He was formerly professor of law and associate dean at Brooklyn Law School.

CHRISTINE C. WILSON is an associate at Howrey, Simon, Arnold, and White.

ANTITRUST
GOES GLOBAL

1

Antitrust Policy in an Evolving Global Marketplace

SIMON J. EVENETT
ALEXANDER LEHMANN
AND BENN STEIL

That competition policy has acquired a prominent place in discussions on international economic policy is in large part due to the growing interdependence among national economies during the closing decades of the twentieth century. This interdependence blurs the long-standing distinctions between "domestic" and "international" policies, in which competition policy has been the purview solely of the former. A nation's antitrust policies are no longer concerned exclusively with corporate practices within its borders, nor are these policies any longer seen as the sole preserve of national government. The "globalization" of antitrust therefore raises questions about the erosion of national sovereignty, about the potential for intergovernmental disagreements to lead to trade wars, and about the effects of antitrust actions that "spill over" borders.

The merits and practicalities of reconciling national antitrust law and enforcement with an increasingly global marketplace have been discussed in several arenas: regional forums, the World Trade Organization (WTO), the Organization for Economic Cooperation and Development (OECD), and with increasing frequency over the last ten years, in meetings between the United States and

1

the European Union. The chapters in the book analyze the considerable progress made by the United States and the European Union in cooperating, while enforcing their respective antitrust and competition laws. Our analysis focuses on two areas: the economic and legal questions that will arise if the United States and the European Union decide to move beyond the status quo; and the merits of the various outstanding proposals for reform.

Our focus on the intensification of cooperation on antitrust matters by the United States and the European Union in no way denies the importance of the changes in law and enforcement practices that have occurred for other reasons.[1] Nor should our focus on antitrust policy give the impression that EU and U.S. cooperation on economic matters is confined to this important policy area. Indeed the mid-1990s saw considerable momentum grow behind proposals to establish a transatlantic marketplace, including the launching of formal negotiations between the European Union and United States.[2] The failure of this wide-ranging initiative does not appear to have prevented sustained cooperation in a large number of policy arenas, including antitrust, but it does appear to have taken efforts to harmonize laws or to adopt common standards off the negotiating agenda.[3]

The rest of this introductory chapter is organized into seven sections. The next two sections draw the implications for antitrust enforcement of the changes in business strategies that have occurred during the latest phase of international market integration. The third section outlines the issues facing policymakers as they craft an effective strategy of transatlantic cooperation on antitrust policy. The fourth section briefly describes the last decade's cooperation between the European Union and the United States. The fifth section assesses potential future transatlantic initiatives on antitrust policy. The sixth section discusses whether such initiatives could evolve into a blue-

1. A number of recent studies document and examine the consequences of these changes. Goyder (1998) provides a comprehensive legal overview of EU competition law and its enforcement, and Bishop and Walker (1999) and Martin (1998) provide recent economic analyses of EU competition policy. Cini and McGowan (1998) is a general introduction to EU competition policy, and Gerber (1998) and Sauter (1997) provide important historical accounts of the evolution of European competition laws. Kovacic and Shapiro (2000) examine the evolution of legal and economic thinking in the United States during the twentieth century. Baker (1999) outlines how new theoretical and empirical insights have been incorporated into the enforcement of U.S. antitrust laws during the last fifteen years. Viscusi, Vernon, and Harrington (1995) provide detailed theoretical treatments of the economic issues raised by market structures that distort resource allocation, and of the antitrust policies that attempt to prevent, and in some cases reverse, those distortions.

2. Reineke (1996) and Frost (1997) provide analyses of the proposals to establish what was known at the time as the TransAtlantic Business Dialogue.

3. See Eichengreen (1998).

print for a global competition policy agreement. The final section provides an overview of the volume.

Antitrust Enforcement and the Evolving Transatlantic Marketplace

Falling trade barriers, a revolution in communications technology, declining restrictions on foreign investment, ongoing deregulation, and the embrace of market-friendly policies by many governments have wrought significant changes in business strategies on both sides of the Atlantic.[4] The following corporate developments have taken center stage in this new environment:

—A cross-border merger wave of unprecedented scale

—A reevaluation of the benefits of vertical integration, resulting in increased outsourcing and the fragmentation of stages of production across national borders

—The spread of network-based industries.

These developments are in turn altering the context in which antitrust policy is enforced. We describe each of these responses with an eye to the questions raised for antitrust policy, questions that are elaborated upon and taken up in the sections and chapters that follow.

The Current Global Merger Wave

One of the principal differences between the current merger wave and its predecessors is the scale of cross-border mergers and acquisitions (see table 1-1). In just five years the value of completed mergers and acquisitions rose from a worldwide total of $200 billion in 1995 to more than $500 billion by the end of 1999. Measured by their value, American and European firms were parties to more than 80 percent of these transactions. And unlike the merger wave of the late 1980s, which was dominated by British and American firms, during the recent wave numerous French, German, Dutch, and Spanish firms also made substantial cross-border acquisitions (see table 1-1).

One might have anticipated that falling tariff barriers, constraints on the use of nontariff barriers, and improvements in transportation technologies would have shifted firms' strategies for entering foreign markets toward ex-

---

4. The contributors to Garten (2000) describe how business strategies have evolved and how they are likely to change in the future with greater integration of national markets.

Table 1-1. *Cross-Border Mergers and Acquisitions, Valued by Sales of Parties,*
1995–99

	1995	1996	1997	1998 Sales	1998 Share (percent)	January–September 1999 Sales	January–September 1999 Share (percent)
World	199,116	242,965	334,435	586,773	100.0	498,203	100.0
United States	61,796	64,604	89,467	145,861	24.9	93,068	18.7
European Union							
Belgium	4,644	3,500	2,137	2,707	0.5	7,206	1.4
Denmark	160	730	1,565	1,259	0.2	2,880	0.6
France	10,200	15,866	22,363	38,705	6.6	52,241	10.5
Germany	18,548	19,875	13,539	69,998	11.9	45,457	9.1
Ireland	1,157	2,245	1,875	3,335	0.6	1,984	0.4
Italy	4,895	1,668	4,547	14,155	2.4	7,000	1.4
Netherlands	7,456	13,268	19,085	25,543	4.4	34,029	6.8
Spain	1,089	3,506	9,360	17,474	3.0	25,681	5.2
Sweden	5,531	2,342	8,093	16,685	2.8	4,160	0.8
United Kingdom	32,045	37,713	62,746	108,648	18.5	139,930	28.1
Other EU	1,019	2,946	6,027	18,453	3.1	6,491	1.3
Australia	6,368	11,123	13,657	8,144	1.4	4,448	0.9
Canada	12,812	9,066	18,929	36,031	6.1	14,236	2.9
Japan	4,190	6,256	3,578	3,403	0.6	9,905	2.0
Switzerland	10,420	9,731	11,423	41,808	7.1	10,665	2.1
Rest of world	16,786	38,526	46,044	34,564	5.9	38,822	7.8

Source: Thomson Financial Securities Data. Data refers to completed deals only.

porting and away from acquiring local partners. However, in those sectors in which it is costly to establish distribution networks or reputations for supplying high-quality products, firms still find that acquiring or merging with a local partner is often the most profitable mode of entry into overseas markets.[5] The attractiveness of this mode of entry has been further strengthened by the ongoing liberalization of foreign investment regimes and, in some nations, a more relaxed attitude toward foreign takeovers of domestic firms.

5. Gaugan (1999) provides a comprehensive overview of the rationales for corporate mergers and acquisitions as well as a brief history of several merger waves.

Deregulation and privatization, especially in Europe, have played a significant role in stimulating cross-border mergers and acquisitions. As governments have opened public utilities (the electricity, water, gas, and telecommunications sectors, for example) to competition, cross-border transactions have surged, putting these industries among the top ten in terms of total mergers and acquisitions during 1995–99 (measured by the value of sales). Furthermore, the liberalization of the highly regulated financial services industry has resulted in considerable consolidation within this traditionally sensitive sector. Typically, deregulation does not mean the end of regulation, and industry regulators, in addition to antitrust authorities, increasingly review cross-border acquisitions. Gary Doernhoefer (this volume), in his case study on the American Airlines and British Airways alliance, argues forcefully that satisfying multiple regulatory authorities adds substantially to the costs and uncertainty involved in cross-border transactions. This problem extends well beyond the airline industry.

Antitrust enforcement, if not antitrust law, has responded to this surge in cross-border mergers and acquisitions.[6] An increasing number of transactions are reviewed in multiple jurisdictions, and officials regularly discuss their concerns and possible remedies. Most of those concerns appear to be international analogues to the concerns raised by domestic transactions. For example, in the Federal-Mogul and T&N merger, U.S., British, French, Italian, and German antitrust officials were concerned that the merged firm would have an 80 percent market share in the worldwide market for thin wall bearings used in car, truck, and heavy equipment engines.[7] To allay fears about the *current* anticompetitive effects of this horizontal aspect of their merger, the parties were forced to divest T&N's thin wall business, including the intellectual property needed for the divested firm to compete effectively in the future.[8]

The possibility that an international merger or acquisition could result in a reduction in *future* competition, possibly by retarding the development of new products, is another concern of antitrust officials. Mergers and acquisi-

---

6. Pitofsky (1999) argues that "overall, there has been less adjustment in basic American antitrust law in response to the increase in global trade than one might expect. Enforcement goals, measurement of market power, and theories of anti-competitive effect are about the same. If there have been changes…the changes are probably more appropriately traced to new scholarship than changes in trade patterns."

7. This transaction fell below the thresholds for review by the European Commission, so national antitrust authorities undertook their own reviews.

8. See Parker (1999) for a discussion of this and other recent international merger cases involving U.S. antitrust authorities.

tions of firms that are about to launch competing products, or that are assisting other firms in developing potential substitute products, were mentioned in authorities' reviews of ABB's acquisition of Elsag Bailey Process Automation, the Zeneca and Astra merger, and the acquisition of COBE Cardiovascular by Sorin Biomedica.[9]

Increased cross-border transactions give additional prominence to two other antitrust issues. The first is the extent to which import competition can discipline the market power of the entities that result from such transactions. Economists have traditionally argued that vigorous competition from firms, no matter their location, can constrain the exercise of market power by large domestic firms. A number of recent empirical studies have shed further light on the extent of this constraint (the implications of these studies for antitrust enforcement are outlined in the next section).

The second issue concerns the proper antitrust response to a proposed merger, acquisition, or joint venture that creates cross-border efficiencies—that is, that lowers the cost of supplying foreign markets but not the domestic market. Unlike Canadian Merger Guidelines, which can take into account the effect on export performance, U.S. case history and the public statements of senior officials suggest that a merger that claims to balance anticompetitive effects in the United States with procompetitive effects abroad would be poorly received. The chairman of the U.S. Federal Trade Commission, Robert Pitofsky, could not be more explicit on this point:

> If that argument were advanced, we would consider it but our approach would be skeptical. This is not a strictly chauvinistic interpretation of American merger law. First, it is consistent with the basic premise . . . that domestic firms are best able to succeed in international markets if required to compete vigorously at home. . . . Second, balancing anti-competitive effects in a domestic market against efficiencies in a foreign market is unusually difficult. Finally, it is an unattractive prospect to "tax" United States consumers (as a result of the domestic anti-competitive effect) in order to confer benefits on U.S. exporters and non-U.S. consumers.[10]

This remark raises a fundamental issue that recurs throughout this book and more generally in discussions of international antitrust enforcement. How efficient can national antitrust enforcement be, focusing almost exclusively on effects within a nation's borders, in a world in which more and more corporate transactions and practices have effects that are not confined to one nation's jurisdiction?

9. See Parker (1999).
10. Pitofsky (1999).

The International Fragmentation of Production and Vertical Disintegration

The last fifteen years have seen far-reaching changes in the internal organization of businesses and in business-to-business contracting and relationships. Two distinct and not mutually exclusive changes have been at the fore: the fragmentation of multistep production processes across national borders and the sale of corporate subsidiaries peripheral to the firm's principal activities (often replacing intrafirm transactions with transactions between firms). One significant consequence of these changes is that production components often cross many international borders before reaching the purchaser of the finished product.[11] The total value of imported components embodied in exports accounts for approximately 30 percent of current world trade; during 1970–95 the growth of this type of trade accounted for one-third of the growth of world trade.[12]

Liberalization of foreign investment regimes, reductions in tariffs on intermediate products, and improvements in communications have spurred firms to relocate (typically labor-intensive) stages of production abroad.[13] It is no longer uncommon to have a product designed in one country, materials purchased (and even refined) in another country, and assembly undertaken in third countries. This multiple crossing of borders implies that even small reductions in international transportation costs and tariffs can have significant effects on trade volumes.[14] Furthermore, multinational sourcing decisions respond vigorously to exchange rate changes.[15]

The effects of international market integration on the vertical structure of firms is more subtle. When suppliers produce specialized inputs, they can be "held up" by buyers who may try to renegotiate the terms of their contract after the inputs have been produced.[16] Such ex post renegotiation is more likely to occur when the seller cannot find other potential buyers for its product, either because there are none or because the inputs are so spe-

---

11. See Feenstra (1998); Hummels, Rapaport, and Yi (1998); and Hummels, Ishii, and Yi (forthcoming) for specific examples of industries engaged in these practices.

12. See Yi (1999). Yeats (1998) provides additional evidence on this phenomenon.

13. This phenomenon is not confined to manufacturing as many service industries have established customer service centers in lower-wage English-speaking countries, such as Ireland.

14. A theoretical demonstration of this claim, with supporting evidence, can be found in Yi (1999).

15. Rangan and Lawrence (1999) found this to be the case for the sourcing decisions of U.S. multinational corporations.

16. Williamson (1971, 1989). An overview of the incentive to engage in vertical integration, and the economic consequences of such integration, can be found in Carlton and Perloff (1994).

cialized that there are only a small number of potential buyers. To cover the losses associated with reduced payments on some of their sales, this hold-up problem causes suppliers of inputs to raise prices, which in turn raises the costs of production of input buyers. These higher input prices lie at the heart of the incentive to vertically integrate: by owning the producers of inputs, the downstream buyer of inputs pays only the marginal cost of producing the inputs and so avoids the premium charged by independent input suppliers to cover expected losses created by the hold-up problem. It should be noted that the incentive to vertically integrate is reduced if there are larger governance costs associated with running a vertically integrated firm. Finally, once vertical integration begins in an industry it creates a dynamic that reinforces the incentive for further vertical integration: as more and more input suppliers and buyers vertically integrate, the set of available input buyers whom the remaining independent input suppliers can sell to shrinks, exacerbating the hold-up problem and reinforcing the incentive to vertically integrate.

Falling impediments to international commerce reduce the incentive to vertically integrate by increasing the number of potential overseas buyers for an input, diminishing the severity of the hold-up problem. Furthermore, as suppliers of inputs are less susceptible to the hold-up problem they charge a lower premium over marginal costs, which in turn reduces the cost savings from vertical integration. Indeed some integrated firms may now find the cost savings (which induced them to vertically integrate in the first place) no longer compensate for the higher governance costs of running both the input producer and its downstream purchaser and so may sell off one of these two activities. Such vertical disintegration further increases the number of potential buyers for any one input seller's output, further ameliorating the hold-up problem and reinforcing the incentive for other firms to vertically disintegrate. It is through this mechanism that falling impediments to international trade are reshaping the vertical structure of firms.[17]

Vertical disintegration has several implications for antitrust enforcement. First, to the extent that arm's-length agreements between firms have been subject to more antitrust investigations than supply management within firms, vertical disintegration can be expected to increase the enforcement activity of antitrust officials. Second, antitrust officials should examine the availability of overseas inputs when assessing claims that a firm is being deliberately denied inputs by a domestic rival. Such claims should be treated with considerable suspicion if the relevant firms are in an industry that is

17. These arguments are developed at length in McLaren (forthcoming).

experiencing considerable vertical disintegration. Finally, although falling trade impediments may mitigate the hold-up problem and reduce the incentive to vertically integrate, other rationales for vertical integration remain—some of which distort market outcomes—and so globalization does not imply that antitrust enforcement in the area of vertical restraints should be abandoned.

The Spread of Network-Based Industries

Although it is fashionable to argue that recent developments in information technology are creating a "new economy," in fact many of the characteristics of today's network industries have historical precedents, such as the spread of the Bell telephone system in the United States during the late nineteenth century. Whether a network is physical (for example, railroads) or "virtual" (for example, compatible software), it has the same principal characteristic: the value any one consumer derives from connecting to a network depends in large part upon the number of consumers already using the network.[18] The antitrust issues raised by the tremendous recent growth of network industries probably merits a chapter of its own, but we focus briefly on a few central issues below.

First, in common with some "old economy" industries, network industries tend to have high fixed costs—reflecting research and development costs and the costs of building a network infrastructure—and very low marginal costs. Firms in these industries thus have an incentive to price-discriminate across consumers, charging higher prices to consumers with price-inelastic demand. Here the critical question is whether this market power is transitory. The fast pace of innovation in these industries suggests that antitrust enforcers should examine not only whether corporate practices and interfirm agreements inhibit the entry of new products but also the effects of these practices and agreements on the rate of innovation and the ability to sustain market power. Another concern, at the center of the recent U.S. federal case against Microsoft, is whether monopoly power in one product market can be used to leverage market power in another product market.

The second characteristic of these industries is the presence of positive network externalities, which complicate antitrust analysis. The source of these externalities is the following: one of the factors that determine how much a consumer values a product is the number of other consumers who are cur-

---

18. For an extensive review of the economics of networks, with its implications for business strategy, see Shapiro and Varian (1999, chap. 7).

rently purchasing or have purchased the product. Firms that sell such products often have an incentive to set prices below marginal cost, expanding sales and so further increasing the demand for their products through network externalities. The likely consequence of this pricing strategy is increasing industry concentration.

In the presence of network externalities, therefore, it is *as if* consumers value concentration, which implies that the traditional techniques for quantifying the effects of horizontal mergers and alleged abuses of dominance need to be modified to take into account the benefits that consumers derive from firms having a large clientele. Furthermore, the magnitude of this benefit to any one consumer may well depend on the worldwide total number of purchasers of the same good. Thus even a national antitrust authority concerned solely with the effects of a firm's actions within its borders ought to consider the effects of company practices on worldwide sales. Network externalities can create international spillovers distinct from those discussed in our earlier section on mergers and acquisitions.

Extensive cooperation on standard setting, product compatibility, and licensing is the third distinctive characteristic of network industries. Whereas any alleged consumer benefits from cooperation between the producers of substitute goods should rightly be viewed with skepticism by antitrust authorities, such skepticism is less warranted for the producers of complements, of which computer software is a leading example. Consumers value compatibility across software programs: being able to convert documents or data supplied by one program into a form manipulable by another program. Cooperation to improve product compatibility, which often involves setting common standards in software design, benefits consumers and ought not to be discouraged by antitrust authorities. This argument extends to patent pooling, in which two or more companies own patents that could block the introduction of each other's products.

An essential precondition for maximizing consumer gains from standard setting is that the adherence to these standards be open to new competitors, irrespective of their nationality. This requires that standards be well publicized and that compatibility with an existing standard can be readily demonstrated. This encourages research and the development of new varieties of products—such as video games, compact discs, and computer applications—that benefit consumers.

Looking forward, there is the potential for intergovernmental disagreement over standard setting by private entities. A critical test will be whether industrial policy considerations trump concerns of allocative and productive efficiency when a national antitrust authority examines foreign complaints of discriminatory standard setting by domestic firms. The merits of this application of industrial policy were examined at length in the 1980s and the early 1990s, and it is worth recalling Paul Krugman's conclusion that, although there are some theoretical circumstances under which government intervention of this sort can raise the national welfare, the preconditions for successful intervention—in particular the information requirements—are so stringent that resisting the temptation to intervene is the best rule of thumb.[19]

Does International Competition Tame Domestic Market Power?

Since antitrust investigations often turn on how much market power a firm (or group of firms) possesses, the extent to which international competition diminishes that power is of considerable interest. In recent years our understanding of exporter behavior and its effects on the pricing behavior of domestic competitors has been enhanced by empirical studies whose methodologies can readily be applied by the antitrust community.

The first research program examines the sensitivity of domestic firms' pricing decisions (specifically the markup of price over marginal cost) to lower trade barriers. Although these studies examine firm behavior in developing countries, the techniques can be applied to firms in industrial countries, such as the United States and the members of the European Union.[20] The principal finding of this research is that, holding other factors constant, the larger the reduction in an industry's protection from imports, the greater the contraction in markups of prices over marginal costs. Furthermore, in response to trade reform domestic firms have increased their productivity levels, reducing costs, which then have in part been passed on to consumers in the form of lower prices. This evidence supports the view that integration into the market economy attenuates domestic market power. However the evidence does not imply that integration eliminates domestic market power, suggesting that a liberal trade policy is not a perfect substitute for national competition policy.

Even though imports from existing overseas suppliers tend to rise in response to a rise in the prices of domestic firms, other empirical studies show

19. See Krugman (1987); for a carefully couched alternative view, see Tyson (1992).

20. Feenstra (1995) surveys these techniques, drawing upon the initial contributions of Levinsohn (1993) and Harrison (1994).

that such price rises are unlikely to induce new foreign firms to start supplying the domestic market. Entering new markets requires considerable start-up costs (establishing distribution networks, tailoring products to the new market, and marketing), and so the assertion of greater market power by domestic firms is unlikely to induce new foreign entrants unless the domestic price increases are so large as to enable those potential entrants to recover these costs over a plausible time horizon.[21] This implies that the short-term constraint on domestic market power is actual, rather than potential, foreign competition.

However, the same studies show that once a foreign firm enters the domestic market (perhaps owing to a favorable exchange rate movement or to falling impediments to trade), then it takes especially unfavorable domestic market conditions for the foreign firm to exit the market. The unwillingness of foreign firms to leave the market in anything other than severe downturns is related to firms' desires to avoid having to reestablish their presence in the market once favorable conditions return. This finding implies that, as global integration unfolds, the extent of foreign competition faced by domestic firms ratchets up over time, posing an ever more serious threat to domestic market power. Finally, one hypothesis that receives little support in recent studies is that foreign exporters learn how to reduce costs by exporting, enabling them to lower prices and so to grind away continuously at what remains of domestic firms' market power.[22]

Taken together these findings imply that, while it is existing foreign rivals that provide the bulk of the restraint on domestic market power, there is a pronounced tendency for the number of these foreign rivals to increase over time. Should these patterns continue into the future—and there is little evidence to suggest that they will not—further development and application of techniques that better account for the discipline that foreign competition exerts on domestic market power is called for.[23]

21. For recent empirical evidence of the importance of start-up (and more generally sunk and fixed costs) for exporters' behavior, see Roberts and Tybout (1997); Clerides, Lach, and Tybout (1998); Bernard and Jensen (1999); and Evenett and Venables (2000).

22. See the references in note 21 for evidence (from several countries' exporters) against the prevalence of this learning-by-doing dynamic.

23. In addition to Feenstra (1995), Goldberg and Knetter (1997) review some of the latest techniques to estimate both the monopoly power of exporters and the extent of international market integration.

Multijurisdictional Antitrust: The Principal Issues

Four important areas require investigation:
—Defining the proper boundaries of "markets"
—The relationship between trade and antitrust intervention
—The "new economy" features of cross-border markets
—The interaction between antitrust and other forms of regulatory intervention.

Defining Markets in an Integrating Global Economy

As markets integrate across national borders, the logic of purely national antitrust policy breaks down. The most immediate problem—and frequently the most critical aspect of antitrust cases, particularly those dealing with monopolization and mergers—is how to define the relevant "market." The market share of the merged parties is scrutinized by competition authorities to gauge potential market power and harm to consumers. The sensitivity of case outcomes to definition of the relevant market is compellingly illustrated in the 1997 case brought by the U.S. Federal Trade Commission against the proposed merger of Staples and Office Depot, two office supply retailers. The combined entity would have accounted for a small percentage of the aggregate sales of office supply products, but the FTC successfully argued for restricting the definition of the product market to "the sale of competitive office supplies through *office superstores*" (italics added). Having been persuaded of the appropriateness of this definition, the judge then granted the FTC's request for a preliminary injunction on the grounds that the combined company would have a dominant 45–100 percent market share in many parts of the country.[24]

The proper geographic scope of a market must include all sellers to whom buyers can turn in order to counteract the effect of a significant and nontransitory price increase by local incumbents. Where imports can play that price disciplining role, then the market should be defined so as to include foreign producers. Thus the proper market definition is itself determined not only by the level of imports but also by trade policy itself, as a measure of the potential for new imports to discipline domestic market incumbents.

24. See Dalkir and Warren-Boulton (1999).

Growing International Trade and Antitrust Intervention

To the extent that antitrust is supposed to promote competition, antitrust enforcement and trade liberalization can logically be seen as substitutes. On this view the 1890 Sherman Antitrust Act represents the political price American big business had to pay in return for protective tariffs.[25] If competition were to be restricted, government intervention would need to increase to offset the loss of market discipline.

If this logic is compelling, the converse should also hold. As import penetration increases, all else being equal, one would expect less need for antitrust activism on the part of a nation's competition authorities. Increased foreign competition can substitute for domestic legal proceedings as a means of keeping prices close to marginal costs. Increased transatlantic trade liberalization should, by such thinking, serve to reduce the scope for antitrust intervention and hence transatlantic antitrust conflict. In fact, the U.S. Justice Department's merger guidelines do require consideration of actual and potential entry by foreign producers in determining the definition of antitrust markets.

Will further trade liberalization therefore mitigate the need for cross-border antitrust cooperation? The answer is almost certainly no, for two reasons. First, as noted, trade liberalization has reduced but not eliminated domestic market power. Second, an alternative logic, backed too by empirical evidence, suggests that cross-border antitrust conflict is actually *more* likely as trade increases.

Antitrust is a political phenomenon and is therefore subject to all the normal interest group pressures that affect policy across the spectrum. As import penetration tends to have a disproportionate negative effect on the profits and market share of smaller domestic enterprises,[26] trade liberalization is likely to be accompanied by increased small-firm lobbying for domestic antitrust intervention. Prima facie supporting evidence would be the resulting rise in domestic market concentration ratios and declining prices, the latter of which may trigger specific charges of predatory pricing. Domestic mergers, motivated by productive efficiency concerns brought on by foreign competition, are also more likely to be challenged by smaller and less viable enterprises. To the extent that trade protectionism is hindered by treaty obligations, antitrust may therefore be used to offset the adverse distributional effects of imports. By this logic, trade stimulates antitrust activity. The latter is a by-product of mercantilism.

---

25. This view has been advanced by DiLorenzo (1985), among others.
26. For example, see Caves (1988); and Chappell and Yandle (1992).

As trade and particularly foreign direct investment increases, the larger firms that will be the actual targets of antitrust intervention are far more likely to be foreign than domestic, as the former will have considerably less domestic lobbying power. Without necessarily impugning the economic case of the European Commission against the Boeing–McDonnell Douglas merger, it is easy to see how compelling the political pressures for antitrust intervention must be in such a case.[27]

Finally, holding constant factors such as the general level of economic activity and agency caseloads, there is a positive relationship between foreign competition and funding for the Federal Trade Commission and the Antitrust Division of the Justice Department.[28] This would appear to indicate that antitrust, rather than being solely driven by consumer welfare considerations, is at the service of domestic firms adversely affected by imports. If trade stimulates antitrust, particularly targeted at foreign firms, the potential for direct conflict of laws and lobbying interests across borders can only grow as economic globalization progresses.

Antitrust in the "New Economy"

Economic efficiency has two components. Allocative efficiency concerns the relation between price and marginal cost and is a function of market power. More competition, or potential competition, reduces market power and increases allocative efficiency. Productive efficiency concerns the unit costs associated with the production of goods and services and is a function of factors such as economies of scale and network externalities. Mergers may reduce the long-run average cost of firms and thereby increase productive efficiency. They may also increase market power and thereby reduce allocative efficiency. It is the task of antitrust analysis to determine which effect is predominant in any given case.

New industries, and new manifestations of old ones, seem particularly likely to exhibit a sharp contrast between the two types of efficiency and thereby pose difficult analytical challenges for antitrust authorities. Computer-based products such as operating systems and trading architectures exhibit enormous network externalities, such that the more users that coalesce around a given product, the more benefit that is conferred on each user. The potential customer reach of such products is frequently global,

27. Fox (1997) analyzes the contentious Boeing–McDonnell Douglas merger and makes several proposals to keep politics out of antitrust enforcement.
28. See the study by Shughart, Silverman, and Tollison (1995), covering the years 1932–81.

even when the owner does not intend it to be: Internet-based applications are the clearest example. Defining the relevant market for both geographic and product identification purposes (What exactly is an "operating system"?) is frequently difficult. Different national competition authorities applying identical principles in identical cases are likely to reach different conclusions or specify different remedies. Where nonefficiency concerns, such as the effects on employment, are allowed to come into play, the potential for cross-border antitrust conflict can only increase as the "new economy" expands. And it is large firms rather than monopolists as such to which political concern is generally directed.[29] Many of the new economy enterprises boast enormous market capitalizations without clearly exhibiting market power, yet they are likely to receive antitrust attention, particularly outside their legal home jurisdiction, merely because of their size of equity base.

Antitrust and Sectoral Regulation

Certain major and growing industries are frequently placed outside the scope of a nation's primary antitrust authority, in particular banks and securities exchanges. Other industries, such as public utilities, fall under the purview of industry regulators as well as national antitrust authorities.[30]

In the euro zone, government agencies not directly concerned with antitrust (that is, central banks and finance ministries) have intervened to inhibit or block cross-border banking mergers that do not appear to raise antitrust concerns, while national bank megamergers have proceeded with little or no formal consideration of domestic competition effects. The promotion of "national champions," which take on a too-big-to-fail status, is likely to lead to transatlantic disagreements, which may or may not take the form of antitrust cases. But at root it is the inconsistent application of antitrust principles across *domestic* industries that sows the seeds for future conflict abroad.

With the rise of cross-border securities trading, U.S. financial market regulators have been subtly transforming themselves into trade negotiators and may themselves be at the center of future transatlantic trade conflicts. The Commodity Futures Trading Commission under former chairman Brooksley Born conditioned direct U.S. electronic access for European derivatives exchanges on reciprocal treatment for U.S. exchanges, notwithstanding the

29. See Posner (1999).
30. In their conclusions Laffont and Tirole (2000) discuss the difficulty of differentiating between antitrust policy and regulatory policy in the telecommunications sector.

fact that Chicago derivatives markets were predominantly floor based and already had functioning after-hours electronic joint ventures in Europe (such as Globex). The Securities and Exchange Commission has steadfastly denied direct electronic U.S. access for European stock exchanges largely on the grounds that their listed stocks frequently did not meet the reporting standards of U.S. GAAP (generally accepted accounting principles). European exchanges offering to limit U.S. trader access to GAAP-compliant stocks have nonetheless been rebuffed. Such apparent protectionism raises costs for U.S. investors without offering them any measure of protection, as they have long traded on foreign exchanges by phone and direct computer link via brokers' terminals (such as Instinet, owned by Reuters). Applying efficiency-based antitrust criteria would logically result in quick regulatory approval for such intermarket access.

Resource Allocation and Multijurisdictional Antitrust

Drawing the foregoing discussion together, we have a clearer idea of the challenges posed by globalization for effective antitrust enforcement. International commercial transactions are altering the allocation of resources—by adjusting investments, outputs, and prices—within and across national borders and are doing so at an unprecedented rate. Markets defined economically are not the same as those defined politically: that is, by national borders. Increased international trade should mitigate the need for antitrust intervention as a matter of economics but is likely to have the reverse effect as a matter of politics. And new computer-based industries feature network externalities that are bound to transcend national borders but are equally bound to face local antitrust scrutiny on the basis of local effects.

These considerations suggest that the following four questions are at the heart of developing an effective transatlantic strategy for antitrust enforcement:

—Are resources allocated away from their most efficient uses when commercial transactions that generate cross-border spillovers are subject to antitrust investigations that only consider the effects within national borders?[31] Alternatively put, in the absence of a mechanism or agency to aggregate effects across nations, to what extent do multiple national vetoes on international transactions affect the allocation of resources?

—What are the consequences for the reallocation of resources, brought about by international commercial transactions, of national antitrust en-

---

31. The notion of efficiency is discussed at length in Richardson (1999).

forcement that is influenced by considerations other than maximizing economic efficiency (such as preservation of competition, employment objectives, and the like)?[32]

—Are there cooperative mechanisms, or common action guidelines, that can minimize the potential for interjurisdictional conflict and improve prospects for welfare-enhancing antitrust intervention across the entire scope of the market, economically defined?

—What are the prerequisites—in terms of shared objectives, information flows, and procedures—for effective antitrust cooperation?

It is tempting for outside observers to call for a broad-based program of harmonized rules and procedures in response to greater cross-border market integration. Of course, substantive and procedural antitrust harmonization is unambiguously beneficial to the extent that harmonized standards are better than the alternatives. But the fact that this criterion is so simply stated merely indicates how difficult it is to satisfy in practice.

Recent Antitrust Cooperation between the European Union and the United States

The increased integration of national markets has led competition agencies on both sides of the Atlantic to review corporate activities that involve foreign firms or firms located outside their national borders. In 1999, 849 mergers notified to the Justice Department and the FTC involved foreign parties, more than a third higher than in the previous three years. In the fiscal year ending in September 1999, the Antitrust Division imposed a record $1.1 billion in fines on cartels, almost all of which had an international dimension.[33]

The much-cited Van Miert report of 1995 provided the foundation for the EU's response to the growing challenge posed by international cases for competition policy enforcement.[34] Based on this report, the European Commission has taken a two-pronged approach: attempting to advance proposals on competition policy within the WTO and enhancing bilateral cooperation. Unlike progress at the WTO, bilateral cooperation has rapidly expanded and deepened. A 1991 agreement with the United States, together with a 1998 agreement on the application of the positive comity principle,

32. See for example Sauter (1997), who documents the relationship between the EU's competition law and its industrial policy.
33. Klein (1999).
34. European Commission (1995).

has facilitated cooperation with the U.S. agencies in a number of notable cases, such as the WorldCom-MCI, Guinness–Grand Met, and Dresser-Halliburton mergers (see Merit Janow, this volume).[35] Occasional confrontations, such as in the 1997 merger of Boeing and McDonnell Douglas, have been much publicized but, as our case studies document, they are the exception rather than the rule.[36]

Bilateral cooperation has therefore become the predominant element of the EU's international competition policy, in part because—unlike the United States—the EU has weaker instruments for the extraterritorial enforcement of its competition laws. In addition to the competition elements contained in the *Europe Agreements* with ten central and eastern European countries, a bilateral agreement was signed with Canada in 1999 and cooperation with Japan and Switzerland is being deepened further.

The ongoing reforms within Directorate General IV (DGIV) of the European Commission should be supportive of foreign parties' interests in European competition law enforcement. Through the block exemption of vertical restraints and the planned streamlining of the notification process, DGIV will free up more resources for the prosecution of infringements of its competition rules. The objectives set out in the recent white paper, in particular the introduction of private enforcement before national courts and the strengthening of controls on state aid, should further focus the work of DGIV's very limited staff.

On the U.S. side, in part as a response to these developments, the Justice Department in 1997 established the International Competition Policy Advisory Committee (ICPAC). This committee examined the procedures for review of multijurisdictional mergers, the potential need for closer coordination between trade and competition policies, and the means to improve enforcement cooperation. The committee's *Final Report*, released in February 2000, recommends concentrating efforts on bilateral cooperation and is cautious with regard to further initiatives at the WTO.[37] Therefore, on both sides of the Atlantic at present there appears to be little appetite for initiatives to harmonize competition policy standards or to adopt core minimum standards. Instead, initiatives are confined to securing closer bilateral cooperation on enforcement actions.

---

35. "Positive comity" involves one agency investigating at the request of the other, with the latter subsequently refraining from conducting its own investigation. The positive comity agreement was applied during the investigation into Amadeus Global Travel Distribution; see the case study by James Rill, Christine Wilson, and Sarah Bauers (this volume).

36. See the case study on Boeing–McDonnell Douglas by Thomas Boeder (this volume).

37. International Competition Policy Advisory Committee (2000).

What has this transatlantic cooperation on competition policy enforcement yielded? James Venit and William Kolasky (this volume) document considerable substantive convergence, illustrated in particular by the European Union's adoption of the FTC's "SSNIP" approach to market definition (see also Merit Janow, this volume).[38] However, as Venit and Kolasky emphasize, the EU has displayed considerably less appreciation for merger defenses based on efficiency arguments, in spite of the compelling logic advanced in favor of the efficiency defense as the most direct means of addressing consumer welfare concerns.[39] Whereas the United States has been far from consistent in its consideration and application of the efficiency defense, and in many court cases has rejected it outright, its place in contemporary U.S. antitrust policy is more secure than in that of the European Union.

Although they document promising transatlantic convergence in substantive standards, Venit and Kolasky also document persistent procedural dissonance. In particular, review thresholds are much lower in the United States, and the timing and nature of information requirements differ. Consideration of "best practice" on procedural matters is exceptionally complex, although in principle clearly subject to rational cost-benefit analysis. However, the importance of harmonizing around "optimal" procedural standards is arguably less compelling than for substantive standards. The transaction cost reduction benefits of procedural harmonization for multinational mergers would justify moving more rapidly on this front, political barriers to achieving optimal convergence standards notwithstanding.

What Future for Transatlantic Cooperation on Antitrust Enforcement?

The overriding goal of U.S. and EU cooperation on competition policy ought to be to lower the resource misallocation created by multijurisdictional antitrust enforcement. Achieving this goal requires taking measures to

—Reduce the transactions costs associated with cross-border corporate practices

—Reduce the likelihood of corporate transactions that will improve global resource allocation being rejected by either the European Union or the United States

38. The "SSNIP" approach defines the relevant market as the smallest product and geographic market in which a hypothetical monopolist could impose a "small but significant and nontransitory increase in price."

39. See for example Bork (1978); Posner (1999).

—Increase the likelihood that corporate transactions that would result in resource misallocation are rejected by either the European Union or the United States.

Admittedly, some practitioners may regard the avoidance of transatlantic disputes as an objective in and of itself, but from the economic perspective specific proposals for bilateral cooperation should be judged solely on their expected effects on resource allocation. The economic benefits of the current "gently-as-it-goes" approach to bilateral cooperation, however, are largely limited to reductions in transaction costs. By retaining the multiple national vetoes of antitrust and the discretion to adopt nonefficiency standards during antitrust decisionmaking, the current approach does not tackle the other two sources of resource misallocation in multijurisdictional antitrust enforcement.

Of course, proposals to reduce the costs of notifying antitrust authorities about cross-border transactions and practices are useful. Measures to reduce the costs of complying with the different information requests of antitrust agencies are also to be welcomed. Indeed, the ICPAC *Final Report* contains a whole chapter of recommendations that, if implemented, will reduce the legal costs of international transactions.[40] However, the case for measures that reduce the discretion of authorities is less clear-cut. It is true that such measures may reduce the uncertainty associated with international transactions, but this is cold comfort if discretion is substituted for by a rigid decision rule that worsens the allocation of resources.

In addition to transaction costs, the interaction among the following three factors accounts for the potential of national antitrust enforcement to misallocate resources in the global economy:

—International spillovers created by corporate activities and transactions,

—National antitrust authorities that take into account (at most) the effects of these activities on producer and consumer interests within their country's borders, so generating the multiple-veto problem described earlier,

—The application of criteria by national antitrust authorities that are inconsistent with the efficiency standard.

In light of this interaction, how can one evaluate the effect on resource allocation of the current approach to U.S.-EU cooperation? One of the grounds upon which this approach has been defended is that further procedural cooperation may lead to substantive convergence in standards. Kolasky and Venit argue that some convergence in the implementation of U.S. and EU antitrust policy has already occurred. However, as long as their legal

---

40. International Competition Policy Advisory Committee (2000).

standards differ, convergence in implementation will not eliminate uncertainty in antitrust enforcement. The private sector cannot discount the possibility that the discretion allowed by law will be exercised in the future. Moreover, such convergence is likely to be fragile: changes in the composition or approach of the European Commission, changes in U.S. federal administrations, and changes in the interpretation of antitrust laws by the courts could upset this convergence.

Perhaps the more telling criticism is that even if the current approach led to the adoption of a common efficiency standard in the United States and the European Union, this is unlikely to eliminate the resource misallocation created by multijurisdictional antitrust enforcement. As long as U.S. and EU antitrust authorities retain a national veto—a step that the current approach does not call into question—then corporate transactions that lead to welfare losses in *either* the European Union or the United States will be blocked, even if the activities are welfare improving from the world perspective. In sum, the gains from the present approach to U.S. and EU antitrust cooperation are principally confined to the improvements in resource allocation created by reductions in transaction costs.

The foregoing discussion suggests the two key building blocks of an alternative strategy for antitrust enforcement across the Atlantic: the adoption of explicit efficiency standards and a move away from national assessments of the effects of corporate practices toward one that emphasizes their effects on total welfare in the United States and the European Union.[41] Asserting the primacy of an efficiency standard would involve decisionmakers' giving up any discretion permitted by existing case law, with the added benefit that the uncertainty faced by the private sector would decline. The move toward transatlantic assessment of corporate practices need not involve the creation of a supranational agency, although such an agency might be better shielded from political pressures than a national antitrust body. Instead, national antitrust agencies could undertake transatlantic investigations of cases, evaluating each case on an agreed efficiency standard that takes into account the effects of the corporate practice within the entire U.S.-EU area.[42] These two building blocks are not alternatives to each other; both must be in place before substantial reductions in the resource misallocation created by multijurisdictional antitrust enforcement are achieved.

41. Fox (1999) also makes a strong case for the "internationalization of competition law" (as she puts it). Fox advocates a "borderless" conception of the world in which "the treatment of a market problem [is] as if there were no national boundaries, or conceived differently, as if all harms and benefits fell within the geographical boundaries of the same polity" (17).

42. Of course, ensuring that each national antitrust authority adopts the same substantive standards and pursues the same analyses is a requirement for this approach to work effectively.

One important caveat is that corporate transactions that improve resource allocation across the United States and the European Union may actually reduce welfare in the rest of the world. Given the magnitude of these transactions, the effects on third parties may be substantial, highlighting the relevance of multilateral initiatives to competition policy

Transatlantic Cooperation as a Blueprint for a Global Agreement on Competition Policy

Closer antitrust cooperation between the European Union and the United States has run parallel with efforts to launch substantive talks on competition policy at the WTO. For the foreseeable future, the nature and the scope of U.S.-EU antitrust cooperation will remain much more advanced than cooperation within the multilateral forums. Still, experience in bilateral agreements may hold important lessons for what may be achieved in the WTO.

Three broad trends explain the renewed interest in including competition issues at the WTO. First, allegations that anticompetitive practices within national markets are impeding foreign market access are being made with increasing frequency and have led to a number of high-profile trade disputes, such as the 1996 Kodak-Fuji case. Second, efforts by both the United States and the European Union to apply their national competition laws on an extraterritorial basis are regarded with increasing concern by countries that have no well-established ties with either jurisdiction. Finally, several WTO agreements negotiated during the Uruguay Round contain provisions on competition policy. There is a clear dichotomy between services industries, in which the conduct of monopolistic providers is circumscribed, and the goods sector, in which it is not. Moreover, several WTO agreements are due for a review in the next multilateral trade round, with a view to possibly including elements of competition policy.

Against this background, the 1996 WTO ministerial meeting launched a working group on trade and competition that until now has had only an "educational" mandate. To date there has been only a limited convergence of views regarding a future negotiating agenda. The European Union has perhaps been most ambitious, calling for the application of a number of "core principles" to the procedures and the substance in national competition laws. A number of Asian countries, both developing and developed, have focused on ways to mitigate the application of antidumping policies through national competition law enforcement, an idea that the United States strongly opposes. Developing countries on the whole view the inclusion of provisions on restrictive business practices as a quid pro quo for the further liberalization of foreign direct investment, another possible item for negotiation during the next round.

Although no consensus for a negotiating agenda is in sight, the broad trend toward the adoption of competition laws in the developing and transition economies certainly helps to put the institutional prerequisites in place. More than eighty countries now have competition laws, and many developing and transition economies have benefited from technical assistance provided by the European Union or the United States. Still, the presence of an enforcement agency is by no means indicative of the stance of the national authorities with regard to competition enforcement. Several small and open economies, such as Hong Kong, view international trade as the best enforcer of competition standards.

Given national governments' skepticism about further multilateral trade liberalization following the Seattle failure, competition policy is unlikely to figure prominently in the next trade round. Should a consensus emerge on an agenda for negotiations on competition policy, it is likely to be limited to the application of long-standing principles of international trade, such as nondiscrimination and transparency, to existing competition laws.[43] However, as was demonstrated by the OECD ban on "hard-core" cartels, there might even be a consensus on certain substantive issues.

U.S.-EU antitrust cooperation is unique in the way enforcement procedures are coordinated between the two jurisdictions. This level of trust in, and familiarity with, the other side's practices has been built up over many years and is epitomized by the positive comity principle. This coordination may serve as a model for the emerging network of bilateral cooperation agreements. As in the fields of taxation or direct investment regulation, these bilateral competition treaties may at some point lead to negotiations on a multilateral framework for a strictly limited set of issues.

One (optimistic) scenario is that a network of bilateral competition policy agreements grows over time, covering more and more international commerce. In this manner a de facto global agreement on the enforcement of competition policy could emerge, organized around the principles employed by the major economic powers (which will inevitably focus on the United States and the European Union). Yet the concerns raised in the last section also apply to this evolutionary approach to forging global competition policy: cooperation may not lead to harmonization of substantive standards, and even if harmonization occurs it may not be to the efficiency standard.[44] Fur-

43. Should this consensus emerge it will call for agreements that fall short of those advocated by Graham and Richardson (1997); Morici (2000); and Scherer (1994).

44. Graham (1999) too evaluates the likely consequences of a growing web of international agreements on competition policy.

thermore, even though such an expanding web of agreements may eventually cover the vast bulk of all international commerce, there is a concern that those nations that are not members at a given point in time will be discriminated against. Although this gradual path to global competition policy reform has its attractions (especially to those nations that craft the initial enforcement standards), the overall effects on global resource allocation are at best unclear and at worst may be negative if inappropriate standards are adopted or if discrimination against nonmembers becomes the norm.

Overview of This Volume

To examine the lessons from almost ten years of formal U.S.-EU antitrust cooperation, the Brookings Institution in Washington and the Royal Institute of International Affairs (Chatham House) in London launched a study that commissioned both academic papers and legal case studies. With the generous support of sponsors from both sides of the Atlantic, we convened international antitrust lawyers, academics, and officials from U.S. and EU antitrust agencies at two conferences; in December 1998 at Brookings and in January 1999 at Chatham House.[45] The papers and case studies discussed at these conferences are published in this volume.

The next chapter, by Merit Janow, sets the stage by reviewing the institutional framework for transatlantic cooperation with an analysis of the two U.S.-EU agreements on antitrust enforcement. Janow discusses the use of innovative intergovernmental mechanisms and the considerable potential for expanding cooperation within the current institutional and legal framework.

Mergers and acquisitions have taken center stage in the recent discussion on transatlantic antitrust cooperation. As Monty Graham (chapter 3) points out, this is in no way the first merger wave, though the current wave stands out because of the unprecedented volume of transatlantic merger and acquisition activity. Graham sets out the economic objectives pursued in national antitrust enforcement and then examines the challenges posed by cross-border cases. A review of the economic trade-offs inherent in such cases leads him to a number of projections as to where the United States and the European Union are likely to be too restrictive—and too lenient.

James Venit and William Kolasky (chapter 4) demonstrate that there has already been considerable substantive transatlantic convergence, in part stimulated by both parties learning how better to deal with cross-border

---

45. The sponsors are listed and their generosity acknowledged in the foreword to this volume.

mergers. These findings broaden a discussion that has tended to center on the adoption of harmonized minimum standards for national competition laws. As the authors show, disagreements are most likely to arise from the methodologies used in merger investigations and from the remedies posed by enforcement agencies, highlighting two possible areas for future procedural convergence.

The depth of U.S.-EU cooperation on merger enforcement contrasts with a surprising absence of formal contacts in the area of cross-border cartels. Spencer Weber Waller (chapter 5) argues that this comes in spite of an unprecedented history of cross-border cases. He finds that this is largely due to inadequate coordination of investigation procedures, not least because cartel behavior has very severe criminal consequences under U.S. law.

In chapter 6, on the treatment of vertical restraints, Philip Marsden finds not only procedural but, more important, substantive gaps between the enforcement practices of the two sides. Such differences have been a recurring, and in Marsden's opinion mistaken, basis for calls for international antitrust standards.

We close the volume with a series of studies of major antitrust cases, written by legal practitioners, which have involved considerable cooperation between the antitrust authorities on both sides of the Atlantic.

References

Baker, Jonathan B. 1999. "Policy Watch: Developments in Antitrust Economics." *Journal of Economic Perspectives* 13:181–94.

Bernard, Andrew B., and J. Bradford Jensen. 1999. "Exceptional Exporter Performance: Cause, Effect, or Both?" *Journal of International Economics* 47:1–26.

Bishop, Simon, and Mike Walker. 1999. *The Economics of EC Competition Law.* London: Sweet and Maxwell.

Bork, Robert H. 1978. *The Antitrust Paradox: A Policy at War with Itself.* Free Press.

Carlton, Dennis W., and Jeffrey M. Perloff. 1994. *Modern Industrial Organization.* 2d ed. HarperCollins.

Caves, Richard E. 1988. "Trade Exposure and Changing Structures of U.S. Manufacturing Industries." In *International Competitiveness,* edited by A. Michael Spence and Heather A. Hazard. Ballinger.

Chappell, William F., and Bruce Yandle 1992. "The Competitive Role of Import Penetration." *Antitrust Bulletin* 37: 957–69.

Cini, Michelle, and Lee McGowan. 1998. *Competition Policy in the European Union.* St. Martin's Press.

Clerides, Sofronis, Saul Lach, and James Tybout. 1998. "Is Learning-by-Exporting Important? Micro-Dynamic Evidence from Columbia, Mexico, and Morocco." *Quarterly Journal of Economics* 113: 903–47.

Dalkir, Serdar, and Frederick R. Warren-Boulton. 1999. "Prices, Market Definition, and the Effects of Merger: Staples–Office Depot 1997." Case 6 in *The Antitrust Revolution: Economics, Competition, and Policy,* edited by John E. Kwoka Jr. and Lawrence J. White. 3d ed. Oxford University Press.

DiLorenzo, Thomas J. 1985. "The Origins of Antitrust: An Internet-Group Perspective." *International Review of Law and Economics* 5:73–90.

Eichengreen, Barry, ed. 1998. *Transatlantic Economic Relations in the Post–Cold War Era.* New York: Council on Foreign Relations.

European Commission. 1995. "Competition Policy in the New Trade Order: Strengthening International Cooperation and Rules." July. (Van Miert report).

Evenett, Simon J., and Anthony J. Venables. 2000. "The Geographic Spread of Exports: How Argentina's Trade Has Grown since 1970." Mimeo. Department of Economics, Rutgers University.

Feenstra, Robert C. 1995. "Estimating the Effects of Trade Policy." In *Handbook of International Economics,* edited by Gene M. Grossman and Kenneth Rogoff. Vol. 3. Amsterdam: North-Holland.

———. 1998. "Integration of Trade and Disintegration of Production in the Global Economy." *Journal of Economic Perspectives* 12:31–50.

Fox, Eleanor M. 1997. "Lessons from Boeing: A Modest Proposal to Keep Politics out of Antitrust." *Antitrust Report* (November): 19–24.

———. 1999. "Antitrust Law on a Global Scale–Races Up, Down, and Sideways." School of Law, New York University.

Frost, Ellen L. 1997. *Transatlantic Trade: A Strategic Agenda.* Washington: Institute for International Economics.

Garten, Jeffrey E., ed. 2000. *World View: Global Strategies for the New Economy.* Harvard Business School Press.

Gaugan, Patrick A. 1999. *Mergers, Acquisitions, and Corporate Restructurings.* 2d ed. John Wiley and Sons.

Gerber, David J. 1998. *Law and Competition in Twentieth Century Europe: Protecting Prometheus.* Clarendon Press.

Goldberg, Pinelopi Koujianou, and Michael M. Knetter. 1997. "Good Prices and Exchange Rates: What Have We Learned?" *Journal of Economic Literature* 35:1243–72.

Goyder, D. G. 1998. *EC Competition Law.* 3d ed. Clarendon Press.

Graham, Edward M. 1999. "Trade, Competition, and the Seattle Agenda." Mimeo. Washington: Institute for International Economics.

Graham, Edward M., and J. David Richardson, eds. 1997. *Global Competition Policy.* Washington: Institute for International Economics.

Harrison, Ann. 1994. "Productivity, Imperfect Competition, and Trade Reform: Theory and Evidence." *Journal of International Economics* 36:53–73.

Hummels, David, Jun Ishii, and Kei-Mu Yi. Forthcoming. "The Nature and the Growth of Vertical Specialization in World Trade." *Journal of International Economics.*

Hummels, David, Dana Rapaport, and Kei-Mu Yi. 1998. "Vertical Specialization and the Changing Nature of World Trade." *Federal Reserve Bank of New York Economic Policy Review,* 4:79–99.

International Competition Policy Advisory Committee. 2000. *Final Report.* Government Printing Office.

Klein, Joel. 1999. Speech before the International Cartel Enforcement Conference, September 30 (www.usdoj.gov/atr/public/speeches/3727.htm).

Kovacic, William E., and Carl Shapiro. 2000. "Antitrust Policy: A Century of Economic and Legal Thinking." *Journal of Economic Perspectives* 14:43–60.

Krugman, Paul R. 1987. "Is Free Trade Passé?" *Journal of Economic Perspectives* 1:131–44.

Laffont, Jean-Jacques, and Jean Tirole. 2000. *Competition in Telecommunications.* MIT Press.

Levinsohn, James. 1993. "Testing the Imports-as-Market-Discipline Hypothesis." *Journal of International Economics* 35:1–22.

Martin, Stephen, ed. 1998. *Competition Policies in Europe.* Amsterdam: North Holland.

McLaren, John. Forthcoming. "'Globalization' and Vertical Structure." *American Economic Review.*

Morici, Peter. 2000. *Antitrust in the Global Trading System: Reconciling U.S., Japanese and EU Approaches.* Washington: Economic Strategy Institute.

Parker, Richard G. 1999. "Global Merger Enforcement." Speech. International Bar Association, Barcelona, September 28.

Pitofsky, Robert. 1999. "The Effect of Global Trade on United States Competition Law and Enforcement Policies." Speech given at the Fordham Corporate Law Institute, October 15.

Posner, Richard A. 1999. "Natural Monopoly and its Regulation." Cato Institute.

Rangan, Subramanian, and Robert Z. Lawrence. 1999. *A Prism on Globalization: Corporate Responses to the Dollar.* Brookings.

Reinicke, Wolfgang H. 1996. *Deepening the Atlantic: Toward a New Transatlantic Marketplace.* Gutersloh, Germany: Bertelsmann Foundation Publishers.

Richardson, J. David. 1999. "What Is Competition Policy and What Should It Be?" Paper prepared for International Workshop on Current Issues in Competition Policy, Ministry of Trade and Industry, Copenhagen, November 19.

Roberts, Mark J., and James R. Tybout. 1997. "The Decision to Export in Columbia: An Empirical Model of Entry with Sunk Costs." *American Economic Review* 87:545–64.

Sauter, Wolf. 1997. *Competition Law and Industrial Policy in the EU.* Clarendon Press.

Scherer, Frederic M. 1994. *Competition Policies for an Integrated World Economy.* Brookings.

Shapiro, Carl, and Hal R. Varian. 1999. *Information Rules: A Strategic Guide to the Network Economy.* Harvard Business School Press.

Shugert, William F., Jon D. Silverman, and Robert D. Tollison. 1995. "Antitrust Enforcement and Foreign Competition." In *The Causes and Consequences of Antitrust: The Public-Choice Perspective,* edited by Fred S. McChesney and William F. Shugert. University of Chicago Press.

Tyson, Laura D'Andrea. 1992. *Who's Bashing Whom? Trade Conflict in High-Technology Industries.* Washington: Institute for International Economics.

Viscusi, W. Kip, John Vernon, and Joseph E. Harrington. 1995. *Economics of Regulation and Antitrust.* 2d ed. MIT Press.

Williamson, Oliver. 1971. "The Vertical Integration of Production: Market Failure Considerations." *American Economic Review* 61:112–23.

———. 1989. "Transaction Cost Economics." In *Handbook of Industrial Organization,* edited by Richard Schmalensee and Robert Willig. New York: North Holland.

Yeats, Alexander J. 1998. "Just How Big Is Global Production Sharing?" Policy Research Working Paper 1871. World Bank.

Yi, Kei-Mu. 1999. "Can Vertical Specialization Explain the Growth of World Trade?" Division of International Research, Federal Reserve Bank of New York.

2

Transatlantic Cooperation on Competition Policy

MERIT E. JANOW

B y many measures, economic relations between the United States and the European Union have seen some of the deepest forms of economic interaction that the United States has experienced with any region. Two-way trade and corporate sales amount to approximately $2 trillion. Europe accounts for approximately 45 percent of total U.S. foreign direct investment, while nearly 60 percent of total European foreign direct investment is found in the United States.[1] The aggregate data suggest that there is a domestic merger wave under way both in the United States and in Europe and that cross-border activity represents a modest but important part of that overall story.[2] In the 1998–99 period alone, U.S.-EU megamergers in several industries changed the profile of global competition: Daimler Benz–Chrysler, Deutsche Bank–Bankers Trust, British Petroleum–Amoco, Ford-Volvo, among others.

1. TransAtlantic Business Dialogue (1998), "Statement of Conclusions" (www.tabd.com/recom/charlotte.html).
2. The global market for mergers and acquisitions in 1999 reached $3.4 trillion. There were approximately $1.7 trillion worth of U.S. deals and approximately $1.2 trillion of announced deals in the EU. See Judy Radler Cohen, "Blockbusters, Nonstop! Global Mergers and Acquisitions Hit $3.4 trillion as Europe Takes off and Telecom Soars." *Investment Dealers Digest,* January 17, 2000. See also Wambold (1998).

The importance of the U.S.-EU economic relationship suggests that the reduction or elimination of remaining obstacles to trade and investment between the United States and Europe, especially if coupled with effective cooperation between authorities, could produce significant gains on both sides of the Atlantic. This chapter considers that proposition through an examination of cooperation in the field of antitrust, or competition, policy, in which national authorities are responsible for reviewing and acting independently on cases that can involve foreign-based firms or markets that are global.

U.S.-EU Bilateral Antitrust Cooperation Agreements

The United States and the European Commission (EC) entered into a bilateral antitrust cooperation agreement in 1991.[3] This agreement embodies two themes—enforcement cooperation, on the one hand, and the avoidance or management of disputes, on the other.[4] Under U.S. law the 1991 accord is considered an executive agreement: a binding international agreement that does not however override domestic law since it has not been ratified by the U.S. Senate.

Interestingly, U.S. government documents point to the following three developments in Europe that made the need for a bilateral agreement especially compelling to the United States at the time negotiations began. First, the European Court of Justice in the *Wood Pulp* case had recently confirmed the application of EU antitrust law to offshore conduct deemed to have adverse competitive effects within the European Union.[5] This case suggested that U.S. and EC approaches to the question of subject matter jurisdiction were becoming more similar. It also suggested the possibility of greater en-

3. Agreement between the Government of the United States of America and the Commission of the European Communities Regarding the Application of Their Competition Laws, September 23, 1991, 30 I.K. M. 1491 (November 1991), reprinted in 4 *Trade Regulation Report* (CCH)13,504; and OJ L 95-45 (27 1995); corrected at OJ L 131-38 (June 15, 1995).

4. The earliest bilateral agreement in this field was entered into between the United States and the Federal Republic of Germany in 1976. Later agreements involved Australia (1982) and Canada (1984, superseded by a new agreement in 1995). Japanese press reports indicate that the United States and Japan are currently negotiating a bilateral accord.

5. In this case, the European Commission brought proceedings against forty wood pulp producers from the United States, Canada, and Finland and three of their trade associations for concerting on price and on price announcements. This foreign-based export cartel sold its products within the EC, thereby subjecting them to EU law. See cases 89-85, etc., *A. Ahlstrom Osakeyhtio* v. *Commission*, 1988 E.C.R. 5193 (1987–88 transfer binder) Common Market Report (CCH) 14, 491 (1988).

forcement cooperation and the potential lessening of disputes over jurisdictional principles. Needless to say, the case also served as a reminder that another important jurisdiction was willing to apply its laws to offshore conduct, thus underscoring the need for developing additional ways of addressing differences that could arise from such overlapping jurisdiction.

Second, this period was characterized by an expansion of EC-level regulation under the 1992 program, aimed at the completion of the internal market. Although this campaign did not extend the EC's antitrust powers, it did highlight the importance of European integration and hence antitrust enforcement. And third, the Council of Ministers of the EC had recently adopted a new merger control regulation. It was evident that both U.S. and EC authorities would regularly be examining the same mergers under their respective laws. As a result, an established channel of communication between the two authorities was necessary for those cases of overlapping review.[6]

For a period of time, internal legal requirements and politics within the EC cast some doubt on the validity of the 1991 agreement. However, in 1995, the procedural features were remedied by a joint decision of the Council of Ministers as well as the commission approving the agreement and deeming it applicable from the date it was first signed.[7]

In June 1998, the United States and the EC entered into a separate, positive comity agreement, which supplements the 1991 agreement.[8] The 1998 accord, while separate, built on the positive comity provisions contained in the 1991 agreement. The exact mix of factors that led to the negotiation of this agreement is not fully known. However, the policy decision by the U.S. Department of Justice to remove so-called footnote 159 was a significant development in the intervening period and may have been a relevant factor.

This famous footnote in U.S. antitrust policy can be summarized as follows. As a matter of prosecutorial discretion, the Justice Department during the Reagan administration chose to enforce actions against those export restraints that harmed only U.S. consumers and not those that harmed only

6. For a fuller discussion of these three points, see World Trade Organization (1997).

7. France sued to annul the agreement on the grounds that the EU lacked the authority to enter into such an agreement. The European Court of Justice held in August 1994 that it was up to the EC, not the commission, to conclude such an agreement under article 228 of the treaty. See case C-327-91, *France* v. *Commission* (1994), ECR 1-3641.

8. Agreement between the Government of the United States of America and the European Communities on the Application of Positive Comity Principles in the Enforcement of Their Competition Laws. June 4, 1998 (www.usdoj.gov/atr/public/international/docs/). Article 6 states that "this agreement shall supplement and be interpreted consistently with the 1991 agreement which remains fully in force."

U.S. exports. In 1992, during the Bush administration, the Antitrust Division of the Justice Department repealed footnote 159 (which had expressed this policy). In so doing, James F. Rill, assistant attorney general for antitrust, also made clear the Justice Department's intention to undertake enforcement action restraining U.S. export commerce, if the conduct was having a "direct, substantial and reasonably foreseeable effect" upon U.S. exports. In other words, direct consumer harm was not going to be the only focus of Justice Department enforcement action. A number of foreign officials voiced their concern regarding this shift in policy and expressed opposition to U.S. assertions of extraterritorial jurisdiction. Not long into the first Clinton administration, Justice Department officials affirmed their intention to continue this policy, which was later incorporated in the 1995 international guidelines issued by the Antitrust Division.[9]

A rash of foreign commerce or export restraint cases did *not* follow upon the heels of this decision. However, the announced shift of policy created anxiety and suspicion in Europe and Asia regarding U.S. intentions. The negotiation of a positive comity accord may have addressed some of those concerns.

Analysis of the Agreements

The key features of the 1991 U.S.-EC agreement essentially cover four areas:

—Notification of enforcement activities that may affect "important interests of the other party" (article 2)

—Exchanges of information, including through regular meetings between officials (article 3)

—Cooperation and coordination in enforcement activities "to the extent compatible with the assisting Party's laws and important interests and within its reasonably available resources" (article 4)

—Traditional comity procedures and positive comity procedures (articles 5, 6).

The notification and cooperation provisions apply both to enforcement matters and to multijurisdictional mergers.

The 1991 agreement was the first accord related exclusively to competition law to include a provision covering the notion of positive comity. Positive comity refers to the principle that a country should give serious consideration to another country's request to investigate and remedy anticompetitive conduct occurring within its borders that is harming an-

---

9. U.S. Department of Justice–Federal Trade Commission (1995).

other country's important interests.[10] This differs from the notion of traditional comity, which refers to the general principle that a country should take other countries' important interests into account in its own law enforcement in return for their doing the same.

Put simply, positive comity means that either the United States or the EC can request the other jurisdiction to enforce its laws with respect to conduct occurring within its borders that is harming the other jurisdiction. Most important, such cooperation remains voluntary and discretionary. Specifically, article 5 states that "if a Party believes that anticompetitive activity carried out on the territory of the other party is adversely affecting its important interests," the requesting party may request the other party "to initiate appropriate enforcement activities." The requested jurisdiction is required to "consider" the matter and inform the requesting jurisdiction of its decision and any resulting investigation. The agreement also speaks to traditional comity notions: article 6 (3) itemizes six comity factors that will be taken into consideration when it "appears that one Party's enforcement activities may adversely affect important interests of the other Party."

Building on these features of the 1991 agreement, in June 1998 the United States and the EU entered into a separate positive comity agreement that supplements the 1991 agreement and sets forth principles for implementation in particular kinds of cases.[11] In this sense, it clarifies the situations that would presumptively call for referrals between agencies and seeks to further articulate the report-back and consultation mechanisms that are triggered once a referral is made.

Article 3 of the 1998 accord provides that either party may request the other to "investigate and, if warranted, to remedy anticompetitive conduct in accordance with the Requested Party's competition laws." Article 4 (1) provides that the parties "may agree" that the requesting country will defer or suspend activities during the pendency of enforcement activities by the requested party. These provisions apply to all competition violations other than mergers, which are excluded. The agreement does not apply to mergers because of the short statutory deadlines on both sides of the Atlantic.[12]

---

10. For example, the antitrust guidelines state that "in determining whether to assert jurisdiction to investigate or bring an action, or to seek particular remedies in a given case, each Agency takes into account whether significant interests of any foreign sovereign will be affected." See U.S. Department of Justice–Federal Trade Commission (1995).

11. Agreement between the Government of the United States of America and the European Communities on the Application of Positive Comity Principles in the Enforcement of Their Competition Laws, June 4, 1998.

12. Klein (1997).

The presumption that a requesting jurisdiction defer or suspend its own enforcement activities in favor of enforcement activities by the requested jurisdiction is narrowly drawn. It applies to cases in which the requesting country's exports are affected and circumstances in which the conduct occurs principally in—and is directed principally toward—the requested country's territory. The agreement also specifies additional conditions that need to be satisfied before the presumption can apply in a particular case. According to article 4 (1) (b), it must appear that the adverse effects on the requesting party can be and are likely to be fully and adequately investigated, eliminated, or remedied pursuant to the laws or procedures of the requested jurisdiction. Further, according to article 4 (1) (c), the requested jurisdiction must agree to a variety of conditions regarding the conduct of their enforcement efforts, including commitments that it will

—Devote the necessary resources to investigate the anticompetitive activities

—Use best efforts to pursue all reasonably available information

—Inform the competition authorities of the status of the enforcement activities as well as the results of an investigation

—Use best efforts to complete the investigation within six months; among other undertakings.

Even when all the considerations for deferral or suspension are met, article 4 (1) (b) provides that the parties may still decide to pursue separate enforcement activities when "anticompetitive activities affecting both territories justify the imposition of penalties within both jurisdictions." The agreement does not preclude the requesting party from later initiating or reinstating its own investigation. In this way a positive comity referral does not oblige the antitrust agencies to relinquish their rights to pursue their own investigations should they conclude that their interests are not adequately being served by the investigation under way in the foreign jurisdiction.[13]

Inherent in the very structure of positive comity undertakings are significant limitations and protections. Neither the 1991 agreement nor the more elaborated 1998 agreement permits the sharing of confidential information without the provider's consent, and both agreements exclude mergers. Neither agreement provides a mechanism for resolving disputes that continue after the end of consultations in the event that a positive comity referral is seen as unresponsive to the identified problems. Neither of these agreements implicates substantive law nor seeks to reach a formal procedural harmonization between the two jurisdictions. Furthermore, jurisdictions retain their

13. Pitofsky (1998a).

full sovereign rights to accept or reject a referral. Thus both agreements allow the requested party to take its own national interests into account in determining whether and to what extent to provide cooperation in any given matter. In this way, a jurisdiction is not obliged to accept a request it deems inappropriate under its own law.

Both U.S. and European officials have praised the 1991 and 1998 agreements as facilitating the expansion and deepening of effective communication between the two jurisdictions. Given the degree of cross-border mergers and acquisitions activity between U.S. and European firms, increased cooperation and interaction between antitrust officials would appear to be a natural—indeed a market-driven—development and one that does not even require an underlying accord. After all, bilateral communication could legally have occurred, and presumably did occur, before 1991. Yet whether as a result of the increased economic and merger activity between U.S. and European enterprises over the last decade or of the initiative and enthusiasm on the part of U.S. and European competition authorities, the agreements have provided a useful context for the competition agencies to cooperate in a more structured and proactive fashion than in earlier periods.

Interagency Cooperation and Positive Comity

Three forms of cooperation could, hypothetically, occur between competition authorities, each of which might also reflect varying degrees of mutual trust between authorities. First, at the request of another jurisdiction or because of information shared by one jurisdiction with officials in the other jurisdiction, a jurisdiction might use its compulsory or investigatory powers to look into allegations of anticompetitive practices occurring within its own territory. Such cooperation might take the form of the proverbial "dawn raid," undertaken at the request of another jurisdiction. Information obtained through that action could in theory then be provided to the foreign jurisdiction so that it can prosecute the case under its domestic laws.

Second, a jurisdiction might undertake a parallel investigation with a foreign authority, apply its own compulsory or discovery powers within its own territory, and thereafter apply its own relevant domestic remedies.

Third, jurisdiction A might undertake an investigation at the request of jurisdiction B, and jurisdiction B would then forgo its own investigation because it believes that the requested jurisdiction (A) is willing and better able to effectively investigate the case. This example of positive comity is a relatively untested concept; it has its roots in the Recommendations of the Organization for Economic Cooperation and Development (OECD) Council on Cooperation between Member Countries on Restrictive Business Practices. Unlike traditional or negative comity, in which deference tends toward less enforcement action, positive comity is intended to result in more action.[14]

In the U.S.-EC context, the number of notifications made by each jurisdiction and at least several instances of enforcement cooperation are a matter of public record.[15] For example, in 1997 the EC notified the United States with respect to forty-two nonmerger cases and the United States notified the EC with respect to thirty-six matters. However, because neither accord permits U.S. and European authorities to exchange confidential information, the first archetype of cooperative enforcement action mentioned above is not legally permissible and would not occur unless the affected party voluntarily waives its right to protect information obtained by authorities in its jurisdiction.

The United States is, however, a party to bilateral mutual legal assistance treaties (MLATs) with several member states of the European Union; some of these include antitrust matters. Hence U.S. officials have received assistance from some EU member states on antitrust enforcement matters, and there have been cases in which affected parties chose to waive their rights to restrict exchanges of confidential information between U.S. and EC authorities. This transpired in 1994 in the context of parallel investigations by the Department of Justice and the European Commission's Directorate General IV (DGIV) of exclusionary restrictive licensing practices by Microsoft.[16] That case resulted in a single, jointly negotiated and coordinated remedy, implemented by a U.S. court decree and an undertaking in Europe that were virtually identical. Because of the waiver, the staffs on both sides of the Atlantic were able to coordinate their investigations to a degree that could not have been achieved otherwise. The specific reason that Microsoft granted a waiver to U.S. and European authorities is not a matter of public record; presumably, it was adjudged a means of

14. Atwood (1992, 84).

15. The European Commission has issued two informative reports on cooperation under the 1991 U.S.-EC agreement: October 8, 1996 (COM[96]479 final) and July 4, 1997 (COM[97]346 final), both available on the World Wide Web homepage of the EC's antitrust authority, DGIV. These reports contain statistics on number of notifications and a discussion of the nature and mechanics of the cooperation between EC and U.S. authorities.

16. The U.S. complaint alleges that Microsoft's requirement that PC manufacturers pay a fee to Microsoft for each computer shipped meant that it was using its monopoly power to levy a tax on PC manufacturers, that Microsoft's contracts were unreasonably long, and that it had introduced overly restrictive nondisclosure agreements. The EU complaint identified similar concerns. See Department of Justice, press release, July 16, 1994; DGIV, press release, July 17, 1994.

securing a faster resolution of the case and perhaps minimizing the adverse impact on the firm's ongoing operations.

Positive comity, if it proves robust in application, is a significant step toward enhanced cooperation between U.S. and European competition authorities. As practical matter, it offers the possibility of surmounting some of the obstacles that can stymie effective prosecution of transnational cases. Difficult issues of jurisdiction, service of process, discovery, availability of witnesses, and enforcement of judgments can be lessened if the foreign jurisdiction where such information is located undertakes the investigation. Invoking positive comity can also potentially be used by the requesting jurisdiction to put pressure on the requested jurisdiction to undertake an investigation; the 1998 agreement imposes some structure on the reporting and consultations that then occur. Since EC action is supreme to inconsistent law of member states, positive comity may also offer the prospect of preempting inconsistent national blocking legislation of the member states, if EC authorities choose to undertake the investigation.[17]

Positive comity offers some possibility of reducing tensions between countries with respect to the exercise of jurisdiction over a case. This may be especially important in the context of so-called footnote 159, or market access cases, in which the United States exercises jurisdiction with respect to foreign-based conduct that is adversely impacting U.S. exports (and presumably also European consumers).

Indeed, some European officials have stated that "for the Commission, an Agreement on the use of positive comity was essentially a means to restrict the extraterritorial use of antitrust legislation by the United States. . . . The application of positive comity not only represents a commitment to cooperate rather than seeking to apply antitrust laws extraterritorially, it also reduces the possibility of conflicting decisions being made by different competition authorities."[18] Both U.S. and European officials stress in their public remarks that positive comity can serve to enhance cooperation and reduce sources of tension. U.S. officials also stress its potential as a means of overcoming impediments to prosecution of transnational cases, while European officials often place equal (if not greater) emphasis on its utility (in their view) in curbing the United States in its extraterritorial enforcement efforts.

By its very structure, the application of positive comity requires a degree of confidence by the requesting jurisdiction in the ability and willingness of the requested jurisdiction to undertake an investigation. This trust is par-

17. Waller (1977, 369).
18. Devuyst (1998, 467).

ticularly important in those cases in which the requesting jurisdiction has jurisdiction over the case and yet defers its own investigation during the pendency of the referral. Positive comity, in some circumstances, may also be the only available competition policy instrument for focusing the attention of a foreign jurisdiction on a matter that the requesting jurisdiction deems important but cannot reach.

Positive Comity Referrals, Informal and Formal

Although the formal invocation of positive comity has occurred in just one instance, this single example may underemphasize its effect on the overall environment of cooperation between U.S. and European authorities. The concept has reportedly been applied in at least three other cases in which it has not been formally invoked. In 1996 the Justice Department conducted an investigation of A. C. Nielsen, a U.S. firm that tracks retail sales, to determine whether Nielsen offered customers more favorable terms in countries in which the firm had market power if those customers also used Nielsen in countries in which it faced significant competition. The European Commission also investigated the matter, since most of the conduct occurred in Europe and had a direct impact on European consumers. According to press releases issued by both competition agencies, there was close contact between the staffs of both agencies in the form of discussion of legal and economic theories and, with the consent of the parties, exchange of confidential information.[19] Joel Klein, acting assistant attorney general, indicated that it made sense to let the European Commission take the lead in the investigation because it was clear that "the European Commission had a firm intention to act."[20] The Department of Justice closed its investigation when Nielsen signed its undertaking with the European Commission.

Similarly, Robert Pitofsky, chairman of the Federal Trade Commission, has indicated that the FTC informally encouraged "the Italian antitrust authority to end a production quota agreement by a consortium of ham producers that exported to the United States, harming U.S. consumers with supracompetitive prices."[21] Because the Italians had an investigation under way that would result in a decision by a date certain, the FTC decided to stay

19. Department of Justice, press release, December 3, 1996; European Commission, press release, December 4, 1996.

20. European Commission, press release, December 4, 1996.

21. Pitofsky (1999).

its hand. The Italian authority's decision and remedy addressed the FTC's concerns; consequently, the FTC closed its investigation.[22]

A further matter, involving Marathon Oil, has also been referenced as an informal positive comity referral to the EC. The company, which took its complaint to EC authorities, alleges that anticompetitive behavior by European concerns was costing the company hundreds of millions of dollars in losses. A novel feature of this dispute is that the company is alleging disruption in its sales from Norway to Europe, and hence the case might not even come under the jurisdictional reach of the Sherman Act. U.S. authorities may have no choice but to rely on EC authorities for appropriate enforcement measures.[23]

Let us now consider the circumstance and reactions within the United States to the first formal referral, since that record may prove instructive for the future. In April 1998, the Department of Justice announced that earlier in the year, on January 20, it had made its first formal positive comity request to the EU under the 1991 agreement. The Antitrust Division asked the European Commission's DGIV to investigate possible anticompetitive conduct by Amadeus (the dominant computer reservation system in Europe, owned by three of Europe's largest airlines) to determine whether that conduct might be preventing the U.S.-based SABRE computer reservation system from competing effectively in certain European countries. The matter was referred to the commission because it occurred in the commission's home territory and because European consumers were those principally harmed. Nearly two years after the referral was made public, in March 1999, the EC announced that it decided to open a formal procedure against Air France for possible abuse of a dominant position.[24]

By then Sabre had made some progress in the European market and had entered into new arrangements with SAS and Lufthansa, designed to enhance SABRE's distribution in those jurisdictions. In the intervening period, the case generated considerable interest and concern among some members of Congress. In hearings in the fall of 1998, when the EC's re-

22. Consorzio del Prosciutto di San Daniele—Consorzio del Prosciutto di Parma (Rif. I138) Delibera del 19.06.96—Boll. N. 25-1996, available on the homepage of the Italian Competition Authority; Pitofsky (1998b).

23. Pitofsky (1999).

24. The Statement of Objections is a confidential document, disclosed only to the parties. However, the EC objected "to Air France's having provided Amadeus with more accurate information and on a more timely basis than it did to other CRSs, thereby putting the latter at a competitive disadvantage." See press release IP-99-171 (www.europa.eu.int/comm/dgo4/pressre.htm).

sponse to the positive comity referral appeared to be getting off to a slow start, an executive from the SABRE Group noted that the DGIV seemed to treat the referral as a new matter, hence "much of the benefit of the near two-year investigation by the Justice Department into Amadeus was lost."[25] SABRE's representative also raised concerns about investigatory and evidentiary features of EC practices that differ from U.S. practices, among them the EC's limited discovery procedures, the absence of criminal penalties for filing incomplete or false responses, its limited resources, and its different and higher standards of proof. The implication was that the United States should not only retain its authority to undertake unilateral action but be willing to exercise jurisdiction, possibly even in this case.

From a distance, it seems that the features of the European system identified as problematical were neither new nor exceptional. Indeed, EC practices may be closer to those of the United States than is true for many other jurisdictions. Nevertheless, the consequences of the existing differences may be more meaningful in the context of a positive comity referral than in the context of national litigation procedures.

This early record of positive comity also suggests that more experience with actual cases may require additional procedural refinements to ensure that all parties have a clear and shared understanding about the communications that will occur after a referral has been made.

Positive Comity, an Early Evaluation

These developments raise fundamental questions about positive comity referrals. What are reasonable expectations for coordination between authorities? And what are reasonable expectations with respect to results?

Clearly, expectations about the benefits as well as the risks of positive comity should not be inflated. This is a point that U.S. authorities have cautioned about from the outset. Robert Pitofsky, chairman of the FTC, has stated that U.S. agencies should not "expect that the EC or other countries' competition authorities will always be able or willing to receive and pursue

---

25. Steinberg (1998). Andrew Steinberg, senior vice president, general counsel, and corporate secretary of the Sabre Group, suggested certain changes to improve the referral process, including intensive monitoring by the United States and more frequent communications between governments; formal updates to private complainants on the status of their pending matters and on a time frame for resolution; enhanced convergence of investigative procedures, such as joint evidence gathering to address the EU's inability to compel discovery; imposition and adherence to a strict timetable; and reservation of a unilateral right to act when positive comity does not work.

a positive comity request. Nor should agencies—or companies bringing the complaints—expect that foreign authorities will always succeed in investigating and prosecuting a complaint."[26] European officials for their part have cautioned that the U.S. Congress and U.S. firms not be hasty in their evaluation of the potential of positive comity. Positive comity, some warn, would die on the vine if authorities were constantly being second-guessed by affected parties and obliged to testify or appear before the nation's legislative body about the status of pending matters.

Positive comity has inherent limitations given that cooperation could be constrained by the ban on sharing of investigatory information and given that the doctrine applies only to conduct that is illegal in the requested jurisdiction. Positive comity is unlikely to prove an antidote to those market access cases that reflect conflicting national policies or in which there are substantial differences in law. The benefits of positive comity referrals that appear achievable between the United States and the EC may not be generally available between jurisdictions that do not have the resources, the experience, or the legal infrastructure to undertake an investigation or consider a referral. A referral, especially if it involves a suspension of a domestic investigation by the requesting jurisdiction, requires a degree of confidence between authorities that may not be present in all bilateral cooperation environments.

But these concerns and limitations should also not be overblown. The early record suggests that positive comity is an important doctrine and that it can go some way in ameliorating tensions associated with extraterritorial enforcement and in facilitating enforcement cooperation. The practical application of positive comity is likely to prove particularly useful in those cases that a competition authority would naturally have investigated had it known of it. Positive comity is also useful in two other instances: when the requesting jurisdiction is unable as a practical matter to pursue unilateral remedies because of foreign-based evidence or other impediments to effective prosecution; and when the requesting jurisdiction has no jurisdiction over practices that are nevertheless affecting the overseas activities of their firms. Positive comity can put pressure on the requested jurisdiction to investigate a claim and then offer a structure for the cooperation that ensues. As such there are few risks associated with positive comity and some significant potential gains. It is cannot, however, address all sources of competition-related friction between jurisdictions.

The *Final Report* of the International Competition Policy Advisory Committee (ICPAC) concludes that "positive comity can be an important ve-

---

26. Pitofsky (1998a).

hicle for minimizing conflict and enhancing enforcement of law in market access violations. Positive comity, however, can succeed only if the international antitrust community maintains a full understanding of its ultimate goals and potential. It is imperative that both parties to an agreement set realistic goals for what positive comity can and cannot accomplish."[27]

Multijurisdictional Merger Control

There is now a steady stream of transnational merger activity involving U.S. and European firms, a trend that shows little sign of abating. Although the precise number is not known, a large number of mergers have been reviewed by U.S. and EC authorities and have raised no competition policy concerns in either jurisdictions.[28] There is also a substantial track record of notifications pursuant to the 1991 agreement. For example, in 1997 the EC notified the United States of thirty-one merger investigations that met the threshold of implicating important interests of the other jurisdiction. During that same period, the United States notified the EC of twenty merger investigations. FTC officials suggest that at any given time about half of the merger matters before the FTC involve some level of interaction with foreign competition authorities.[29] As the data suggest, there is a rich case record for scholars and experts to examine. Let me offer but five observations about this recent record.

First, cooperation between U.S. and European competition authorities appears to have deepened and broadened and become regularized. Such cooperation has not, however, become formulaic. Interaction between officials at all levels is now commonplace. Discussion can include a review of product markets, timing of respective procedures, and consideration of relevant geographic markets. In a number of cases, DGIV and FTC staffs share their views on the appropriate definition of product and geographic markets, possible competitive effects, and potential remedies.[30]

27. International Competition Policy Advisory Committee (2000, 239, 241).

28. Neither U.S. nor European authorities keep data on mergers by nationality of the merging parties.

29. Baer (1998, 15); Pitofsky (1998a): "Today, 50 percent of the mergers that we take a careful look at—I mean that we go beyond the initial investigation—involve more than one jurisdiction."

30. For example, in the initial phase of FTC and EC investigations of the *Shell-Montedison* case, a merger of the world's largest polypropylene producers, in addition to the routine discussion of review process and timing, questions concerning U.S. and European intellectual property and contract law (particularly joint venture contracts) were discussed and explanations exchanged. See *Shell-Montecatini*, commission decision 94-811-EC, June 8, 1994, case 4-M.0269, OJ L 332-48 (November 22, 1994); *Montedison-Shell*, FTC docket C-3580 (May 25, 1995). See also Starek (1996). In the Kimberly Clark–Scott merger, relevant markets were a

Second, cooperation between authorities appears particularly effective in cases in which the parties granted waivers to the exchange of confidential information. Two mergers, WorldCom-MCI and Halliburton–Dresser Industries, illustrate this point, but there are others. Both of these mergers involved a proposed combination of two U.S. firms. The result of WorldCom-MCI was the largest divestiture in U.S. merger history—of MCI's $1.75 billion Internet assets to Cable and Wireless. According to A. Douglas Melamed, principal deputy assistant attorney general, bilateral cooperation worked as follows:

> Division staff and DGIV staff worked closely to share their independent analyses of the transaction as they evolved, and we and the EC Commission ultimately reached essentially the same conclusions. With the parties' consent, obtained through written waivers of confidentiality, the agencies shared confidential information with one another and held joint meetings with the two U.S. companies to discuss the issues and possible solutions. In addition, before announcing its approval of the transaction in July, the European Commission formally requested, pursuant to the 1991 U.S.-EU antitrust cooperation agreement, the Division's cooperation and assistance in evaluating and implementing the proposed divestiture.[31]

The Halliburton–Dresser Industries merger also involved independent but coordinated investigations, which culminated in a proposed U.S. consent decree whereby Halliburton agreed to sell "a key part of its worldwide oilfield service business. In this matter, too, Division and DGIV staffs shared views and information about the transaction, pursuant to written waiver . . . and again, the Commission relied on Halliburton's divestiture commitment to the Division to resolve competition issues that might have arisen for the Commission."[32]

The singular features of these two mergers that may contain the indicia of successful multijurisdictional merger reviews include the following:

—The authorities were able to preserve their independent decisionmaking authority.

---

subject of early discussion; the authorities came to different conclusions about divestiture requirements with respect to the geographic market. The United States obliged Scott to divest its facial tissue and baby wipes business; in Europe, the DGIV obliged the parties to divest KC's Kleenex brand toilet tissue. See Hawk and Lewis (1997).

31. Melamed (1998).

32. Melamed (1998).

—Staffs were able to interact effectively, perhaps because of waivers.

—Issues were resolved with both U.S. and European staffs at roughly the same time.

—Divestiture results satisfied the completion concerns of both authorities.

Third, cooperation between enforcement agencies and communication between investigating staffs does not always result in agencies arriving at coordinated or even similar outcomes. For example, in the proposed merger of two Swiss pharmaceutical firms, Ciba-Geigy and Sandoz, U.S. and EC antitrust authorities held quite similar views on what markets would be affected by the $3 billion merger, namely the world market for certain types of gene therapy research and development. Yet the two authorities reached different conclusions on the question of competitive effects. European authorities concluded that potential anticompetitive effects in this market were too speculative to warrant antitrust relief. The FTC, on the other hand, determined that the merging firms were the leading commercial developers in a highly concentrated gene therapy market and that new entry was not expected to deter or counteract the merger's anticompetitive effects. As a result the FTC consent order required the merged firm to license certain gene therapy patent rights and other technology to Rhone-Poulenc Rorer.

In an elegant discussion of multijurisdictional merger review, an FTC official suggests that "even if the transaction needs to be addressed somewhat differently on both sides of the Atlantic because of differing market conditions and competitive realities, we reach solutions involving divestitures and licensing that neither conflict nor force firms to choose between complying with U.S. or EC law."[33]

Fourth, direct conflicts in the form of incompatible remedies, while rare, can occur. The Boeing–McDonnell Douglas merger is probably the best-known example of a parallel antitrust investigation resulting in a conflicting outcome regarding the competitive effects of the merger. This was a merger between two U.S. companies that had no production assets in the EU. It provoked nationalistic responses in both the United States and Europe, with politicians accusing each other of supporting their own national champion. The dispute nearly escalated into a trade war, as European authorities threatened to impose very high fines if the merger went forward and some U.S. officials threatened to bring the case to the World Trade Organization (WTO).

In hindsight, the case proves quite instructive, dramatically illustrating that in a global market the "effects" doctrine is going to be applied. Shortly after this case, for example, Japan amended its antimonopoly act to permit

33. Valentine (1998).

it to review offshore mergers. Since then, the European Court of First In-stance in another case confirmed its *Wood Pulp* judgment with respect to the issue of jurisdiction as applying to a merger decision.[34]

Further, the case demonstrates that when important interests are involved (and nationalistic sentiments invoked) interagency cooperation may not be sufficient to avoid conflict and surmount differences. Interestingly, neither U.S. nor EC antitrust authorities took issue with the right of the European authorities to review the merger, given the global market for aerospace. Given differences in underlying law between the United States and the EU, one should expect that direct conflicts will periodically arise. Some draw from this case a further implication: that an international or global organization is needed to mediate or adjudicate when conflicts arise. I do not see the WTO as currently well suited to address such a conflict but can imagine that there will be instances in which mediation or arbitration mechanisms could be useful to resolve merger disputes. Generally, however, the press of time is likely to make mediation both unwieldy and unattractive to the parties to the merger.

The fifth and more speculative observation about transatlantic merger cooperation is that, the occasional conflict notwithstanding, the market is itself creating incentives for interagency cooperation, which may keep brinkmanship in check. Game theorists have long argued that the incentives for cooperation or accommodation are greater in so-called repeat interac-tion games than in interactions that are one-offs. The fact that competition authorities are likely to be dealing with one another on a frequent and regu-lar basis will not eliminate the probability that officials may reach different conclusions as a matter of law or that some cases may trigger political or nationalistic responses; yet on balance one suspects that repeat interaction is creating new incentives for cooperation.

One might challenge that proposition by pointing to U.S.-EU trade policy relations, which have been replete with many tough trade disputes and no shortage of brinkmanship. Yet there are distinctions between trade disputes and competition policy disputes. Trade disputes often center on allegations of discriminatory and less-favorable treatment. If the source of a dispute, be it trade or merger review, is perceived as discrimination in the treatment of the foreign product or firm by a foreign government, then it is not surpris-ing to see tensions escalate and little difference in the degree of brinkmanship

34. See the decision by the European Court of First Instance concerning the commission's negative decision in the proposed merger between South Africa's Gencor and Lonrho's plati-num mining interests (curia.edu.int/jurisp).

between trade or competition policy disputes. However, in the absence of such discrimination concerns, mitigating influences in merger review often operate from the start. Many transnational mergers that are reviewed by both U.S. and European authorities involve firms from one or both of these jurisdictions that are themselves trying to make the adjustments necessary to get the deal cleared. Thus while some regulatory friction may arise from differences in law or policy, the merging parties themselves are countervailing influences, working to bring the transaction to a close.

The Road Ahead

As this chapter shows, U.S. and European competition authorities have come to work more closely despite substantive and procedural differences between their competition laws. Former EC competition commissioner Karel Van Miert notes that this cooperation is producing "soft harmonization" and a spirit of deference, as non-U.S. competition authorities see that U.S. responses sometimes address the same competition policy concerns as those of foreign jurisdictions. These developments bespeak a spirit of cooperation that is a far cry from the earlier history of international antitrust enforcement—the days of blocking statutes and uranium cartel cases.

Looking ahead, there are a number of steps that could be undertaken by U.S. and European authorities to enhance cooperation still further. Some imply legislative steps and thus more formalized efforts at enhancing procedural convergence; others may be possible without amending national laws and presumably are therefore easier to implement. Substantive adjustments could imply the application of comity doctrines. The discussion that follows is not intended to be advocacy for any single approach, because several of these steps could facilitate more efficient coordination between authorities.

The magnitude of cross-trade and investment occurring between the United States and the EU makes that economic relationship a particularly likely testing ground for creative initiatives in the field of competition policy. This was recognized at the EU-U.S. summit in London in May 1998, when it was agreed to "explore the scope for further cooperative dialogue on greater compatibility of procedures between our competition authorities as part of the Transatlantic Economic Partnership."[35] U.S.-EC antitrust cooperation is

---

35. Transatlantic Economic Partnership, May 18, 1998, para. 13.

not, however, the only bilateral forum that is seeing increased consultation and cooperation.[36] What then might be considered?

An Agreement on Confidential Information Exchange

One logical next step to enhance effective communication and cooperation between antitrust authorities might be for the United States and the EC to negotiate and enter into an agreement that permits the intergovernmental exchange of confidential information in antitrust matters, along the lines of the International Antitrust Enforcement Agreements Act (IAEAA) in place between the United States and Australia. The advantage to both jurisdictions of such an agreement is that it can facilitate cooperation and enforcement efforts. Given the strength of U.S. discovery and investigatory procedures, the IAEAA could provide Europe with especially strong tools for obtaining U.S.-based evidence—which would require some legal amendments in Europe.

Notwithstanding such legal adjustments, if the United States and the EC were to enter into an IAEAA-type agreement, authorities would need to address the concerns about leakage that have frequently been raised by business groups on both sides of the Atlantic. For example, the TransAtlantic Business Dialogue (TABD) issued a statement in 1997 on the draft positive comity accord; the statement welcomed cooperation but requested that authorities ensure that no confidential business information be disclosed without business consent.[37]

U.S. and European legal and business groups are concerned that authorities provide advance notice to the person whose information may be disclosed and, because downstream protection is extremely important, that foreign authorities be able to protect confidential information from downstream disclosure. From a U.S. perspective, this latter point often takes the form of a concern that foreign authorities may (intentionally or unintentionally) disclose confidential information about U.S. firms to their competitors and that the very structure of the EC system may make it difficult to limit access to confidential information. The often-voiced foreign concern is that U.S. authorities may be unable to protect such information from disclosure to private third parties, thereby making foreign firms susceptible to

36. Canadian-U.S. antitrust cooperation has been particularly close with respect to both merger matters and enforcement cases, and Australia has concluded a bilateral antitrust agreement with the United States covering the exchange of confidential information.

37. www.tabd.com/recom/charlotte.html.

the use of their information in private U.S. treble-damage suits. It is also argued that the lack of convergence between substantive laws and treatment of privileged information can lead to disparities in treatment of confidential information.

Although the fear about leakage is understandable, the record suggests that it may be exaggerated.[38] Hearings undertaken by the ICPAC asked officials and practitioners to identify instances in which leaks had occurred. This question produced no referenced cases in either the United States or the EC.[39] If U.S. and EC authorities should wish to expand instruments of cooperation with respect to confidential information exchanges, it may be useful to broaden public discussion and also to consider what additional measures would be necessary to increase public and business confidence. The ICPAC, for its part, recommends that steps could be taken to increase transparency concerning enforcement matters.[40]

The Harmonization of Merger Control Procedures

The logic behind efforts at procedural harmonization is straightforward. One proposal is to develop common forms, which, to the extent that parties are able to prepare and present substantially the same information to authorities of more than one jurisdiction, could reduce transaction costs and increase the efficiency of review. This is doubtless especially true with respect to mergers unlikely to raise serious competition policy issues, which are the vast majority. A second proposal is that jurisdictions should undertake continuing efforts to correct defects in their own merger control procedures that are unduly burdensome and serve no necessary competition policy objective. A third proposal argues in favor of an overall reform notion, namely, that given that there are now as many as sixty jurisdictions applying merger control regulations, international efforts are needed to reduce the volume

38. At the November 1998 ICPAC hearings, Karel Van Miert of the EU, Dieter Wolf of Germany, and Allan Fels of Australia stressed that they knew of no instance in which confidential business information had been leaked. Joel Klein of the United States argued along similar lines in a speech to the TransAtlantic Business Dialogue in November 1998.

39. Transcript of the November 1998 and April 1999 ICPAC hearings (www.usdoj.gov/atr/icpac).

40. The committee recommends that authorities consider providing notice, either before or after the fact, of their intent to disclose information to authorities in other jurisdictions, unless such notice would violate a U.S. treaty obligation or court order or jeopardize the integrity of any U.S., state, or foreign investigation. It was thought that increased transparency in the use and management of confidential information may increase confidence on the part of firms as to how their information, including that produced pursuant to a waiver, might be handled. See International Competition Policy Advisory Committee (2000, 194).

of applicable law. The second and third proposals may be mutually reinforcing, given that some jurisdictions may need to be induced to forgo applying
their laws absent a substantial threshold of economic effects within their
country.[41]

Each proposal has considerable merit, could be pursued simultaneously,
and probably should be considered specifically in the context of U.S.-EC
cooperation. For example, a frequently voiced argument by advocates of the
"learning from abroad" perspective calls for reducing up-front information
requests under EC procedures, since few transactions are likely to raise serious competition issues. Similarly, when a U.S. merger review goes into the
second-request phase, authorities could try to reduce or more narrowly frame
the information requests required under Hart-Scott-Rodino (HSR) procedures. Adjustments along these lines are likely to be well received by firms in
both jurisdictions and do not require a coordinated or harmonized effort.

A number of other useful but more ambitious steps might require more
formalized and harmonized steps.[42] It is beyond the scope of this chapter to
discuss these in detail. Suffice it to say that harmonizing any single element
is unlikely to be a simple proposition and may require a comprehensive harmonization of elements, which then can make the prospects of such reform
more challenging.[43]

41. One report recommends the development of model filing forms that "would request
common information in a single format and use different country annexes as appropriate."
See Whish and Wood (1994). A further report recommends harmonization of the timing and
content of various premerger reporting requirements. See American Bar Association (1991).

42. Establishing an international merger treaty (either opt-in or mandatory) is one of the
more ambitious proposals. Alternatively, there is some international discussion of harmonization of key elements of merger control procedures such as timing or triggering events. In
the EC, antitrust filings can be made only after the signing of a definitive merger agreement,
acquisition of control, or announcement of a public bid. However, once one of these triggering events occurs, a notification must be made within seven days (although extensions may be
granted). The European Commission also is bound by stringent time requirements for the
completion of a merger investigation (maximum five months from filing). EC Merger Control Regulation, 4064-89 OJ 1990 L 2S7-14, art. 10 (December 21, 1989). By contrast, there is
no notification deadline for submitting an HSR form. Notification may be made as early as
the time an agreement in principle, letter of intent, or contract has been entered into. Further,
the final review period in the United States is triggered by substantial compliance with the
agency's request for additional information and may be extended by the parties.

43. For example, adjusting timing is not simple and may implicate other adjustments, such
as harmonizing triggering events and review periods. These changes would necessitate legislative amendment of existing law. Some experts suggest that this problem can be surmounted
by the parties if they were to first file in the United States on a letter of intent (which they
cannot do in the EC) and begin prenotification consultation with the EC. The longer the
parties delay in notifying the United States after notifying the EC (which starts an unstop-
pable five-month clock), the more difficult coordination becomes. See discussion papers prepared for ICPAC meeting, December 16, 1998.

Another potentially useful dimension of merger cooperation could occur with respect to the handling of confidential information. Since an IAEAA agreement excludes mergers, developing agreed upon procedures for the handling of confidential information produced voluntarily in the merger context may serve to instill confidence on the part of the merging parties providing such information and also facilitate effective cooperation between authorities. Experience on both sides of the Atlantic with voluntary waivers is increasing. Further steps along these lines do not necessarily require legislative action. It could, for example, take the form of a model protocol or policy statement produced by each jurisdiction that delineates how agencies will handle confidential information disclosed pursuant to voluntary waivers.

This was an important ICPAC recommendation. It argued that "cooperation among reviewing authorities can be enhanced if all jurisdictions establish a transparent legal framework for cooperation that contains appropriate safeguards to protect the privacy and fairness interests of private parties."[44] In sum it appears that much by way of procedural harmonization could be considered. Of course, to the extent differences in national laws reflect "real differences in countries' views on how their premerger notification system should run, complete harmonization can occur only when and if the underlying policy differences are resolved."[45]

Substantive Harmonization: Steps toward Enhanced Comity

Few see formal harmonization of competition laws as likely, either as a general proposition or in the U.S.-EC context. Formal international negotiations to harmonize substantive law are not likely to be productive. At the same time, some cross-fertilization does seem to be occurring. Recent years have brought modifications to European law in the area of vertical restraints and merger control. These modifications include both the EC's adoption of the SSNIP (small but significant and nontransitory increase in price) approach to market definition, used in the United States, and the decision in the *Kali und Salz* case, which officially sanctions the EC's challenge of mergers on an oligopolistic coordination theory.[46] The United States has also

---

44. International Competition Policy Advisory Committee (2000, 83).

45. OECD, Notification of Transnational Mergers, 2.

46. The 1992 U.S. merger guidelines offer that the relevant market is the smallest product and geographic market in which a hypothetical monopolist could impose an SSNIP, generally around 5 percent but possibly larger or smaller depending on specific facts.

moved somewhat in the direction of the EC by placing emphasis on single-firm dominance ("unilateral effects"), which has long been an important focus of EC merger review.[47] EC authorities have also created a new cartel unit, which may itself be a reflection of interest in the U.S. experience, the large numbers of U.S. international cartels cases (a number of which involve European defendants), and the ongoing coordination on hard-core cartels between the United States and other jurisdictions as part of OECD consultations.

Such cross-fertilization is constructive and important. However, it seems unlikely to ever be complete. For this reason, a more interesting question than whether substantive harmonization is fully possible is the extent to which U.S. and European antitrust authorities can develop the spirit of deference alluded to above. Few national authorities (or legislative bodies) are willing to sign away authority to review a transaction if domestic competitive effects are implicated or local firms are potentially affected.[48] Thus we should assume that neither the United States nor the EC will abdicate jurisdiction. What degree of deference to another agency is feasible in instances of multijurisdictional merger review to reduce the burden on merging parties and resolve or avoid disputes? For example, could a jurisdiction with a comparatively lesser interest in investigating a transaction defer to those more substantially concerned?

It is interesting to consider how much of an integrated or work-sharing approach to an investigation is possible between the United States and the EC. As experience with cooperation increases, might it be possible, for example, for one or another agency to become the de facto lead agency, which would then be responsible for investigating the transaction, possibly with participation or monitoring by staff from the other authority—and in some circumstances pursuant to waivers by the parties? Can remedies be fashioned that take into consideration the concerns of another jurisdiction? Could a single consent agreement be negotiated that would incorporate remedial provisions sufficient to satisfy the other jurisdictions concerned?

These are important questions and point to possible future directions for cooperation between competition authorities. To a limited extent, efforts along these lines may already be occurring. For example, in *Federal-Mogul Corp.–T&N Plc.* the FTC coordinated review efforts closely with enforce-

---

47. Some also argue that this case reflects additional convergence in that the court endorsed a form of the failing firm defense, which has long been recognized in the United States. See Kolasky and Greenfield (1998).

48. Baker (1998).

ment agencies in the United Kingdom, Germany, France, and Italy. The German Federal Cartel Office raised concerns that the merger threatened competition in dry bearings. The FTC included in its consent agreement a provision for divesting dry bearings units partly to satisfy German concerns and to allow Federal-Mogul to avoid entering a separate divestiture proceeding in Germany.

There are many challenges to this approach. A lead agency could reach different results on the merits, or the remedy undertaken by one jurisdiction may not be deemed appropriate by another. Given the short deadlines under which, for example, the United States and the EC operate, it is difficult for a jurisdiction to defer an investigation, particularly if there is a perceived risk that consumers and important interests may not be adequately protected. Complicated issues of law and policy are raised by these considerations, namely, to what extent are authorities able, as a matter of domestic law, or willing, as a matter of policy, to consider negative externalities in their own decisions? Fuller consideration of these questions may be part of the next phase of cooperation between U.S. and European competition authorities.

The ICPAC's final recommendation helps to unbundle a number of steps that could be taken to deepen cooperation still further along these lines. The suggestions contained in that report may be particularly relevant for cooperation between the United States and the EU. The suggested first step in coordination and cooperation in the area of merger review is already evident; it takes the form of several jurisdictions reviewing a transaction and participating in the formulation, if not the negotiation and implementation, of remedies.

The ICPAC report argues that, in appropriate cases, cooperation could be taken to the next level, which could be to limit the number of jurisdictions conducting independent second-state reviews of a proposed transaction.[49] This approach may not, of course, be feasible in circumstances with statutorily mandated review periods if the agency could lose the right to review the transaction at all. But where there is no available remedy to the reviewing jurisdiction or there is a sufficient level of confidence in the reviewing jurisdiction, this approach may be possible.

At some point, given sufficient substantive and procedural convergence among merger review regimes, the ICPAC considered whether the coordinating agency could accept the "mantle of parens patriae for world competition. Accordingly, it would endeavor to evaluate procompetitive and

49. International Competition Policy Advisory Committee (2000, 84).

anticompetitive effects of a proposed transaction on a global scale, taking into account all of the merger's costs and benefits to the competition, not only the net effects within its borders." This type of multimarket balancing would allow the coordinating agency to account for what had been viewed as externalities, thereby enabling it to assess the net effects of a proposed transaction on a global scale. The ICPAC notes (properly, in my view) that this is a distant vision.[50]

Conclusion

The record suggests that U.S.-EU economic relations offer a fertile field to consider ways that bilateral relations in the field of competition policy can be strengthened to the benefit of consumers and business interests. The policy steps that U.S. and EC competition authorities undertake together will have a significant impact on the global competition policy landscape.

U.S. and EC competition authorities have significantly expanded their formal and informal cooperation in recent years. The agreements discussed above are designed to facilitate bilateral cooperation on case matters of practical value to officials and affected parties. And they appear to be working quite well. As economic globalization continues to propel the United States and the EU down the path of greater economic interaction, antitrust cooperation whether it works well or badly is likely to leave the realm of the specialist and become a matter of more general interest and scrutiny.

Is the U.S.-EC experience in antitrust cooperation transferable to arrangements between other jurisdictions? Both EC and U.S. authorities are entering into similar, although in some cases less elaborated, arrangements with other countries (like U.S. arrangements with Israel, Japan, and others). Differences between these arrangements notwithstanding, this pattern or web of bilateral arrangements is a positive development. Unlike bilateral trade agreements, which can connote special arrangements with trade-distorting potential, bilateral antitrust arrangements seem unlikely to introduce economic distortions. As many experts note, they provide a means of building shared experience and confidence between authorities on matters that can be highly sensitive and that are usually seen as essentially domestic. As we

---

50. Indeed, the report argues that "while no agency should be obligated to take into consideration competitive harm or benefits that may be achieved outside the reviewing jurisdiction, competition authorities should consider that the transactions they review also have the potential to generate spillover effects in other jurisdictions." International Competition Policy Advisory Committee (2000, 81).

saw in the discussion of positive comity, antitrust enforcement is a matter of political concern as well.

I believe that bilateral cooperation arrangements should be looked upon as building blocks, not stumbling blocks, to broader antitrust and economic cooperation. As the United States (or the EC) enters into bilateral accords with other jurisdictions that have less experience with enforcement, fewer resources, less legitimacy within their own policy environments, or more limited experience with protection of confidential information, officials will have to tailor their bilateral arrangements accordingly. Yet bilateral arrangements cannot solve all problems of a competition policy nature. Small or underdeveloped economies may not be parties to bilateral antitrust agreements and thus may be unable to effectively address competition problems of a cross-border nature. Moreover, as this chapter suggests, a considerable range of anticompetitive or exclusionary private or governmental conduct can remain unaddressed even when bilateral accords are in place. Examples include discriminatory enforcement or—even more difficult to challenge—nonenforcement by government agencies; the use of antitrust measures to mask industrial policy objectives; and collaborations between governments and their domestic firms to exclude foreign products or participants.

These types of problems require the development of other building blocks, including initiatives by international organizations such as the OECD and the WTO. The OECD has been an effective forum for discussion among competition authorities and between competition and trade authorities. At the present time, the OECD has the greatest depth of analytical experience among international organizations on competition policy as well as competition-trade interface issues. The WTO has, since the Singapore ministerial, established a Working Group on the Interaction between Trade and Competition Policy, which has benefited from participation by a diverse group of countries. While I do not believe that the compelling next step for the WTO is the negotiation of a comprehensive multilateral competition policy agreement subject to dispute settlement, there is still much that can be done at the WTO, the OECD, and elsewhere to expand public awareness and cooperation on competition policy matters.

There is, for example, a considerable need (and in many countries a significant desire) for further institution building or capacity building in developing or transition environments. Recent years have seen the introduction of new competition laws and institutions around the world. For many countries, the introduction of competition laws or policies appears to reflect an interest in ensuring a greater role for market forces in the domestic economy. This is a direction of economic change that can prove beneficial not only to the liberalizing economy but also to its trading partners. Imagine how much could be accomplished if the United States and the EC, working together with host countries and perhaps with other international organizations, designed and implemented a collaborative work program on these capacity-building challenges for the twenty-first century!

References

American Bar Association. 1991. *Report of the Special Committee on International Antitrust.*

Atwood, James R. 1992. "Positive Comity: Is It a Positive Step?" *Fordham Corporate Law Institute* 4: 84.

Baer, William J. 1998. "Address." American Bar Association, Antitrust Section, April 2.

Baker, Donald I. 1998. "Merger Review in an Era of Escalating Cross-Border Transactions and Effects." Second Annual Competition Seminar, International Bar Association, Florence, October 2.

Devuyst, Youri. 1998. "The International Dimension of the EC's Antitrust Policy: Extending the Level Playing Field." *European Foreign Affairs Review* 3:467.

Hawk, Barry E., and Cynthia R. Lewis. 1997. "The Future of International Antitrust: The Twenty-First Century Belongs to the World of Cross-Border Mergers." In *Competition Law for the Twenty-First Century.* Juris Publishing.

International Competition Policy Advisory Committee. 2000. *Final Report.* Government Printing Office.

Klein, Joel. 1997. "Remarks." Twenty-Fourth Annual Conference on International Antitrust Law and Policy, Fordham Corporate Law Institute, October 16–17.

Kolasky, William J., and Leon B. Greenfield. 1998. "Merger Review in the EU and the U.S: Substantive Convergence and Procedural Dissonance." *Global Competition Review* (October-November): 22–25.

Melamed, A. Douglas. 1998. "Statement." Twenty-Fifth Annual Conference on International Antitrust Law and Policy, Fordham Corporate Law Insitute, October 22.

Pitofsky, Robert. 1998a. "Statement." Senate Judiciary Committee, Subcommittee on Antitrust, Business Rights, and Competition, October 2.

———. 1998b. "Statement." Annual Meeting of the American Bar Association, Toronto, August 4 (www.ftc.gov/speeches/pitofsky/canada.sp2.htm).

———. 1999. "Statement." Senate Judiciary Committee, Subcommittee on Antitrust, Business Rights, and Competition, May 4.

Starek, Robert. B. 1996. "Remarks." Illinois State Bar Association, May 10.

Steinberg, Andrew. 1998. Testimony before Senate Judiciary Committee, Subcommittee on Antitrust, Business Rights, and Competition, October 2.

U.S. Department of Justice–Federal Trade Commission. 1995. *Antitrust Enforcement Guidelines for International Operations.*

Valentine, Debra A. 1998. "Building a Cooperative Framework for Oversight in Mergers: The Answer to Extraterritorial Issues in Merger Review." *George Mason Law Review* 6:525.

56   MERIT E. JANOW

Waller, Spencer W. 1977. "The Internationalization of Antitrust Enforcement." *Boston University Law Review* 77:343–404.
Wambold, Ali. 1998. Testimony before the International Competition Policy Advisory Committee, November 3.
Whish, Richard, and Diane Wood. 1994. "Merger Cases in the Real World: A Study of Merger Control Procedures." Organization for Economic Cooperation and Development.
World Trade Organization. 1997. "U.S. Experience with Antitrust Cooperation Agreements." Submission from the United States to the Working Group on the Interaction between Trade and Competition Policy, November 24.

3

Economic Considerations in Merger Review

EDWARD M. GRAHAM

Merger review is an important, indeed arguably the most important, application of competition policy. Mergers and acquisitions are a very large force in the economies of both the United States and Europe, and competition law in both jurisdictions grants considerable authority to enforcement agencies to scrutinize and regulate this activity. Mergers and acquisitions are one of the prime means by which modern economies "restructure" themselves to adapt to new technologies and to changing circumstances that inevitably occur with the advancement of time. The decision of a competition authority to intervene or not to intervene in a merger and acquisition case can have lasting and important consequences for an economy.

At present, both the United States and Europe are in the midst of a boom in mergers. The level of merger activity has waxed and waned over the past one hundred years or so. In the United States there have been five periods when such activity has been frenetic: during the mid to late 1890s, the late 1920s, the late 1960s, the second half of the 1980s, and the second half of the 1990s.[1] Dur-

1. One might argue that the 1980s and 1990s booms have been in fact one prolonged phenomenon. However, there was a lull of several years between the two. Both booms spilled over into the following decade.

ing both of the latter two periods there were also booms in Europe, albeit the first such boom, during the 1980s, was more a British phenomenon than a continental European one. The 1990s boom, by contrast, has been a truly European one, with significant numbers of transactions taking place in Germany, France, and other continental countries. Even so, however, the United Kingdom remained the locus of a disproportionate share of European mergers.

The mergers and acquisition booms in the United States of the 1890s, 1920s, and 1960s had characteristics that set them apart from other booms. For instance, the 1890s boom witnessed the emergence of large trusts that created near monopolies in certain markets. Some analysts argue that the passage of the Sherman Act in 1890 helped to fuel this boom, because of its strong anticartel provisions. It was noted in the business press of the day that, by merging into a single firm, erstwhile rival firms then could undertake actions that would have been ruled illegal had the firms remained independent. Such sentiment may have motivated in part the "trust busting" prosecutions mounted by the U.S. Justice Department against the Standard Oil and tobacco trusts during the following decade (both of these resulted in the trusts being broken) and the unsuccessful effort to break apart the United States Steel Corporation.

The 1920s boom was characterized by consolidation of many firms operating in the public utilities sectors and saw the emergence of regional monopolies in the electric power and distribution sectors (for example, Consolidated Edison in New York) and the creation of a national telecommunications monopoly (American Telephone and Telegraph). Unlike in the aftermath of the 1890s, there was no effort to break apart the emergent monopolies. Rather, the authorities recognized that most of these mergers were driven by considerations of efficiency. Over the next decades, however, laws and governmental agencies were created to regulate these so-called natural monopolies. The 1960s boom witnessed a large number of conglomerate transactions, in which a number of firms selling in distinct and unrelated markets were combined into a single organization. With hindsight, these combinations often did not seem to make commercial sense, because they created neither market power nor organizational or operational efficiencies that might increase returns on investment. Indeed, many of these combinations were later undone by the market itself, rather than by competition authorities. In particular, during the early 1980s, "corporate raiders" took over numerous conglomerate firms and were able to make substantial profits by selling off individual business units, thus demonstrating that many of these conglomerates suffered from organizational inefficiencies.

The two most recent merger and acquisition booms are difficult to characterize as neatly as the earlier three. In recent times, merger and acquisition activity has extended across numerous industries, and the motivations for these transactions have varied from case to case. Attainment of efficiency within a defined market or sector has clearly been the motive for some transactions, whereas diversification has motivated other transactions.[2] It cannot be ruled out that achievement of market power motivated at least some transactions, albeit this issue is greatly complicated by the fact that a number of so-called horizontal mergers took place in declining sectors and, indeed, often in ones in which incumbent sellers face new competition from firms offering products embodying new technologies that have rendered older products obsolete. Unlike the earlier booms, the two most recent have witnessed a large number of cross-border transactions, including some of the largest. Indeed the largest announced merger to date is between a British firm and a German firm. Unusually, this particular transaction started as an effort at a hostile takeover of the German firm Mannesmann by the British firm Vodafone; in the end the two parties agreed to the merger.

What is the magnitude of the current boom? It is difficult to put exact figures on the value of transactions for a number of reasons, the most important of which is that no figures are publicly released for a significant number of transactions.[3] Also, for a minority of reported transactions, the figures are based on book values of the parties. Furthermore, neither the European Union nor the United States has implemented reporting requirements for statistical purposes for mergers and acquisitions, even though in both areas transactions meeting certain threshold requirements must be reported to the competition enforcement agencies (which are mandated not to reveal information collected in this manner). Nevertheless, the total market value of the assets involved in the current mergers and acquisitions boom is well into the trillions of U.S. dollars. Indeed, during the early part of the year 2000, two transactions have been reported with combined market values exceeding $160 billion.[4]

Private estimates of the total value and volume of mergers are indicated by the following figures: in 1999, the announced total was $3.4 trillion, com-

2. As was the case of conglomerate mergers during the 1960s, some mergers of the 1980s that were motivated by diversification have subsequently been undone by the market.

3. No figures are released in deals in which one of the parties is privately held or, more commonly, in which the transactions involve subsidiary firms held by one parent investor that are sold to another parent.

4. These were the mergers of America Online with Time Warner (U.S. firms), whose combined market value was about $160 billion; and of Vodafone (United Kingdom) with Mannesmann (Germany), whose combined market value was about $180 billion.

pared with $2.5 trillion in 1998.[5] In the United States, the number of deals in 1998 totaled 12,279, with a combined value of about $1.7 trillion. In 1999, the number of deals declined to 10,892, but the total value remained approximately $1.7 trillion, suggesting a larger average size of individual deal. In Europe, the value of deals in 1999 was estimated at $1.2 trillion, more than double the amount of the year before. More important, the number of cross-border deals increased. During the 1980s boom, for example, approximately 15 percent of the merger filings with U.S. authorities under the requirements of the Hart-Scott-Rodino Act—which typically affects only the largest 40 percent or so of transactions—involved a foreign acquiring or acquired firm. This percentage grew to more than 50 percent in 1997.[6] According to transatlantic merger estimates prepared by the private firm Linklaters and Alliance, in 1990–99 U.S. firms acquired European firms in 5,673 mergers, for a value of $273.4 billion; European firms acquired U.S. firms in 3,039 mergers, for a value of $552.3 billion.

Another indicator of the magnitude of the boom is fees paid to investment bankers, lawyers, and accountants who help put the mergers together. In both 1998 and 1999, the value of bonuses—that is, compensation in addition to regular salaries and fringe benefits—paid to such persons working in New York was well over $1 billion; indeed, in both years more than 1,000 individuals working on "The Street" received bonuses of $1 million or more. If nothing else, the arranging of mergers and acquisitions itself is very big business.

The Goals of Merger Review by Competition Policy Enforcement Agencies

As with other aspects of competition policy, the ultimate economic goal of merger review should be to enhance efficiency, in order that the value created by merger and acquisition activity be maximized given resource constraints.[7] Alas, however, there is no unequivocal general case to demonstrate whether mergers or acquisitions result in increased or diminished efficiency. A merger review must deal with a tension between the possibility that a merger or acquisition will enhance technical or organizational efficiency at

---

5. International Competition Policy Advisory Committee (2000).
6. International Competition Policy Advisory Committee (2000).
7. *Should be* is used in lieu of *is* because there is not a complete consensus on this matter; see below.

the level of the firm and the intrinsic fact that mergers and acquisitions typically reduce the number of sellers in a market, resulting in some degree of monopolization of that market and associated loss of allocative efficiency. In addition, of course, monopolistic pricing creates distributional concerns that result from transfer of consumer surplus from purchases to producers, either because these products themselves are monopolistically priced or because inputs are monopolistically priced.[8]

Somewhat surprisingly, only recently has a broad consensus emerged that the ultimate goal of competition policy is the enhancement of efficiency (or almost equivalently, the maximization of consumer welfare). Even now, this goal is not fully reflected in law. In the United States, for example, merger review was initially conducted as a means to prevent "incipient" monopoly, which is to say that the goal was to minimize or eliminate the distortions created by monopolistic pricing and output decisions.[9] Until the late 1970s, this was done pretty much without regard to whether these distortions might be offset by factors that would enhance efficiency and hence improve consumer welfare. Thus during the 1950s, 1960s, and 1970s, significant numbers of mergers in the United States were blocked in the name of preventing incipient monopoly.[10] This unwillingness to consider efficiency defenses, however, changed during the 1980s, when these enforcement agencies—the Federal Trade Commission and the Antitrust Division of the Department of Justice—upgraded their analytical techniques to recognize that mergers could create offsetting efficiencies.

In Europe, merger review was rather haphazard until passage of a merger regulation in 1989.[11] This regulation attempts to codify criteria under which a merged entity might be deemed to be in violation of Treaty of Rome article 82 strictures on "abuse of a dominant firm position."[12] Thus the regula-

---

8. If an input for some final good or service is monopolistically priced, the price of that final good or service must be raised above the level that would prevail if input markets were competitive, again resulting in lost consumer surplus, and this is true even if the market for the final good or service is itself competitive.

9. Although the basic U.S. antitrust laws date from the late nineteenth century (the Sherman Act) and the early twentieth century (the Clayton Act), and the latter act explicitly authorizes merger review, enforcement agencies did not begin systematic review of mergers until after World War II. The view that the goal of merger review was to prevent incipient monopoly was incorporated into U.S. policy under U.S. Assistant Attorney General Thurman Arnold. For a concise history of the economic rationale behind U.S. merger policy, see Scherer and Ross (1991).

10. Scherer and Ross (1991).

11. Council Regulation 4064/89.

12. The history and objectives of the EU merger regulation are provided in Neven, Nuttall, and Seabright (1993). Article 82 refers to the relevant article under the new numbering system.

tion seems, like pre-1980s U.S. policy, to be directed toward preventing incipient monopoly rather than toward enhancement of efficiency. However, the regulation does explicitly mention efficiency as one factor the authorities may take into account when making their determinations, but without giving any indication with respect to how this factor is to be considered against other factors. Thus it would seem that this balancing is left to the enforcement agency of the European Commission, the Directorate General IV (DGIV).

Related to the tension between monopoly and efficiency is another tension: that between dynamic efficiency, which determines the long-run rate of improvement in productivity, and static efficiency, the maximization of short-run output given a finite amount of resources.[13] This second tension largely derives from organizational complementarities that can give the merged entity greater capabilities to generate and implement new technologies than either premerged entity could achieve alone. Thus these capabilities can result in long-run efficiency gains, which would not be realized in the absence of the merger, even if little or no immediate efficiency gain were to be achieved. The implication is that authorities should in some instances be tolerant of mergers that create dynamic efficiencies even if these create static welfare losses due to increased market power.

Indeed, some Schumpeterian economists would argue that an element of monopoly is actually desirable in order to achieve these long-run dynamic gains. This is because some rents are necessary to give a firm an incentive to undertake costly research and development, the results of which are subject to both uncertainty and, if the undertaking is successful, appropriation by rival firms. In fact, research and development expenditures tend to be sunk costs: that is, they must be incurred before any return can be realized and, once incurred, are not recoverable. Because future returns are uncertain, there is a disincentive to undertake these investments, and this disincentive is magnified by the appropriation problem. Not only can rival firms imitate new technologies and hence appropriate at least some of the returns that might otherwise go to the innovator, these rivals might be able to do so without incurring all of the initial sunk costs. Market power can reduce the threat of appropriation of returns to research and development expenditures. Likewise, sheer scale might enable a firm to underwrite a portfolio of research and development activities that can reduce the risk of such under-

---

13. By standard duality theorems, maximization of output given a resource constraint is equivalent to minimization of use of resources to produce a given output objective. The latter is exactly maximization of static efficiency.

takings (because losses incurred from unsuccessful undertakings are compensated by high returns from successful undertakings).[14] Both of these considerations might argue for leniency in merger review.

However, there is considerable empirical evidence that monopolies or near monopolies are rarely innovators. A plausible reason that this is so is that monopolist sellers, or at least some subset of these, hold market positions that are virtually unassailable by rival firms. Further, the threat of a rival firm introducing new technologies that results in a loss of market share for the noninnovator provides a strong incentive for a firm in an industry characterized by rivalry to innovate.[15] Thus the case can be made that too much monopoly will suppress dynamic efficiency, not enhance it. In addition, it is equally true that sectors in which competition is highly fragmented often are not characterized by high rates of innovation. This might be because all rents from innovation are bid away, and hence there is no incentive for any firm to sink resources into research and development. However, other explanations have been advanced: in a fragmented sector no one firm might achieve the organizational scale necessary to undertake profitable research and development. Therefore it is difficult to say how much monopoly power is too much, especially given that some degree of market power is desirable, if the objective is to maximize innovation.

In sum, whether or not a merger will result in dynamic efficiencies is a difficult issue to address. At a theoretical level, there are arguments both for and against increases in market power creating more favorable conditions for dynamic efficiency. However, it is difficult to develop from these theoretical considerations operational tests to determine whether a particular merger will have a positive or negative effect on the realized rate of technological advance.

These considerations notwithstanding, in recent years in the United States and implicitly in the EU, merger and acquisition review has operated largely

14. But must this portfolio diversification effect require that these research undertakings be performed under one organizational roof? After all, investors looking for returns from new technologies can hold diversified portfolios of financial securities issued by separate firms undertaking different research and development projects and, in doing so, achieve the same benefits of diversification. It would thus seem that, for this diversification effect to be of benefit to investors, there must either be organizational or technical complementarities to be realized by having all such undertakings conducted within the same organization or that there exist financial market imperfections that create barriers to effective portfolio diversification.

15. In fact, neither theory nor empirical evidence supports the contention that monopolistic industries are more innovative than ones in which competition prevails. However, neither does the evidence support the opposite contention, that the more competitive an industry (in the sense of the larger the number of sellers in the relevant market), the more innovative. See Scherer and Ross (1991, chap. 17), for a review of the evidence.

under the premise that market concentration is in most circumstances a self-correcting distortion. In other words, it is largely held that, if monopoly rents are created by merger or acquisition, in the absence of greater efficiency of the merged enterprise, these rents will in most instances draw new entry into the market. This entry, in turn, will correct the inefficiencies created by market power held at the outset by the merged firm.[16] Thus based on this view, in both jurisdictions the thresholds for challenging a merger or acquisition on grounds that the merger creates a monopoly, or an incipient monopoly with unacceptably high probability of success, have been quite high. This is revealed in the fact that, as a percentage of the total number of such transactions, very few mergers or acquisitions have been challenged in either the United States or Europe.[17] Indeed, it is rather rare for a merger to be fully investigated, and most mergers that must be reported under thresholds established in Europe under its merger regulation or in the United States under the Hart-Scott-Rodino Act are cleared only after a preliminary investigation (and transactions that do not have to be reported are, for all practical purposes, never investigated at all).[18]

There have of course been cases in which transactions have been challenged by the authorities and, indeed, cases in which the authorities on opposite sides of the Atlantic have reached opposite conclusions with respect to whether a particular merger or acquisition should be challenged. The differences in these cases have, at least in part, been due to differences in the way authorities on the two sides of the Atlantic view efficiency defenses. U.S. doctrine in particular seems to be, in most circumstances, de facto quite tolerant of an efficiency defense for a merger that has the potential to in-

16. However, the U.S. Justice Department case against Microsoft demonstrates that U.S. authorities are not wholly unconcerned about monopolization of a market, and the preliminary ruling by the judge in this case suggests that there are circumstances in which U.S. courts will require remedial action in the face of such monopolization.

17. Some observers however see the recent challenge by the U.S. Federal Trade Commission of the proposed takeover of Atlantic Richfield (ARCO) by British Petroleum–Amoco as marking the end of the era of leniency in U.S. merger review. The FTC's reason for the challenge is that the combined firms will control virtually all of the Alaskan oil fields and thus possibly enable monopoly pricing on the U.S. West Coast. Private analysts have already concluded that such pricing is unlikely given that the local market for crude oil could be economically supplied from non-Alaskan sources of crude oil and thus that the challenge brings back the old concerns of incipient monopoly in a market defined overly narrowly, as evidenced in U.S. merger review before the 1980s. However, at the time of this writing, the full dimensions of this case had yet to reveal themselves, and a rush to pronounce the significance of this case would appear to be premature.

18. Both the thresholds for reporting and the specifics of the information that must be provided if the threshold is reached differ greatly between Europe and the United States, a matter of considerable consternation to firms that must meet the requirements.

crease market power, while European doctrine is more ambiguous toward such a defense.[19] But these differences have been comparatively rare, and most transactions considered by both sets of authorities have been allowed to proceed with little or no modification.[20]

Despite the fact that most mergers are cleared in both jurisdictions, at a formal level the procedures used to determine whether to allow an efficiency defense in the United States and the EU are quite different (for details, see chapter 4, this volume).[21] In Europe the DGIV Mergers Task Force holds a certain amount of discretionary authority to decide whether a particular merger poses problems for competition. In contrast, U.S. authorities have in recent years attempted to make their procedures more explicit and to indicate when considerations involving efficiency can override concerns about

19. The most conspicuous of these was the merger between Boeing and McDonnell Douglas, which was cleared in the United States but subjected to intense scrutiny in Europe. In the end, the merger was cleared by the EU after conditions were imposed on the merged firms to end certain practices deemed to constitute anticompetitive vertical restraints. In the United States, these same practices had been cleared on grounds that they were efficiency enhancing. It has been suggested in the business press that DGIV was in favor of blocking the merger altogether but that it relented in the face of pressure from political levels not to create what might have been a major transatlantic row over the merger.

One factor that the American authorities were prepared to consider in this case that European authorities apparently were not was what has been termed a flailing firm defense. U.S. authorities took into account the likelihood that McDonnell Douglas, as an independent seller of large passenger aircraft, would never be a robust rival to Boeing or Airbus, even if McDonnell Douglas were to survive in this market. Thus to these authorities potential efficiencies resulting from the merger outweighed any additional market power that would have accrued to Boeing. European officials, by contrast, sought undertakings to end vertical restraints (noted above), apparently as an offset to this potential additional market power.

An earlier case in which there was disagreement across the Atlantic also involved Boeing: a proposed sale of a subsidiary, de Haviland, to the French-Italian firm Aérospatiale Alenia was blocked by the EU after being cleared by both U.S. and Canadian authorities. Again, efficiency considerations entered into the case. In particular, EU authorities were concerned that the merger would create a firm with a "dominant" position in commuter aircraft, with no offsetting efficiencies. North American authorities were apparently prepared to accept an efficiency defense (see Addy 1991).

20. Thus for example authorities on both sides of the Atlantic reviewed the WorldCom-MCI merger and reached similar conclusions, allowing both authorities to clear the merger.

21. James Venit and William Kolasky in fact note three specific instances in which U.S. and EU merger review procedures are convergent. The first is the acceptance in Europe of a doctrine similar to that of the United States regarding market dominance via oligopolistic collusion; ceteris paribus, U.S. doctrine argues against certain mergers that could lead to a small group of firms dominating a market. The second is the acceptance in Europe of something like the U.S. failing firm defense, whereby a merger of two firms is allowed if one of these otherwise would most likely exit the market, even if the merger leads to a situation in which the combined entity might dominate (monopolize) the market. The third is the definition of a market. The EU has moved toward use of price cross-elasticity as a means of determining whether two products should be deemed to be in the same or different markets.

monopoly. Thus the 1997 U.S. merger guidelines emphasize that such a defense rests on three criteria. The efficiency must be

—Specific to the merger or acquisition (that is, would not be realized in the absence of the merger)

—Tractable, or cognizable (that is, can be recognized and measured)

—Sufficient (that is, must result in greater consumer surplus than that which is lost due to market monopolization).

In the EU, by contrast, in spite of some recent cases revealing an apparent willingness of DGIV to accept an efficiency defense, the official attitude toward this defense is ambivalent. James Venit and William Kolasky (chapter 4) argue that, to their knowledge, the commission has never taken an efficiency defense into explicit account "as the basis for approving a merger it would not otherwise have approved." Indeed, they argue that in some instances the very fact that a combined firm might realize an efficiency that would give the firm greater dominance (and hence, under European doctrine, a greater potential to abuse a dominant position in the market) has led the commission to challenge a particular transaction.[22] To the extent that this is true, European authorities would seem to believe that harm to competitors, as well as harm to consumers, is a valid criterion for establishing abuse of a dominant firm position.

Nonetheless, the EU Commission has, since enactment of the merger regulation, de facto taken a rather tolerant view toward most mergers.[23] In 1998, for example, DGIV received 235 merger notifications pursuant to the 1989 merger regulation. As noted earlier, this regulation establishes thresholds for mandatory merger notification to the commission, and thus the 235 notifications represent all mergers or acquisitions that fall above these thresholds. There were also 238 decisions by DGIV on cases involving the regulation's main provisions.[24] Only two decisions blocked mergers follow-

22. If Venit and Kolasky are correct, it would follow that the leniency revealed by the EU in clearing mergers and acquisitions (see below) is based on quite high thresholds for establishing potential for abuse of a dominant position. However, it is also possible that European policy toward an efficiency defense is de facto more tolerant than the formal merger review procedures would suggest.

23. But might there be a similar nascent tendency in Europe toward closer scrutiny of mergers, as some observers believe is happening in the United States? DGIV is, at the time of this writing, examining the proposed merger of Swedish truck makers Volvo and Scania, and press reports indicate that the authorities are indeed worried about the possibility of a local monopoly in certain national truck and bus markets. Several articles suggest that DGIV will require both divestitures of certain assets held by Volvo and undertakings to end some exclusive dealing relationships between the producers and their distributors as conditions for clearing the merger.

24. Kemp (1999).

ing detailed phase 2 investigations. Nine decisions required or accepted merging firms' undertakings to remedy possible competition problems under phase 1 investigations.[25] Twelve cases were taken to full-blown phase 2 investigations, suggesting that potential competition problems had been identified. Seven cases already under phase 2 investigations were cleared, and in five of these cases undertakings were required to remedy identified competition problems.[26] Counting the 7 phase 2 investigations in which the merger either was prohibited or was cleared with undertakings required, and adding the eight phase 1 decisions requiring undertakings, only 15 of 235 notified transactions, or less than 7 percent, were identified as posing problems for competition.[27] And of course only 2 cases were actually blocked—less than 1 percent of all cases notified—which in turn are only a fraction of all transactions. Indeed, in the ten years since the merger regulation has been in existence, only 11 mergers in total have been blocked.

However, there is some evidence that European policy toward mergers is becoming less lenient. During 1999, for example, the fraction of mergers notified to DGIV that were subject to phase 2 investigations increased to 20 percent, up from well under 10 percent two years earlier. And as already noted, the commission reportedly is considering blocking one very visible merger, between Scandinavian truck makers Scania and Volvo.[28]

Another factor that potentially could change European mergers policy is the rise of subsidiarity in the application of competition policy. Since publication in early 1999 of a competition policy white paper by DGIV, it has become known that the European commissioner in charge of this policy, Mario Monti, will seek a greater role for national and regional authorities (that is, greater subsidiarity) in the application and enforcement of European competition law.[29] Although specific proposals thus far have been limited to the areas of state aid and cartels policy, there could be a push for greater subsidiarity in merger review if for no other reason than to ease caseloads on the DGIV Mergers Task Force. Monti's reason for seeking greater

25. That is, changes in business structure or practice, including in some cases divestiture of certain operations.

26. Nine decisions were thus rendered in phase 2 cases, including, however, some decisions on cases that had been notified during the previous year. Thus of the twelve cases taken to a phase 2 investigation in 1998, resolution of a number of these was still pending in 1999.

27. Only quite large transactions must be notified to DGIV. The vast majority of mergers and acquisitions in Europe fall below the thresholds for notification. Thus what these figures reveal is that in 1998 EU authorities identified problems with competition in 7 percent of all sizable transactions, not 7 percent of all transactions.

28. See "Monti Shows His Tough Streak," *Financial Times*, March 6, 2000.

29. Commission of the European Union (1999).

subsidiarity in the enforcement of European competition law stems from the observation in the white paper that national and local officials might often be better placed to spot, evaluate, and remedy anticompetitive practices than a centralized agency in Brussels.

Whatever the merit of this proposal, it has been subject to a lot of critical comment. Most criticism has been that, because enforcement of competition law necessarily has a discretionary component, decentralized enforcement of competition policy could lead to divergent and even contradictory outcomes. At the extreme, a practice ruled legal in one state might be ruled illegal in another, even if the underlying law is the same. But even short of this, interpretations of law could vary widely across jurisdictions.

As noted, the merger regulation itself already embodies the concept of subsidiarity, because only those mergers that meet certain threshold tests qualify for EU-level review to begin. Although there has been no change yet, a number of proposals have been put forth to raise the thresholds so as to reduce the number of mergers reviewed at EU-level. But even without a formal change in policy, there has been a trend in recent years for the commission to encourage review even of certain mergers and transactions that do meet threshold tests at the national level. One worry that has been expressed is that national review of mergers and acquisitions could lead to blockages of cross-border transactions for nationalistic reasons.[30]

This all leads to the following potential dilemma for merger review authorities. Let us make the following convention. If competition authorities in any jurisdiction allow a merger or acquisition to pass review without objection or challenge, but the result is that the combined entity does in fact have enough market power to diminish consumer surplus, we shall say that the authorities have made a "type 1 error." Under this nomenclature, the goal of prevention of incipient monopoly, or of prevention of abuse of a dominant firm position, is to prevent a type 1 error. On the other hand, if authorities block such a transaction, in which the combined entities would have realized sufficient efficiencies that would have increased long-run consumer surplus, we shall say that these authorities have made a "type 2 er-

---

30. For example, following the Vodafone launch of its hostile takeover bid for Mannesmann, there were calls in Germany for new legislative safeguards to protect incumbent firms from such takeovers. In France, the January 2000 decision to block the takeover of the local soft drink producer Orangina by Coca-Cola was seen by some observers as motivated by nationalistic concerns. However, French officials, in announcing the decision, noted that the combined firms would have had a dominant position in soft drink distribution that might have enabled them to foreclose any new entry. Thus some commentators have concluded that the decision was taken for sound reasons of protection of competition in this market.

ror."[31] Given these conventions, the potential dilemma is as follows: whenever authorities act to block or to impose conditions on a merger or acquisition, they run a risk of a type 2 error. But whenever they allow such a transaction to be completed without imposing any condition, they run the risk of a type 1 error.

Can an Optimal Regulation of Mergers Be Achieved?

The taxonomy of errors suggests that an optimum degree of merger control could be achieved under certain conditions. In principle, if total social costs associated with type 1 errors decrease monotonically as regulation of mergers becomes more stringent but, also, total social costs associated with type 2 errors increase monotonically, then there is a level of stringency at which total social costs associated with both types of errors are minimized.

However, determining exactly what this level would be is at best a difficult empirical exercise. One reason for difficulty in determining the optimal level of merger control is that, as discussed, it is difficult to determine whether or not a merger likely will result in efficiency gains or increases in market power. In practice, with respect to the former, regulators tend to rely on information and projections regarding possible efficiency gains supplied by the firms themselves and to judge whether this adds up to a credible story. With respect to the latter, the current emphasis is to try to determine whether, as a result of the merger, the combined firms would be able to raise prices in an uncontested manner. Although by all accounts the techniques for making this determination have become highly sophisticated, at the end of the day this analysis comes down to an informed judgment.

Is there a better way for determining whether or not a merger is likely to create rents or efficiencies? One indicator in principle is a change in the total value of the shareholders of the firms that are parties to the merger. In an efficient equity market, if a merger generates an increase in the total shareholder value of the combined firms, one can assume that this reflects a change in the expected value of future earnings.[32] In such an efficient market, if a

31. Also classed as a type 2 error will be a merger that is challenged but subsequently allowed under restrictive conditions, when these conditions have the effect of reducing net long-run consumer surplus over what would have been realized in the absence of those conditions.

32. The word *efficient* is now used in the sense as understood by financial economists, which differs somewhat from the sense as used earlier. A financial market is termed efficient if new information affecting the value of a financial security is quickly transmitted to all actors in the market and if the market itself is competitive such that rents that might accrue to a

combined firm is able to earn rents because of monopoly power that neither of the parties to the merger could achieve in the absence of the merger, one would expect that the shareholder value of the combined firm exceeds the sum of the shareholder values of the separate, unmerged firms. This additional shareholder value results from the nearly perfectly competitive nature of the stock market, whereby, adjusting for risk, returns are equalized across all securities.[33]

The higher shareholder value will not, however, necessarily be realized immediately. Rather, it will be realized some time between the date when the merger is announced ("new information") and the date when the merger is realized. The reason that the full increase in shareholder value might not be realized until this latter time is that investors might be uncertain whether the merger will in fact proceed to completion. Merger review itself can, of course, add to that uncertainty.

Thus stock market data can shed insight on whether or not mergers will create rents. But alas, exactly the same reasoning can be applied to efficiency gains, where we now revert to the earlier meaning of *efficiency*. If these gains, for example, were to reduce the combined firm's total costs but not affect revenues, the firm's profits would increase. Thus again, in order to equalize risk-adjusted returns on securities, the shareholder value of the combined firm must increase.

A further theoretical point is warranted: if the market for corporate control is competitive, most of the shareholder gain from a merger would fall on the shareholders of the target firm and not those of the bidding firm.[34] This is because excess returns to the acquiring firm would be bid away. The market for corporate control might, of course, not be competitive. For ex-

---

particular security are quickly bid away. The result of much analysis of the behavior of stock markets is that such markets do seem to be quite efficient, or at least this is true for the largest markets (such as the New York Stock Exchange, the NASDAQ, the London Stock Exchange, and the major European bourses).

33. This equalization occurs because, holding risk constant, an investor should not be able to achieve a higher expected return on any one security than on any other. If such a higher expected return could be achieved, the investor could increase his or her claim to expected future earnings simply by selling the lower expected return securities and buying the higher expected return ones. Also, the arrival of any new information that would cause the investor to reevaluate the expected return on any security or set of securities would trigger such an action. But the action itself would tend to bid down the price of the low-return security or bid up the price of the high-return security, until the returns were again equalized. Adjustments must be made, of course, for changes in the financial structure of the enterprise, including issuance of long-term debt to finance the merger and changes in total number of shares outstanding due to stock swaps and so on.

34. See Weston, Chung, and Siu (1998, chap. 5).

ample, if two firms were the only sellers in a market for a particular good or service and if potential rents were to be gained by merger of these two firms to form a monopoly, then each firm is the only bidder for the other, and in this case the market for corporate control is noncompetitive.[35] Even so, the expectation is that the shareholders of the target firm in a merger will receive greater value from a merger than shareholders of the bidding firm.

In sum, stock market data can be utilized to determine whether or not a merger creates expected rents or efficiencies. Unfortunately, these data cannot easily separate the one from the other. Put another way, although stock market data can yield information on whether or not a merger creates additional shareholder value, this information is not sufficient to enable regulators to determine the source of the increase. Nor is this information sufficient to enable an overall judgment as to whether the current wave of mergers is, on net, creating welfare-enhancing efficiencies or welfare-subtracting monopolization of markets.

Empirical Studies of the Economic Consequences of Mergers

A 1983 survey of thirteen empirical studies on whether mergers increase shareholder value concludes that on average the target firm's shareholders register significant gains whereas the bidder's shareholders typically do not lose.[36] Thus most mergers in fact increase total shareholder value, and most of the increased value is indeed realized by the target firm's shareholders, as theory would predict. Such studies, of course, do not include those transactions that occurred during the merger booms of the 1980s and 1990s. However, a number of later studies tend to confirm these earlier findings.[37] It is also the case that, even if most mergers and acquisitions that have been studied have increased total shareholder value, by no means all mergers have this effect. For example, in a relatively recent study of 330 transactions, 76 per-

---

35. The market for corporate control, a financial market, is not the same as the market that the two firms would monopolize. Also, the statement that each is the only bidder for the other assumes, of course, that there is no bidder from an unrelated industry that would seek to merge with either firm.

36. Jensen and Ruback (1983).

37. Weston, Chung, and Siu (1998) in fact state that "there is no doubt that the returns to target shareholders are positive." But they indicate that "it is less clear whether or not the excess returns to shareholders of bidder firms are positive." They also note that the evidence would suggest that returns to target firms have generally increased over recent decades, while returns to bidder firms have decreased.

cent of the sample resulted in increased total shareholder value.[38] This implies, of course, that 24 percent did not.

Another study suggests that, consistent with remarks made in the beginning of this chapter, conglomerate mergers are especially unlikely to create total shareholder value increases.[39] This study reports that in 260 pure U.S. stock-for-stock mergers during the period 1963–96 there were "significant net synergistic gains" in nonconglomerate mergers (that is, security holder wealth, including that of bondholders, did increase) but that "insignificant net synergistic gains" were found for conglomerate mergers. In the latter case, the shareholders of the bidding conglomerate firms tended to lose, whereas other security holders at least broke even. These findings suggest that nonconglomerate mergers do tend to increase shareholder value but that conglomerate mergers do not (or at least not to a statistically significant degree) and that, in the latter case, it is the shareholders of the bidding conglomerate who lose. This makes sense, in that a conglomerate merger (the merging of two firms whose businesses are unrelated) would expect to create neither market power nor efficiency.[40]

The use of the term *synergistic* would seem to imply that the gains result from efficiencies, not increased market power. However, the source of increases in shareholder value was not addressed. Do such increases reflect the creation of undesirable rents or of desirable efficiencies? In particular, do shareholders benefit because merger review has produced type 1 errors, such that anticompetitive mergers are being cleared too easily? Or does increased shareholder value indeed generally reflect enhanced efficiency, such that any tightening of policy would result in type 2 errors, which result in reduced welfare to society? Alas, further search of the empirical literature does not provide a conclusive answer to this last question. Some studies do look at this issue from several perspectives, but their results are not conclusive, and much of the work is now quite dated.

For example, a study published in 1976 examined stock price movements of firms that were defendants in antimerger complaints in the United States before 1973, when the regulation of mergers in the United States was enforced zealously. This study finds that, following the filing of a complaint, the residual return on stock prices of the defendant became negative—but

---

38. Berkovitch and Narayanan (1993).

39. Maquiera, Megginson, and Nail (1998).

40. However, Ravenscraft and Scherer (1987) find that conglomerate mergers do create high returns for shareholders of the bidding conglomerate firms for those shareholders who invested in the conglomerates early on. Thus returns to shareholders in these firms were highly skewed.

only slightly.[41] The explanation for these negative residuals is, apparently, that rivals of the merged firm were engaging in harassment tactics and that the negative residuals represented market assessments of the positive probability that such tactics would succeed—and not that the merger review stripped away rents.[42]

Two prominent studies look at the effects of merger announcements and merger blockages in the United States on the residuals both of the merged firms' stock prices and those of rival firms' stock prices.[43] The studies examine the hypothesis that, if a merger were to increase rents because increased seller concentration facilitated collusion, then both merged firms and their rivals would benefit. R. S. Stillman finds no evidence that merger announcements create positive residuals for firms that are rivals to merged firms, whereas B. E. Eckbo does find positive residuals. However, Eckbo also finds that rivals are not subject to negative residuals if and when it appears that a merger will be blocked. If a merger of two competing firms were to create rents for rival firms that remain independent, then blockage of the merger obviously should nullify those rents, and so these results do not appear consistent.

A study of postmerger performance of firms involved in the fifty largest U.S. mergers between 1979 and 1984 finds some evidence of efficiency gains.[44] On several measures the merged firm outperformed (or at least performed differently from) the average firm in the merged firm's industry. For example, the merged firm reduced employment faster than the industry, suggesting that following the merger there was significant corporate restructuring. Although the cash flow margin on the merged firm's sales was not significantly different than for the industry, returns on assets were higher. These two findings suggest that improved performance came primarily through better asset management rather than through reduction of employment expense (because such a reduction should have created higher margins on sales, which were not found). Significantly, this study shows that positive residuals associated with merger announcement events correlate positively

---

41. See Ellert (1976). The residual is the difference between a predicted normal return that would have prevailed had there been no "event" affecting the stock price movement (in this case, the event is the filing of the complaint) and the return actually realized. There are several accepted methods for calculating a normal return, all based on historic (pre-event) data, but they yield in most cases similar results. See Weston, Chung, and Siu (1998, chap. 5, app. A).

42. Ellert (1976) bases this conclusion on the small size of the residuals. However, the presence of the residuals is also consistent with the hypothesis that rents were generated.

43. Eckbo (1981); Stillman (1983).

44. Healy, Palepu, and Ruback (1992).

with improved performance following the merger, suggesting that markets do effectively evaluate whether a merger will lead to improved performance.

The finding suggesting that mergers do create efficiency gains appears at first to be inconsistent with other studies that find that shareholders of merged firms subsequently lose asset value.[45] However, it is possible to reconcile these different findings if the merger activity being studied takes place predominately in poorly performing industries.[46] More recent evidence suggests that postmerger returns are affected by mode of acquisition.[47] Shareholders of firms acquired during 1970–89 who received stock tended to earn residuals that were not significantly different from zero during the five-year period following acquisition. In contrast, those who received cash earned a positive residual (consistent, of course, with the finding reported earlier that target shareholders receive most of the benefits of a merger or acquisition). Also, total shareholder return would seem to be higher for the transactions for cash than for the transactions for stock.

The Agrawal, Jaffe, and Mandelker finding appears consistent with other findings that the targets of hostile takeovers during the 1980s (all of them on the Fortune 500 list of the largest U.S. corporations) had low Tobin Q ratios (ratio of market value of assets to replacement value) and, furthermore, so did their industries.[48] The latter implies that the stock market took a particularly dim view of the prospects of these takeover targets. Also arguing against mergers creating efficiency is a study of the effect of mergers in the United States on shareholder value during the period 1980–88 (when antitrust enforcement was, in their term, "relaxed") that compares results with those recorded during the period 1948–79. They find no evidence that the mergers in the more recent time period were "more strategic" or greater "value creators" than in earlier time.[49]

---

45. Agrawal, Jaffe, and Mandelker (1992), in a study based on a large sample size, conclude that after certain adjustments are made shareholders of merged firms lose on average 10 percent of their asset value during the five years following a merger. Magenheim and Mueller (1988) find a similar result for mergers of the late 1970s and early 1980s.

46. Weston, Chung, and Siu (1998) make this observation. This follows because Healy, Palepu, and Ruback (1992) report that industry-adjusted performance of merged firms is positive, whereas Agrawal, Jaffe, and Mandelker (1992) report that performance relative to the economy of merged firms is negative. However, the samples on which the two studies are based are not the same, and whether the Healy, Palepu, and Ruback result would obtain for the larger sample used by Agrawal, Jaffe, and Mandelker is unknown.

47. Loughran and Vijh (1997).

48. See Morck, Shleifer, and Vishny (1988) for a study of thirty-one such firms.

49. See Lubatkin, Srinivasan, and Merchant (1997). Their results mirror those of Ravenscraft and Scherer (1987), which were based on an evaluation of nearly 6,000 mergers in the United States consummated between 1950 and 1976. Using various measures, they found the

This last conclusion suggests that earlier merger review in the United States did not create inordinate type 2 errors. If it had, increases in shareholder value would have been more pronounced in the later period than in the earlier one. At the same time, this conclusion and others reviewed here do not suggest that current merger review is guilty of excessive type 1 errors, or shareholder value increases from mergers would themselves have increased in current times.

In sum, the empirical literature on the rent-versus-efficiency issue remains largely unsettled. Indeed, what is striking is that studies based on share price responses to mergers and those based on postmerger performance tend, in the aggregate, to come to opposite conclusions, the former supporting the case for efficiency and the latter generally not. Exactly why this should be is not clear. It could result from a certain amount of euphoria on the part of markets with respect to mergers, which is not wholly justified by the underlying economics. To the extent that this is true, one might place more credibility on postmerger studies as indicative of whether or not efficiencies generally result from mergers. However, a problem in this regard is that postmerger studies tend to be more dated than share price response studies. Indeed, the most definitive of the former covers only pre-1967 mergers and, as noted, the 1960s boom in mergers was characterized by conglomerate mergers, many of which were later discredited.[50] Thus it is not clear that the conclusions regarding efficiency implications of mergers during this period are valid for the recent merger booms.

The very fact that merger and acquisition activity has been so robust in recent years serves, all by itself, as a beacon for further research. For example, serious attention needs to be paid to the issue of whether the current surge of transactions qualitatively differs from earlier surges, as a reading of the daily financial press suggests might be the case. Indeed, certain differences are quite apparent. The current surge extends far beyond the English-speaking world, for example, whereas the 1980s surge was largely confined to the United States and the United Kingdom (or at least the target firms were largely headquartered in these areas), and the 1960s surge was largely confined to the United States. Worldwide, the institutional and regulatory

---

postmerger performance of firms generally to be quite disappointing (but with "occasional successes"). Their evidence suggests that, in fact, inefficiencies might result when smaller firms are absorbed by bigger firms. Similarly dim overall conclusions are drawn from studies of the European experience of the 1970s (Mueller 1980) and the United Kingdom (Meeks 1977). Mueller (1985) published findings from the United Kingdom that generally are consistent with the Ravenscraft and Scherer (1987) results.

50. Ravenscraft and Scherer (1987).

framework in which mergers and acquisitions take place has changed since the earlier surge periods. Finally, the current surge seems to involve more cross-border mergers, and more megamergers, than in earlier periods. Future research on the current surge needs to focus less on whether these mergers create shareholder value (although this issue remains of importance, again to determine whether there is a major difference between current activity and that of earlier periods) and more on the sources of any enhanced shareholder value.

Should Merger Review Change?

The regulation of mergers should focus solely on how mergers and acquisitions affect competition and efficiency. As stressed repeatedly, the criterion as to whether competition is harmed by a particular transaction can rest on whether the transaction creates a net efficiency gain or loss. Alas, the empirical studies do not reveal as conclusively as one might hope whether or not this is the case. In particular, recent merger activity has not been subject to the level of empirical inquiry that the volume of this activity would seem to warrant. In the end, whether or not a change in policy by merger review authorities is warranted largely rests on the results of such inquiry. In particular, it would be rash to suggest at this point that merger review needs tightening, although there does seem to be some slight trend in this direction.

One thing that is clear in spite of this last point is that divergence in both substantive standards and procedures among national and regional authorities can lead to increased costs for firms trying to comply with the requirements of these authorities. This point is stressed in the *Final Report* of the International Competition Policy Advisory Committee (ICPAC), which calls for increased cross-border cooperation among competition enforcement agencies in the area of merger review, including

—Greater transparency through, for example, publication of merger review guidelines (as is done in the United States but not in Europe)

—The adoption of work-sharing arrangements among enforcement agencies, whereby in most cases remedial steps taken by the agency in the jurisdiction having the greatest interest in a particular merger will be deemed sufficient to satisfy competition problems in all jurisdictions having an interest in the transaction

—The creation of protocols by enforcement agencies indicating how these agencies will act to cooperate with other agencies, including creation of waivers whereby officials will be permitted to engage in discussions or share information with other officials that otherwise would be statutorily prohibited.[51]

Whether or not the problem of overlapping jurisdictions and the resulting possibility of inconsistent (and perhaps unsound) outcomes will be solved by the measures recommended by the ICPAC remains to be seen. It has been noted in the legal press that the ICPAC report identifies the potential problems created by international proliferation of competition law but that it is timid in terms of proposed solutions.[52] What is clear is that the jurisdictional conflict is greatest between the United States and the EU, the locus of the vast majority of current merger activity, including cross-border transactions. The ability of authorities on both sides of the Atlantic to resolve conflicts that occur because of overlapping jurisdiction will thus be a prime test of whether current procedures require reform.

References

Addy, George N. 1991. "International Coordination of Competition Policies." Speech, October 9.

Agrawal, Anup, Jeffrey E. Jaffe, and Gershon N. Mandelker. 1992. "The Post-Merger Performance of Acquiring Firms: A Re-examination of an Anomaly." *Journal of Finance* 47 (September): 1605–21.

Berkovitch, Elazar, and M. P. Narayanan. 1993. "Motives for Takeovers: An Empirical Investigation." *Journal of Financial and Quantitative Analysis* 28 (September): 347–62.

Eckbo, B. E. 1981. "Examining the Anti-Competitive Significance of Larger Horizontal Mergers." Ph.D. diss., University of Rochester.

Ellert, J. C. 1976. "Mergers, Antitrust Law Enforcement, and Stockholder Returns." *Journal of Finance* 31 (May): 715–32.

Commission of the European Union. 1999. *Livre Blanc sur la Modernisation des Règles d'Application des Articles 81 et 82 du Traité.* Brussels.

Healy, Paul M., Krishna G. Palepu, and Richard S. Ruback. 1992. "Does Corporate Performance Improve after Mergers?" *Journal of Financial Economics* 31 (April): 135–75.

International Competition Policy Advisory Committee. 2000. *Final Report.* Government Printing Office.

Jensen, Michael C., and R. S. Ruback. 1983. "The Market for Corporate Control: The Scientific Evidence." *Journal of Financial Economics* 11 (April): 5–50.

Kemp, John. 1999. "Mergers: Applications of Council Regulation 4064/89." *Competition Policy Newsletter.* February. Commission of the European Community.

---

51. International Competition Policy Advisory Committee (2000).

52. See for example Mark A. Warner, "Thin ICPAC: Report on International Antitrust Enforcement Doesn't Dare Enough." Legaltimes.Com (www5.law.com.de-shl/display.cfm?id=2978 [April 3, 2000]).

Loughran, Tim, and Anand Vijh. 1997. "Do Long-Term Shareholders Benefit from Corporate Acquisitions?" *Journal of Finance* 52 (December): 1765–90.

Lubatkin, Michael, Narasimhan Srinivasan, and Hemant Merchant. 1997. "Merger Strategies and Shareholder Values during Times of Relaxed Antitrust Enforcement: The Case of Large Mergers during the 1980s." *Journal of Management* 23 (1): 61–84.

Magenheim, Ellen B., and Dennis C. Mueller. 1988. "Are Acquiring-Firm Shareholders Better Off after an Acquisition?" In *Knights, Raiders, and Targets: The Impact of Hostile Takeovers*, edited by John C. Coffee, Louis Lowenstein, and Susan Rose-Ackerman. Oxford University Press.

Maquiera, Carlos P., William L. Megginson, and Lance Nail. 1998. "Wealth Creation versus Wealth Redistributions in Pure Stock-for-Stock Mergers." *Journal of Financial Economics* 48 (April): 3–33.

Meeks, Geoffrey. 1977. *Disappointing Marriage: A Study of the Gains from Merger.* Cambridge University Press.

Morck, Randall, Andrei Shleifer, and Robert W. Vishny. 1988. "Characteristics of Targets of Hostile and Friendly Takeovers." In *Corporate Takeovers: Causes and Consequences*, edited by Alan J. Auerbach. University of Chicago Press.

Mueller, Dennis C., ed. 1980. *The Determinants and Effects of Mergers.* Cambridge, Mass.: Oelegeschlager, Gunn, and Hain.

Mueller, Dennis C. 1985. "Mergers and Market Share." *Review of Economics and Statistics* 67 (May): 259–67.

Neven, Damien, Robin Nuttall, and Paul Seabright. 1993. *Merger in Daylight: The Economics and Politics of European Merger Control.* London: Centre for Economic Policy and Research.

Ravenscraft, David J., and F. M. Scherer. 1987. *Mergers, Sell-Offs, and Economic Efficiency.* Brookings.

Scherer, F. M., and David Ross. 1991. *Industrial Market Structure and Economic Performance.* 3d ed. Houghton Mifflin.

Stillman, R. S. 1983. "Examining Antitrust Policy towards Horizontal Mergers." *Journal of Financial Economics* 7 (April): 225–40.

Weston, J. Fred, Kwang S. Chung, and Juan A. Siu. 1998. *Takeovers, Restructuring, and Corporate Finance.* 2d ed. Saddle River, N.J.: Prentice Hall.

4

Substantive Convergence and Procedural Dissonance in Merger Review

JAMES S. VENIT AND
WILLIAM J. KOLASKY

As the integration of the global economy continues, the number of major merger transactions with multijurisdictional dimensions has also increased. The growth of mergers with multinational dimensions has given practitioners considerable opportunity to compare the procedural and substantive features of the systems of merger control in effect in the United States and the European Union and has also posed new challenges both for antitrust regulators and practitioners. The experiences of private counsel in cases that have been reviewed in both jurisdictions has led to considerable reflection about the comparative advantages and disadvantages of the two systems of merger control. It also led to an initiative launched by Joel Klein, the U.S. assistant attorney general for antitrust, to appoint an International Competition Policy Advisory Committee (ICPAC) to study, among other things, how the United States might better coordinate its merger clearance process with that of other jurisdictions, especially the European Community. Two of the principal issues covered by the final ICPAC

The authors would like to thank Leon B. Greenfield and Jayant V. Prabhu for their invaluable assistance in the preparation of this chapter.

report are the need for, or desirability of, procedural harmonization and substantive alignment.

Although there are still several important areas in which significant differences remain, in general it is fair to say that the substantive standards applied by EC and U.S. antitrust agencies for reviewing horizontal mergers are increasingly converging. However, as has become clear in some cases, even where the substantive standards are close, there can be appreciable differences in the assessment of factual and economic issues and, therefore, in outcome. The Boeing–McDonnell Douglas is the most famous (or infamous) instance, but in the nonmerger area there has also been a substantial difference concerning the appropriate antitrust remedies applicable to at least one major transatlantic airline alliance—Lufthansa-United-SAS—which suggests that, even where the technical approach to market definition or other antitrust issues is similar, different policy objectives may lead regulators to very different results.[1] Such cases suggest that substantive harmonization, which is generally thought to be an unattainable Holy Grail, may not be the central issue. Indeed, a strong argument can be made that substantive harmonization already exists to a large extent but that agreement over the nuts and bolts of antitrust analysis, while a necessary element of reaching uniform results, is not sufficient to guarantee a uniform outcome because of fundamental policy-based differences in the assessment of commonly accepted facts and principles of antitrust economics.

Significant procedural differences between the two systems continue to have an important impact on the practical outcome of cases. Some of these result from differences in timing; others result from the resources available to the agencies, the way they allocate them, and the differences in the legal tools at their disposal for challenging mergers. While there appears to be a growing consensus among U.S.-based practitioners who have handled mergers in both jurisdictions that the EU merger clearance process has some ad-

---

1. The Lufthansa-United alliance was granted antitrust immunity by the Department of Transportation in 1996, subject to one major condition, a "carve out," which excluded cooperation between the parties in respect of capacity and fares on the two hub-to-hub routes, Chicago to Frankfurt and Washington to Frankfurt. Underlying the remedy was a recognition of the overall consumer benefits of airline alliances but a concern that the alliance might be able to raise prices in respect to time-sensitive nonstop passengers on two routes linking the alliance partners' respective hubs. Faced with exactly the same facts, the European Commission published a notice in July 1998 (OJ n. C239-5 of July 30, 1998) announcing its intention to require reductions on the two hub-to-hub routes in order to encourage entry; major slot surrenders on a large number of routes, again to facilitate entry; and measures designed to limit the use of frequent flyer plans, corporate discounts, and travel agency incentives as marketing tools.

vantages over the U.S. system, European practitioners have been critical of the procedures employed under the EU's Merger Regulation 4064-89 and believe that there are elements of the U.S. system that might well improve the EU model.[2]

Substantive Convergence

The divergent positions taken in 1997 by the European Commission and the U.S. Federal Trade Commission toward the Boeing–McDonnell Douglas merger caused many to question whether EU and U.S. antitrust agencies share common substantive standards or whether the authorities bring substantially different notions to mergers touching both sides of the Atlantic. Although, as well illustrated by the *Boeing–McDonnell Douglas* case, the European Commission and the U.S. agencies may reach different conclusions in a particular case, the substantive criteria applied by both authorities are very similar. Two developments in the EU have contributed to this convergence: the judgment of the European Court of Justice in *Kali und Salz* in March 1998, which established that the EU merger regulation applies to coordinated effects ("oligopolistic dominance," in EU parlance); and the European Commission's 1997 notice on the definition of relevant market.

Single-Firm and Oligopolistic Dominance

The most fundamental way in which EU and U.S. merger standards have converged is their increasing agreement concerning single-firm dominance and oligopolistic coordination. In *Kali und Salz*, the European Court of Justice endorsed the EC's power to challenge mergers on the basis of coordinated effects, thus embracing the concern about oligopolistic coordination that has traditionally been a major focus of U.S. merger review. Conversely, U.S. agencies have moved significantly in the EU's direction by placing increased emphasis on single-firm dominance, which has been the principal focus of EU merger review.

Kali und Salz resolved the long-standing uncertainty as to whether the EU merger regulation applies to oligopolistic dominance. Just as important, the Court of Justice also required that the commission apply a nuanced,

---

2. Council Regulation 4064-89 of December 21, 1989, on the control of concentration between undertakings, amended by Council Regulation 1310-97 of June 30, 1997 (OJ 1997 n. L 180/1).

multifaceted microeconomic analysis to determine the potential for coordinated behavior in the market under review, thereby rejecting reliance on a laundry list of factors that could, in theory and under certain circumstances, lead to coordinated effects.[3] Although the commission's decision had looked beyond mere concentration levels and considered several structural market characteristics, the Court of Justice rejected the commission's somewhat superficial economic analysis, finding that other microeconomic factors, which the commission had failed to consider—most important, the substantial postmerger asymmetries between the allegedly jointly dominant companies—indicated that postconsolidation collusion was in fact unlikely.

The agency checklist for cases in which coordinated effects may be suspected is not appreciably different. In the *Degussa-DuPont* case, U.S. authorities identified the following factors, which gave rise to a risk of coordinated effects in respect to the market for hydrogen peroxide:[4]

—Reduction of the number of North American producers from seven to six and increase in the Herfindahl-Hirschman index by 500 points, to over 2,500

—Homogeneous product, purchased largely on the basis of price

—Reliable pricing information available to producers due to use of delivered pricing, advance announcement of price increases, and meet-or-release clauses in customer contracts

—A history of past collusion

—The ability of producers to maintain large differentials among different end uses, indicating an ability to coordinate and an absence of arbitrage.

In past cases, the commission's checklist has been similar:

—A limited number of participants in a stagnant, "mature" market

3. In its judgment in *Kali und Salz* of March 31, 1998 (cases 68-94 and 30-95, ECR 1998 p.I-1375, OJ 1998 C 209-2), the European Court of Justice also endorsed the commission's version of the"failing company defense," which is similar to the eponymous U.S. doctrine. The commission had applied the defense to permit consolidation in Germany, even though the merger would create a dominant firm there. Under its version of the defense, the commission may approve a concentration it would otherwise disapprove if three conditions are met: the acquired company would in the near future be forced out of the market if not taken over by another company; the acquiring company would, in any event, gain the market share of the acquired company if the acquired company were forced out of the market; and there are no less anticompetitive solutions than the concentration. This formulation is similar to, but more rigorous than, the U.S. version of the defense. Significantly, U.S. agencies do not require that the acquiring firm would have obtained the market share of the acquired company in any event. It remains to be seen, however, whether the commission will apply that requirement in all cases.

4. Decision *Degussa Corp.–DuPont* issued by the FTC on June 10, 1998 (Docket N.C-3813).

—A standardized, commoditylike product or a product based on standard-ized inputs or some other factor yielding similar transport cost structures

—Pricing transparency

—Substantial barriers to entry

—Inelasticity of demand and inability of the oligopolists to shift produc-tion to other products.

As noted above, in its judgment in *Kali und Salz*, the Court of Justice rejected an analysis based on the first three of these factors and also rejected allegations of links between Kali und Salz and Société Commerciale des Potasses et de L'Azote (SCPA), the two largest remaining players in the mar-ket. Rather, the court found that a causal link between Kali und Salz's and SCPA's membership in a previous cartel and the likelihood of anticompetitive behavior in the relevant market had not been established and, furthermore, that distribution links between them involved a different product. Most important, the court concluded that a combined market share of 60 per-cent, with the merged Kali und Salz–MdK having 23 percent and SCPA 37 percent, could not by itself establish the existence of a collective dominant position. Noting that it was necessary to demonstrate to a sufficient legal standard that Kali und Salz and its merger partner, Mitteldeutsche Kulz AG (MdK), and SCPA would be able to act independently of its competitors, suppliers, and customers, the court concluded that the commission's analy-sis failed to satisfy the requisite legal standard because the substantial asym-metries between Kali und Salz and SCPA argued against the likelihood of collusion.[5]

The Court of Justice's insistence on exacting economic analysis in *Kali und Salz* is consistent with the approach of U.S. agencies. Since the Supreme Court's *General Dynamics* decision in 1975 the FTC and the Department of Justice have moved away from a purely structural approach, which relied primarily on market concentration, toward a more rigorous, qualitative ap-

5. In reaching this conclusion, the court cited the following factors. First, although MdK had only a 7 percent market share in the EC apart from Germany, it was the second-biggest potash producer in the community after Kali und Salz and was using only 50 percent of its production capacity. As a result, the addition of MdK would greatly increase the industrial capacity of Kali und Salz, with that company and MdK accounting for 60 percent of total potash production in the EC (35 percent for Kali und Salz and 25 percent for MdK), whereas SCPA accounts for only 20 percent of EC production. Second, there would also be significant asymmetries between the alleged members of the oligopoly in terms of financial resources in that Kali und Salz is a subsidiary of BASF, a leading fertilizer processor, with considerably greater economic power than EMC, the parent company of SCPA. The court found that these factors, coupled with a declining market and competitive pressure from third-country im-ports, meant that the "static" elements relied on by the commission in its decision did not support a conclusive finding of joint dominance.

proach, taking into account all the relevant market characteristics that an economist would consider in determining the likelihood of collusion.

Product Market Definition

A second critical area in which EU and U.S. standards are converging is market definition. The commission's notice on market definition adopts a pragmatic approach to the task of market definition in competition law cases, recognizing that the goal of this exercise is to determine the likelihood that any given structural transaction will enable the merged entity to raise prices to anticompetitive levels.[6] In particular, the notice expressly adopts the SSNIP test that U.S. agencies have long used to define product markets. Under the SSNIP test, two products are deemed to be in the same market if a hypothetical nontransient 5–10 percent increase for product A would cause sufficient numbers of customers to switch to product B to make the price increase unprofitable for the supplier of product A. Although the commission has in the past (in *Nestlé-Perrier* for example) defined markets by examining demand response to price changes, it has often focused on more subjective factors like product characteristics and intended use.[7] The commission's adoption of the SSNIP test signals a clear move toward the U.S.'s more rigorous economic test for product market definition.

The commission's notice on market definition also makes clear that, to determine likely consumer responses to price changes, it will evaluate the same kinds of empirical evidence that U.S. agencies use. This evidence includes historical data about customer responses to significant price changes, econometric studies (including data concerning cross-elasticities of demand among different products), surveys, and other information revealing the views of competitors and consumers about the boundaries of the market and likely responses to price changes.

Notwithstanding these broad areas of agreement, there are some significant substantive differences between the substantive approaches of U.S. and EU agencies. The first and most important of these concerns the treatment of efficiencies. A second important difference, which is partly procedural, derives from the adversarial nature of EU proceedings; the commission's role as prosecutor, judge, and jury; and the consequent significance of the role played by third-party complainants (competitors) in EU merger review proceedings.

6. OJ 1997 n. C 372/5 of 9-12-1997.
7. Commission decision of 22.7.92 n.IV/ M100 (O.J. 1992 n. L 356/1). SSNIP means "small but significant and nontransitory increase in price."

Efficiencies

One key substantive area in which U.S. agencies and the European Commission still appear to diverge is in their treatment of efficiencies. In 1997 the U.S. agencies substantially revised the section of their merger guidelines dealing with efficiencies, intending to integrate efficiencies more fully into their analyses of the likely competitive effects of mergers.[8] Under the revised guidelines, the agencies take into account efficiencies that are *merger specific*, in that they are unlikely to be realized absent the merger; *cognizable*, in that they are measurable, verifiable, and do not arise from anticompetitive restrictions of output or service; and *sufficient* enough to reverse the merger's potential to harm consumers in the relevant market by, for example, preventing price increases in that market.

In contrast, the commission's attitude toward efficiencies is highly ambivalent. The text of the merger regulation suggests that there may well be an efficiency defense, and it certainly does not suggest that efficiencies are irrelevant to the assessment of a merger.[9] Nevertheless, to our knowledge the commission has never explicitly taken efficiencies into account as the basis for approving a merger it would not otherwise have approved; indeed, at times the commission has come close to suggesting that the possibility that a merger may make a firm with a leading position more efficient is itself a reason for challenging the transaction. As a result, some practitioners in EU merger cases have been reluctant to argue that a merger will give rise to significant efficiencies because of concern that the enhanced ability of the merged entity to compete more efficiently than its rivals may be interpreted as a sign of dominance. The more skeptical approach to efficiencies on the part of the commission may be traceable to a number of uniquely European cultural factors vis-à-vis the United States:

—A greater distrust of bigness, which has its origins in concerns about the potentially negative influence that large concentrations of economic power can have on democratic institutions

—Less thorough internalization of the consumer welfare model, under which the sole focus is on whether a merger is likely to restrict output or increase price

—A distrust of synergies due to concerns about unemployment

8. "Horizontal Merger Guidelines," issued by the U.S. Department of Justice and the Federal Trade Commission, April 2, 1992, revised April 8, 1997.

9. Article 2(1)(b) of the merger regulation requires the commission to consider whether a concentration will result in "the development of technical and economic progress provided that it is to consumers' advantage and does not form an obstacle to competition."

—A greater willingness to manipulate the industrial structure, which may have its roots in greater state economic involvement in Europe

—A tendency to equate preserving effective competition with preserving competitors.

While these factors may help explain the commission's reluctance to embrace efficiencies, they leave open the question of whether that reluctance is justified. Since the achievement of efficiencies has arguably been the motor driving many transnational mergers in the 1990s, it is likely that the status of efficiencies in European merger review will be tested with increasing frequency in the future.

The Treatment of Joint Venture Cases

Compared to the European Commission, the U.S. authorities do provide a truly one-stop review of joint ventures, in that when the agencies clear a joint venture they do so with respect to the entirety of the parties' arrangements. In the EU the situation is considerably more complex and less satisfactory. Under the merger regulation adopted in 1989, only full-function joint ventures that did not give rise to a risk of coordination between the parents were treated as mergers. This situation proved highly unsatisfactory both analytically and in practice, since it required drawing economically meaningless distinctions and resulted in the application of very different procedural and substantive approaches to what were essentially structural transactions. Pursuant to amendments to the merger regulation that went into effect in March 1998, the commission now treats all full-function joint ventures under the merger regulation; it still distinguishes between concentrative joint ventures, to which only the market power standards of the regulation apply, and cooperative joint ventures, which in addition are judged under what may amount to the standards of article 85 in respect to their cooperative aspects.

While this approach does resolve the procedural unfairness of treating structural transaction under very different timetables (a rigid one for mergers and an open-ended one for cooperative joint ventures), it has not eliminated the analytic incoherence of applying different standards to the same transaction.[10] Although there is no clear precedent yet in favor of such an approach, it cannot be excluded that, under the EU system, the "structural"

10. As discussed below, a similar problem arises out of the commission's analysis of ancillary restraints, which in theory may provide the commission with a backdoor way of disapproving or limiting the approval of certain of the contractual aspects of a concentration that has been approved.

aspects of a joint venture will be examined under a market power test, while the "cooperative" aspects will be examined under a test that falls into an undefined zone somewhere below the market power threshold.[11] In addition, continuing uncertainty as to what is meant by "ancillary restraints," which are cleared in the context of merger review, has given rise to further uncertainty concerning the scope of merger authorizations and the legal standards applied thereto.[12]

The Role of Competitors in the Review Process

Another very important difference between the U.S. and EU approaches is the far greater importance attached to competitors by the European Commission during the course of its merger investigations. While this difference is as much procedural as substantive, we discuss it in this section since, like the commission's approach to efficiencies, it is related to the commission's tendency to view competition law issues from the perspective of competitors and not solely from the perspective of consumers.

Both U.S. and EU agencies normally attach considerably greater weight to the reactions of customers than to those of competitors. However, although in certain cases (*WorldCom-MCI* being the most dramatic recent example) the Justice Department has paid great attention to competitors' claims, the commission as a general matter attaches greater weight to competitors' claims than do its U.S. counterparts.[13] The importance of the role played by competitors in the EU process is increased by two factors: the commission's shortage of highly trained staff and particularly of skilled antitrust economists; and the adversarial nature of EU procedures, including

11. The court's judgment in *Kali und Salz* does suggest that the market power test should also apply to the coordination analysis under article 2(4).

12. Ancillary restrictions are defined as "restrictions on the parties to a concentration that limit their freedom of action in the market" and that are "directly related and necessary to the implementation of the concentration" and "subordinate in importance to the main object of the concentration." Notice on ancillary restrictions (OJ C 203/5, 1990).The notice states that ancillary restrictions do not include "contractual arrangements which are among the elements constituting the concentration, such as those establishing economic unity between previously independent parties or organizing the joint control by two undertakings of another undertaking." This study suggests that contractual arrangements concerning the creation and operation of a joint venture are inherent in the concentration and thus are *not* subject to separate review. However, the language of the notice, and the examples cited therein, are less than clear. As a result, there has been a tendency for notifying parties to seek clearance as ancillary restrictions for contractual arrangements that are arguably integral to the concentration.

13. Notified to the commission on February 3, 1998 (OJ 1998 n. C 44/8. of Feb. 10, 1998); see n.17.

the pivotal role played by the oral hearing, in which the notifying parties are confronted not merely by the commission's challenges to its transaction but more important by the challenges (and the rebuttals of the notifying parties' defenses) presented by competitors. The organization of the hearing—in which competitors are normally given the better part of a full day to attack the proposed merger, *after* the notifying parties have made their defense to the commission's statement of objections—and the fact that the oral hearing serves as a kind of "trial by combat" of the commission's assessment before a very important body of nonpublic opinion (member state experts and representatives of other services of the commission) magnify the role of competitors far beyond anything in the U.S. system.

Procedural Dissonance

Although substantive standards are converging, there remain fundamental differences in the procedures under which the EU and the U.S. agencies review mergers. Some of these differences result from the different deadlines applicable in U.S. and EU regulatory procedures. Others result from the differences in how the two agencies allocate their scarce investigative resources. Still others can be traced to the fact that the European Commission has the direct power to prohibit or require the substantial modification of a notified transaction by adopting a decision that can then be appealed to the courts. In contrast, U.S. antitrust agencies must sue the merging parties in federal court to prevent a merger they oppose. This latter factor, combined with the time limits imposed on the commission and the need to respect the procedural rights of the notifying parties (and to a lesser extent, competitors), has given rise to a highly structured, transparent, but adversarial proceeding.

This proceeding, once it enters the four-month phase 2 inquiry, becomes hostage to increasingly adversarial procedural milestones: the issuance of the commission's statement of objections, the notifying parties' reply, the confrontational oral hearing, consultation with the member states, and the adoption of a final decision. Such adversarial procedures make the merger review process more transparent than it is in the United States but also considerably more formal and adversarial. We review below the principal procedural differences between U.S. and EU procedures.

Triggering Event, Notification Deadline

In the EU, notification is mandatory within seven days of the first of the following to occur: the signature of an agreement creating a concentration, the announcement of a public bid, or the acquisition of control by one firm over another. Thus in contrast to the United States, where a memorandum of understanding may be notified and where notification is a prerequisite only to closing the transaction but not a legal requirement in itself, the EU merger regulation makes prior notification within a seven-day period itself a legal requirement, whose neglect can result in the imposition of fines. Given the commission's generous approach to extending the notification deadline and its encouragement of extensive prenotification contacts, the legal, seven-day filing requirement has not had substantial practical effects and does not necessarily impose any serious harm to attempts by notifying parties to coordinate the review process.

That being said, many EU practitioners would prefer the system that exists in the United States and, inter alia, Germany, under which clearance is a prerequisite to implementation of the concentration but notification is not itself subject to a legal deadline. Because many mergers, and particularly the largest ones, are kept highly secret during the negotiation stages (which makes it impossible to gather the detailed market information required for an EU notification), the seven-day filing deadline is not realistic or meaningful in many cases. Since the need to gain approval before implementation achieves the legitimate regulatory interest of ensuring that concentrations are not implemented before being reviewed, and since there is probably a virtue in having law and reality coincide, there would appear to be little basis for not modifying the EU system to eliminate the seven-day filing deadline. However, it is unlikely that the EU will drop the seven-day filing requirement; rather, it will more likely continue its practice of taking a flexible and pragmatic approach to the deadline in order to encourage the extensive prenotification contacts that normally characterize the EC merger review process.

Review Thresholds

Thresholds for reporting transactions to the EU are much higher and arguably more appropriate than in the United States, where with certain limited exceptions parties are required to file premerger notifications with both the FTC and the Justice Department for all acquisitions of over $15 million in assets or voting securities. That reporting threshold has remained unchanged since 1976, when Congress established the premerger notification requirement. As a result, although Congress intended to require reporting of only a small number of large transactions, both agencies now review all but the smallest acquisitions. (Based on stock market valuations, a $15 million acquisition in 1976 would be the equivalent of about a $125 million transaction today.) Thus parties bear the burden of reporting—and the agencies must expend tremendous resources reviewing—thousands of transactions a year that are in very small product or geographic markets and that could not possibly pose significant anticompetitive concerns at a national level. As the state attorneys general have become more active in antitrust enforcement, there would appear to be little reason for the federal authorities to review small mergers that have, at most, local consequences.

By contrast, the thresholds for reporting in the EU capture only those acquisitions large enough to justify the burdens imposed on the parties and the commission. Smaller transactions are, of course, often subject to review by antitrust authorities in the individual EU member states.[14] The commission thus sensibly focuses its energies on investigating only those transactions that are large enough potentially to raise significant competition concerns in the EU. In addition, if a transaction is reportable at the EU level, the commission's review preempts review at the national level: individual member states must content themselves with participating in the commission's review process absent a referral by the commission. Many practitioners now believe that the U.S. system would benefit from following the EU model. At present, even when a transaction is reviewed and cleared at the national level by the Justice Department or the FTC, it may still be challenged by any state attorney general under federal as well as state law. Federal preemption, as in the EU model, would prevent mergers being held hostage by individual states (which often act out of parochial political concerns), while still giving the individual states input into the decision at the federal level.

Level of Information Required for the Initial Filing

Low U.S. thresholds are offset by the fact that an initial Hart-Scott-Rodino (HSR) filing requires very little information, including none on market

14. According to article 1(2) of the merger regulation, a concentration is deemed to have EC dimension if any of two sets of turnover thresholds are met. One set requires that the combined worldwide turnover of all the undertakings concerned is more than ECU 5 billion and that the aggregate communitywide turnover of each of at least two of the undertakings concerned is more than ECU 250 million, unless each of the undertakings concerned achieves more than two-thirds of its aggregate communitywide turnover within one and the same member state. The second set requires that the combined worldwide turnover of the parties is ECU 2.5 billion; the parties have a combined aggregate turnover of more than ECU 100 million in each of these member states, with each party having an individual turnover exceeding ECU 25 million in each of these member states; and the aggregate communitywide turnover of each of at least two parties exceeds ECU 100 million.

shares. The dearth of information required in the United States puts a high burden on regulators to spot problematic transactions and has also given rise to what is known as the "file and pray" approach, under which applicants simply provide the bare-bones information required for an HSR filing and then hope that the agency will not take any greater interest in the transaction. While it is unlikely that any significant, well-publicized transaction will slip through the net, there have probably been more than a few cases in which major problems have gone unnoticed, either because the affected market was not known to the agency staff or because the transaction had not been publicized or was too small to attract attention on its own.

In contrast, the EU filing requires, it is said, as much information as a second request under HSR. Strictly speaking, this is not quite true, since the scope of a second request in the United States may vary considerably and, as discussed below, is frequently overly broad and burdensome because it is used by the agency to gain additional time for the review process. However, it is clear to EU practitioners that the commission's form CO can be unnecessarily burdensome with respect to transactions that may involve affected markets but still do not raise substantial competition law concerns. There may be much to be said for eliminating some of the information required in form CO and focusing instead on requiring information on market shares, competitors, customers and suppliers, and recent market entry.[15] The provision of this essential information should be sufficient to ensure that a problematic transaction will not slip through the net, provided the relevant market has been correctly defined.

It would appear that efficiency might be better served if the United States raised its thresholds and if the initial filing required more information than is currently the case (although less than is required by the European Commission on its form CO). And for Europe, resources would be more rationally allocated by excluding much of the narrative from sections 7 and 8 of form CO, requiring instead only market-share data for affected markets, lists of customers, competitors, and suppliers, and a discussion of barriers to entry or recent entry. Further inquiries concerning the role played by research and development, the distribution chain, cooperative agreements, trade associations, and so on could be reserved for phase 2 or second-re-

15. Form CO (section 6) defines affected markets as the relevant product markets in which two or more parties to the concentration are engaged in business activities in the same product market and in which the concentration will lead to a combined market share of 15 percent or more (horizontal relationship); and in which one or more of the parties to the concentration are engaged in business activities in a product market upstream or downstream of a product market in which any other party to the concentration is engaged and any of their individual or combined market share is 25 percent or more (vertical relationships).

quest investigations. Nevertheless, there may be some resistance to paring back form CO, given the tighter EU deadlines and given the fact that some of the information that goes beyond the categories outlined above—such as member state pricing information and information about the way distribution is organized—is relevant to geographic market definition (a major issue in the EU).

The commission clearly should eliminate the need for extensive information about transactions that are wholly unproblematical (either because they have no effects in the EU, or there are no horizontal overlaps or vertical relationships, or such overlaps or relationships are too small to give rise to competition law concerns). According to the head of the Merger Task Force, the commission is considering, in connection with its review of the merger regulation (which must have been submitted to the Council of Ministers in July 2000), a reform of the notification system to address these issues. This reform may include the adoption of a bare-bones notification form (or perhaps a block exemption eliminating the notification requirement for transactions that fulfill certain stipulated conditions); it may even dispense with the need for the commission to adopt decisions in cases judged incapable of raising meaningful competition law issues.

Regulatory Burden

Although initial notification requirements in the EU are quite burdensome in contrast to those in the United States, the EU's merger review process is often more transparent than the U.S. process because of the formality of EU procedures and the need to protect the rights of the defense. This latter requirement forces the commission to make its substantive assessment known to the parties both when the commission opens a phase 2 inquiry and then when it issues its statement of objections some six to ten weeks into the phase 2 proceeding. These requirements tend to narrow the competition issues early in the process, allowing the parties to focus their efforts on the specific areas of concern identified by the commission. However, the formal and frequently adversarial nature of the proceedings can also significantly inhibit the dialogue between the parties and the commission staff, and there is a tendency for the staff to assume an almost prosecutorial attitude toward the notifying parties once a phase 2 investigation has been opened. Moreover, while some noteworthy phase 2 cases have been either dropped or settled without the issuance of a statement of objections, such cases are rare.[16]

16. In its decision of May 20, 1998, *Price Waterhouse–Coopers and Lybrand* (case 4-M.1016, OJ L50-27 of 26-2-99), the commission found no conclusive proof that the merger would

In contrast, U.S. agencies are not required to explain the grounds for their concern at any time during an investigation. Thus although parties are sometimes able to learn the staff's concerns through informal discussions, they often must shape their response to the investigation with little or no direction from the agency. This approach can lead to considerable and unnecessary burden and expense. On the other hand, the less formal nature of these proceedings means that the review process is less driven by formal, procedural milestones, thus permitting more dispassionate evaluation of factual and economic issues.

Time Limits for Review

In contrast to the open-ended nature of U.S. proceedings, merger review in the EU is governed by a very strict timetable; the four- or six-week phase 1 review and the four-month phase 2 are fixed by statute. Although these periods can be extended—by a finding that the original notification was incomplete, or by voluntary withdrawal, or by the failure to provide a complete response to a request for information or a material change—these have been relatively infrequent occurrences, and to date the commission has not systematically made agressive use of the absence of complete answers to its requests for information on material changes to create a pretext for stopping the clock.[17]

---

create or strengthen a dominant position in any of the markets in which these firms were active. In the merger between British Telecommunications and MCI(II), the undertakings proposed by the parties during the proceedings were considered sufficient to satisfy the commission's original concern that the merger would have created a dominant position in the markets for international telephony (commission decision of May 14, 1997, case 4-M.856, OJ L 336-1, 12-8-97). In the AT&T-BT case, the commitments by AT&T to divest some assets in the United Kingdom also cleared the way for the joint venture to be approved without issuance of a statement of objections (commission press release, March 30, 1999, IP-99-209).

17. An example of incomplete notification is the merger between WorldCom and MCI Communications, which first notified on November 20, 1997, and renotified on February 3, 1998. In the case Kali und Salz (4-M308), following the judgment of the Court of Justice annulling the commission decision, the parties were required to submit additional information for a new examination of the concentration (notice 98-C190-03). Regarding parties withdrawing notification of a concentration to avoid an in-depth investigation by the commission, see Total-Petrofina, in which the parties voluntarily withdrew the original notification of December 18, 1998. The parties renotified the concentration on February 11, 1999 (case 4-M1464, 1999-C 47-03). Failure to respond is covered in article 9(1) (information) and article 4(3) (material change) of regulation 4064/89. The review period can in effect be extended under a number of scenarios. Two of these involve incompleteness of the notification, the material changes in the facts of which the notifying parties were or ought to have been aware. In addition, deadlines can be suspended when either information is not provided in response to an article 11 request for information or the notifying parties fail to inform the commission of material changes of the facts contained in their notification.

By contrast, the method used by U.S. agencies to compute the time they have to investigate a merger can also needlessly burden the parties and impose unwarranted expense. Unlike the commission—which subject to the exceptions for incompleteness or material change noted above has a definite four-month period to complete a phase 2 investigation—U.S. agencies must complete their detailed review of a merger within twenty days following the parties'"substantial compliance"with a second request for information. This unrealistically short review period gives the agencies a strong incentive to issue unnecessarily broad and burdensome second requests to ensure that substantial compliance will take long enough for the agency to complete a thorough review. Indeed, compliance with a second request can take many months, produce hundreds of boxes of documents (few of which are ever read), and cost more than a million dollars to review, collect, and file. From the perspective of companies and practitioners, a procedure like the EU's, under which the agencies have a defined—and adequate—period to investigate mergers, seems preferable. Although the adversarial, procedure-driven nature of EU proceedings also has its unattractive side, greater formalization of the U.S. review procedure may be less of a problem since the U.S. agencies can stop a merger only by bringing suit in federal court.

Phase 1 Undertakings

One significant reform introduced in the EU is the six-week phase 1 proceeding, which is designed to enable the commission and the notifying parties to resolve difficult cases (and to avoid lengthy and costly phase 2 proceedings) by agreeing to undertakings (normally in the form of divestitures) during an extended phase 1 examination.[18] Thus although this procedure can work only when the notifying parties and the commission quickly agree on both the substantive competition law problems and the appropriate remedies, and although there is a risk that the commission will impose stricter remedies than would have been the case had there been a thorough investigation (the opposite risk may also exist), the number of cases attests to the popularity of this innovation.

For the reasons discussed above, it is unlikely that such a system would be translatable to U.S. proceedings absent amendments requiring the parties to identify relevant markets and provide market-share information in their initial HSR filing. However, if such an amendment were adopted, cost considerations could make such a procedure attractive as a means of avoiding a

18. Articles 6(2) and 10(1) of the merger regulation.

full-blown investigation, provided that notifying parties are willing to accept strict remedies.

Transparency, Role of Complainants

As noted, complainants tend to play a far more important role in merger clearance in the EU than in the United States. In addition, the fact that the European Commission acts as both prosecutor and judge has given rise to a system more laden than the U.S. system with devices designed to protect the rights of the notifying parties, but these also increase the transparency of the review process for both the notifying parties and their opponents. The principal features of the EU system are

—The right of the notifying parties to have access to the file, to an oral hearing, to receive a copy of the formal decision opening phase 2 proceedings, and to receive the statement of objections setting forth the basis on which the commission is challenging the concentration

—The practice of providing interested parties (that is, competitors) with redacted versions of the statement of objections and the notifying parties' response thereto, allowing them to participate in the notifying parties' oral hearing.

As the foregoing discussion indicates, an EC merger review, although it is not public (neither the commission's decision to open phase 2 proceedings nor the statement of objections is published on any public docket, and the oral hearing is not open to the public at large), is a considerably less private affair than its U.S. counterpart. However, this is unlikely to change as long as the roles of the EU and U.S. agencies continue to be as different as they currently are.

The Availability of Precedent

While many practitioners have criticized the potential for abuse given the European Commission's dual role as prosecutor and judge, at least before judicial appeal, the EU's system does have the virtue of requiring the commission to provide reasoned decisions setting forth the basis on which it has cleared or challenged mergers. As a result, parties considering a concentration (and counsel advising them) have access to a much richer body of precedent in the EU than in the United States. Indeed, in the course of adjudicating merger cases, the commission has developed a copious volume of written decisions. Although, given the importance of economic facts, precedent in merger cases may not always be a reliable guide to the likely outcome, precedent is valuable for issues such as market definition, type of evidence regarded as probative, and the factors relied on by the agency in its analysis.

In contrast to the commission practices, the U.S. agencies do not adjudicate merger cases. Rather, the purpose of their investigation is to determine whether to challenge the consolidation in court. In practice, however, the time, expense, and uncertainty associated with litigating merger cases in U.S. courts means that few cases are actually litigated. The great majority of proposed mergers to which the agencies object either are abandoned or are modified through settlements between the parties and the agencies. Thus although merger cases are (in theory) determined by the judiciary, the courts actually decide very few cases.[19] This sparse precedent gives little guidance to parties contemplating a merger.[20]

Burden of Proof, Power to Oppose

U.S. and EU merger procedures differ significantly in that, whereas the European Commission has the power to adopt a decision prohibiting a merger (which can then be appealed), the U.S. authorities have to go to court and convince a federal judge to issue an order doing so. While this difference may not always be crucial given the infrequency with which merging parties challenge a commission decision and the deterrent effect of a Justice Department or FTC threat to initiate suit, it is fair to say that the commission's dual role as prosecutor and judge puts it in a stronger position than that of the U.S. agencies. This factor, coupled with a perhaps greater predilection to intervention on the part of EU authorities and the other substantive differences noted above—notably the importance attached to competitors' input in the merger review process and a lack of warmth toward efficiency defenses—suggests that the commission, more than its U.S. counterparts, may incline to a more interventionist approach.

19. In the period 1993–98, U.S courts have issued fewer than twenty published decisions on substantive merger issues, and all but a few of those were from trial courts. The U.S. Supreme Court has not decided a substantive merger case since 1975.

20. When a U.S. agency objects to a proposed merger, it publishes a statement of the reasons underlying its decision. But those statements, which generally include only limited analysis, are not binding on the agency in future cases and are not reviewable by the courts. Thus they are poor substitutes for judicial opinions and are of only limited value in determining how the agencies are likely to evaluate future mergers. In addition, there are no written decisions when the agencies decide not to challenge a transaction, even where the agencies and the parties have spent months exhaustively reviewing the merger's likely effect on competition.

Conclusion

Although, subject to certain nontrivial differences, the substantive standards the EU and the U.S. agencies apply to merger review are converging, their procedures remain far apart. The ICPAC report, while reaching similar conclusions, may lead to a round of discussions at the Organization for Economic Cooperation and Development level, in which business and the private bar can participate to harmonize both the substance and the procedures of the merger review process. While substantive harmonization is likely to be thought of as something of a Holy Grail, procedural steps could be envisioned that combine the virtues of the two systems and reduce the transaction costs of completing a multinational merger. As more and more countries adopt merger clearance regimes, these costs are becoming more significant. Procedural harmonization and coordination are, therefore, clearly desirable.

5

Anticartel Cooperation

SPENCER WEBER WALLER

There is an old story about the brand-new newspaper reporter who receives his first assignment—to cover a prominent society wedding. The young reporter drives to the location of the wedding and is back in the newsroom within the hour. When his editor asks him if he covered the wedding, the reporter replies, "There wasn't any story, the bride didn't show up."

Cooperation between the United States and the European Union in cartel cases is a similar story. Unlike other areas of the very fruitful pattern of transatlantic antitrust cooperation, it is virtually impossible to find significant public record information as to how these two leading competition regimes have assisted each other in cartel investigations. The absence of such information would lead the casual observer to make the same mistake as the rookie reporter in the apocryphal story.

The real story is that, despite considerable success by both sides in individual cases, there has been next to nothing that either the United States or the EU can point to by way of significant formal cooperation in the single most important type of case under any competition law regime. What little there is consists of conversa-

I thank Nonna Gushchina and Robert Berry for their research assistance.

tion between officials about publicly known facts. While government secrecy makes it difficult to ascertain the true extent and effectiveness of such conversations, they clearly are not enough. The lack of an institutional mechanism for effective enforcement cooperation is unfortunate given the long and cordial relationship of bilateral and multilateral consultations and a history of increasingly formal institutional cooperation in other areas of antitrust enforcement (primarily mergers and occasional monopolization or abuse of a dominant position investigations).

This is the precise opposite of what one would expect. Both the United States and the EU have a consistent history of vigorous anticartel enforcement, including enforcement aimed at transnational cartels affecting both markets. Both accept, with differing limitations and degrees of enthusiasm, versions of the effects test or its functional equivalent. Both impose significant penalties against proven cartels and accept few if any social welfare defenses to a charge of unlawful cartelization or bid rigging. Both jurisdictions are leaders in trying to establish an international consensus against cartel activity and to require enforcement agencies to consult and cooperate where appropriate. Why then is the record so dismal in the one area in which consensus is so strong and so positive in areas in which consensus is much weaker and the potential for conflict is much greater?

This chapter provides an initial explanation for this paradox by focusing on the institutional mechanisms for investigating cartel behavior in each jurisdiction and by arguing that no current mechanism exists that would permit either easy or significant cooperation in the area of cartel enforcement. Recent transnational cartel cases and investigations illustrate how both the United States and the EU have been forced to go it alone (sometimes successfully and sometimes not) in attacking cartel activity that affected both markets. This frustrating experience is in contrast to the happier recent history of the United States and Canada, which have fruitfully cooperated in several major cartel investigations through a convergence of substantive, procedural, and treaty competition law provisions and mechanisms.

It is unlikely that the United States and the EU will enter into an agreement pursuant to the U.S. International Antitrust Enforcement Assistance Act (IAEAA). But investigatory techniques, and not just the cooperation mechanisms, need to change if better and more realistic transatlantic antitrust cooperation in the cartel area can be realized. New investigatory techniques may permit the kind of effective cooperation that so far has been illusory.

The Way the United States Investigates
and Punishes Cartels

Cartel activity is per se unreasonable under section 1 of the Sherman Act prohibiting contracts, combinations, and conspiracies in restraint of trade.[1] Price fixing and bid rigging normally are prosecuted as criminal offenses punishable by imprisonment up to three years and fines of up to $350,000 for individuals and to $10 million for corporations.[2] Because of the application of criminal sentencing provisions, corporations are subject to fines far in excess of the statutory maximum set forth in the Sherman Act and have agreed to fines in plea agreements up to $500 million, depending on the amount of commerce affected in the conspiracy.[3]

Federal criminal activity of all kinds, including antitrust crimes, is investigated through the grand jury process. The grand jury is an investigative body with the power to subpoena witnesses and documents to determine whether there is probable cause to believe that a crime has been committed.[4] The grand jury investigation is governed by strict secrecy rules embodied in rule 6 (e) of the Federal Rules of Criminal Procedure. More specifically, rule 6 (e) (2) protects "matters occurring before the grand jury," witness testimony, and the identity of witnesses. The key determination is whether disclosure of a particular item of information would reveal something of substance about the grand jury's investigation.[5] Disclosures of matters not even strictly "before" the grand jury, such as a statement to government agents or lawyers in lieu of testimony before the grand jury or a summary of grand jury testimony, are prohibited if they would nonetheless reveal the nature of the grand jury proceedings.[6] Similarly, documents cannot be disclosed if they would tend to reveal something about the grand jury investigation. The burden is on the party seeking disclosure to show that rule 6 (e) does not apply.[7] If rule 6 (e) does apply, a person normally must demonstrate "particularized need," which has proven to be a formidable burden.[8]

---

1. 15 U.S.C. § 1.
2. 15 U.S.C. § 1. In addition, price fixing and bid rigging normally are also the subject of vigorous private treble-damage litigation.
3. 18 U.S.C. § 3571 (d).
4. See generally Beale and Bryson (1998); Waller (1988). If the grand jury indicts one or more individuals or business entities, the defendants stand trial in the federal district and may be convicted only if the government proves the charges contained in the indictment beyond a reasonable doubt.
5. Beale and Bryson (1998, § 5).
6. Beale and Bryson (1998, § 5).
7. In re Grand Jury Proceedings, 851 F.2d 860 (6th Cir. 1988).
8. *United States* v. *John Doe, Inc.* 1, 481 U.S. 102, 116 (1987); *United States* v. *Sells Engineering*, 463 U.S. 418, 445 (1983); *Illinois* v. *Abbott & Assoc.*, 460 U.S. 557 (1983).

The Justice Department can obtain from the courts grants of immunity for witnesses and has set forth corporate amnesty and leniency policies that are closely related to grand jury processes. The government normally agrees to treat communications pursuant to the amnesty or leniency programs as confidential, even if not covered by the secrecy rules of 6 (e). Even if secrecy is not formally required by statute or rule for certain communications with cooperating witnesses, the government normally must promise and maintain confidentiality in practice and may not be able to obtain cooperation without such promises.

The Department of Justice also has the option of investigating any anticompetitive conduct as a civil antitrust violation using the Antitrust Civil Process Act, a statute that is governed by strict confidentiality provisions modeled on rule 6 (e).[9] Finally, the Federal Trade Commission also investigates cartel and other anticompetitive activity under section 5 of the Federal Trade Commission Act, which prohibits "unfair methods of competition" and provides confidentiality for information obtained through compulsory process.[10]

European Union Cartel Rules and Investigatory Procedures

Cartel activity is the classic violation of article 81 of the European Community Treaty, which prohibits agreements and concerted practices that have the purpose or effect of restricting competition and that may affect trade between the member states.[11] There is little chance of individual exemption under article 81 or through the various block exemptions for hard-core cartel activity.

Although violations of article 81 are not crimes, they are punishable by fines of up to 10 percent of the respondent's worldwide annual turnover, with recent fines in cartel cases totaling hundreds of million of dollars. The European Commission investigates potential violations through the procedures and powers set forth in regulation 17.[12] These powers include the abil-

9. 15 U.S.C. § 1313 (c) (3).

10. 15 U.S.C. §§ 45, 57 (b) (2).

11. Consolidated version of the Treaty on European Union and Consolidated Version of the Treaty Establishing the European Community, Maastricht, Rome, and Amsterdam, February 7, 1992, March 25, 1957, October 2, 1996, reprinted in 36 I.L.M. 56 (1998). The competition provisions formerly contained in article 85 of the Treaty of Rome are now set forth in article 81 of the Treaty of Amsterdam.

12. Council Regulation 17-62, 1962 OJ (L 13) 87, as amended.

ity to conduct dawn raids, to demand explanations of documents obtained during a raid, and to request documents from both firms under investigation and third parties believed to have relevant information. In addition, the European Union has initiated a new amnesty-leniency program, with limited results to date. Regulation 17 contains its own strict confidentiality provisions in article 20, which states that "information acquired [pursuant to Regulation 17] shall be used only for the purpose of the relevant request or investigation" and that "the Commission and the competent authorities of their member States, their officials and other servants shall not disclose information acquired by them as a result of the application of this regulation and of the kind covered by the obligation of professional secrecy."

Member states of the European Union have their own competition statutes, most of which track quite closely the substance and procedures contained in the EU treaty. All such statutes contain their own confidentiality provisions, and many member states have enacted enhanced secrecy and blocking statutes specifically to prevent foreign access to documents in competition matters. The continued existence of such blocking statutes appears to have more of a practical, rather than legal, effect on the EU's willingness and ability to cooperate in controversial cases in which a U.S. antitrust investigation affects the important national interests of the member states.

Current Institutional Mechanisms for U.S.-EU Antitrust Cooperation

Antitrust cooperation between the United States and the European Union is based upon a 1991 agreement.[13] The agreement contains traditional provisions requiring notification of any matter affecting the nationals or important interests of the other party and sets forth additional provisions regarding consultation procedures. The agreement also contains the first appearance of so-called positive comity provisions, which allow one party to request the other party to take action against conduct on its territory affecting competition in the requesting party's territory.

The U.S.-EU cooperation agreement got off to a slow start. France successfully challenged the legality of the agreement on procedural grounds before the European Court of Justice, and the agreement was not formally

13. Agreement between the Government of the United States of America and the Commission of the European Communities Regarding the Application of Their Competition Laws, September 23, 1991, E.C.-U.S., reprinted in 30 I.L.M. 1491 (1991).

implemented until 1995.[14] Nonetheless, the parties continued their cordial informal working relationship and actively cooperated with each other in the original 1994 Microsoft investigation, culminating in separate but jointly negotiated settlements with that company.

The transatlantic antitrust relationship was deepened with the signing of the 1998 positive comity agreement.[15] This agreement expanded upon the definitions and procedures contained in this aspect of the 1991 agreement. Under the new agreement, there is a presumption that the requesting party will not proceed with its own case while the other party considers the positive comity request.[16]

Despite the importance of the positive comity provisions, there has been only limited activity under this provision to date, none of which has been related to cartel cases. The phrasing of the positive comity provisions themselves effectively precludes using them to attack export cartels and other arrangements that are not themselves unlawful in the requested country.

The first formal positive comity request was in 1997, when the United States requested that the EU investigate alleged conduct in the EU restricting competition in the computerized airline ticketing services market, which ultimately resulted in the European Commission bringing proceedings against Air France.[17] Earlier, in 1996, there was an informal version of positive comity in action when the United States deferred and ultimately chose not to bring action against A. C. Nielsen following EU action against the same firm.[18]

The lack of powerful institutional arrangements with the EU is mirrored in the antitrust relationships between the United States and EU member states. Only Germany has an antitrust cooperation agreement with the United States.[19] The U.S.-Germany agreement is not even as powerful as the U.S.-EU mechanism and similarly does not allow the exchange of otherwise con-

---

14. Case 327-91, *French Republic* v. *Commission,* 1994 E.C.R. I-3641, I-3678.

15. Agreement between the Government of the United States of America and the European Communities on the Application of Positive Comity Principles in the Enforcement of Their Competition Laws, June 4, 1998 (www.ftc.gov/bc/us-ec-pc.htm).

16. Agreement between the Government of the United States of America and the European Communities on the Application of Positive Comity Principles in the Enforcement of Their Competition Laws, June 4, 1998, art. 4, para. 2.

17. See "EU Opens Procedure" (1999, 276); Klein (1997).

18. Department of Justice, Antitrust Division, press release 1996 WL 692701, December 3, 1996.

19. Agreement between the Government of the United States of America and the Government of the Federal Republic of Germany Relating to Mutual Cooperation Regarding Restrictive Business Practices, June 23, 1976 (U.S.-F.R.G., 27 U.S.T. 1956).

fidential information. Without any such agreement, there is only the limited possibility of letters rogatory or letters of request to national courts as well as informal cooperation with national competition authorities.

The Costs of the Current System

The best illustration of the costs of the current system was an attempt by the United States to enforce its antitrust laws against an alleged international cartel involving producers and distributors of industrial diamonds. The lack of cooperation ultimately prevented effective enforcement against General Electric, DeBeers, and several individual defendants. The U.S. criminal indictment alleged an international cartel in industrial diamonds between U.S., European, and other producers and distributors. The indictment alleged that much of the alleged conduct took place in Europe. Prosecutors believed that much of the evidence also was located in Europe but were almost entirely unsuccessful in obtaining access to documents or witnesses located outside the United States. While this case undoubtedly was the subject of discussions between the Antitrust Division of the Justice Department and the European Commission, the only publicly known assistance came from the Belgian national police, who searched the files of one of the alleged conspirators.[20] The lack of greater cooperation was probably outcome determinative in that the U.S. trial court dismissed all charges against the American defendant, specifically citing the inability of the government to obtain more complete evidence from abroad.[21]

The lack of cooperation also has reduced the effectiveness, or raised the costs, of investigations in other matters, even in those matters in which the United States or the EU was ultimately successful in its enforcement action. There was no known EU cooperation in the U.S. *International Food Additives Cartel* cases. The investigation into the food additive industry was conducted by the Justice Department's Antitrust Division, the U.S. Attorney General's Office, and the Federal Bureau of Investigation. In August 1996, the Antitrust Division obtained guilty pleas and imposed criminal fines on two Japanese subsidiaries and one U.S.-based Korean subsidiary and their executives for their participation in a conspiracy to raise the price of an ad-

---

20. *United States* v. *General Electric Co.*, 869 F. Supp. 1285, 1293 (S.D. Ohio 1994). See also Klein (1996, 4); William M. Carley, "Fatal Flaws: How the Federal Case against GE, DeBeers Collapsed So Quickly," *Wall Street Journal*, December 28, 1998, A1.
21. *General Electric*, 869 F. Supp. at 1300.

ditive called lysine.[22] In October 1996, Archer Daniels Midland (ADM) pled guilty and agreed to pay a $100 million fine, then the largest antitrust fine ever, for participating in a series of international conspiracies to fix prices and allocate sales in the worldwide lysine and citric acid markets. This plea was followed by the subsequent conviction of individual employees and officers of ADM.

During the investigation, the Antitrust Division experienced firsthand the problems with obtaining evidence located outside of the United States. For example, the executives of Ajinomoto ordered the destruction of documents in Japan at the time the search warrant was executed in the United States.[23]

In the beginning of 1997, Haarmann and Reimer, the New Jersey–based subsidiary of the German pharmaceutical and chemical firm Bayer and one of the two largest producers of citric acid, pled guilty and paid a $50 million fine for participating in the conspiracy to fix prices and allocate sales in the citric acid market worldwide.[24] In March 1997, two international Swiss chemical companies, Jungbunzlauer International and F. Hoffmann–La Roche, pled guilty and paid $25 million in fines for the same conduct.[25] Jungbunzlauer International and Haarman and Reimer were investigated by Canadian competition authorities and fined $6.7 million for participation in the citric acid cartel, which affected a large share of the $104 million Canadian citric acid market.[26]

ADM was also investigated and prosecuted in Canada. As a result of an investigation by the Canadian Bureau of Competition, ADM pled guilty to a price-fixing conspiracy and paid a $16 million fine for violations of Canada's Competition Act.[27]

Similarly, there was no publicly known EU cooperation in the U.S. marine construction cases, despite participation by firms and individuals in both markets. Dutch, Belgian, and Texan firms and officials of the Dutch and Belgian companies were charged in the United States with participating in international bid-rigging conspiracies in marine construction and trans-

22. Department of Justice, Antitrust Division, press release 1996 WL 592058, October 15, 1996.

23. See International Competition Policy Advisory Committee, transcript of meeting, February 26, 1998 (www.usdoj.gov/atr/icpac/1772.htm).

24. "Bayer Subsidiary to Plead Guilty" (1997).

25. Scott Kilman, "Two Swiss Chemical Firms Will Plead Guilty, Pay Fines in Price-Fixing Case," *Wall Street Journal*, March 27, 1997, B5.

26. "Two Firms Fined Total of $6.7M for Price-Fixing Scheme," *Financial Post*, October 22, 1998 (1998 WL 19930474).

27. "Two Firms Fined Total of $6.7M for Price-Fixing Scheme," *Financial Post*, October 22, 1998 (1998 WL 19930474).

portation services. The companies involved in the U.S. marine construction conspiracy case ultimately pled guilty and paid a total of $65 million in fines.[28]

The first case charged HeereMac and Meek with violating the Sherman Act by conspiring with unnamed co-conspirators to suppress and eliminate competition. The complaint alleged that, from 1993 until May 1997, they rigged bids for heavy-lift derrick barges (floating cranes with the capacity to lift loads heavier than 4,000 tons used to construct offshore oil and gas production and drilling platforms) and related marine construction services in the United States and elsewhere.[29] The conspirators agreed on prices to be charged for contracts and allocated contracts, customers, and geographical territories among themselves. HeereMac agreed to pay a fine of $49 million; Meek was fined $100,000.[30] In the second case, the Antitrust Division charged Dockwise N.V., Dockwise U.S.A., and two individuals with violating the Sherman Act by conspiring with other unnamed conspirators to suppress and eliminate competition. The division alleged that from 1990 to 1995 the conspirators rigged bids for semisubmersible heavy-lift transport services, a $200-million-a-year industry. In addition to heavy fines, Dockwise N.V. agreed to pay $4 million in damages to the U.S. Navy as a result of contracts charging anticompetitive fixed prices.[31]

Conversely, the United States provided no known assistance to the European Commission in its paper cases. Four European subsidiaries of U.S. paper products companies were among the nineteen enterprises fined a record total of ECU 132.15 million ($145 million) for operating a cartel in the EU's carton board sector between 1986 and 1991. The subsidiaries of U.S. companies Boise Cascade, Stone Container, International Paper, and Manville Forest Products paid approximately ECU 21 million ($23.3 million). Nine of the cartel members were based in Finland, Austria, Switzerland, and Norway. The other ten were based in whole or in part within the EU at the time of the conspiracy. The cartel organized price increases on a semiannual basis over the life of the cartel. The cartel carried out its practices of price fixing and market regulation under the cover of an ostensibly legitimate trade association called the PG (Product Group) Paperboard.[32]

The lack of an effective cooperation mechanism has not, in fairness, al-

28. "Multinational Conspirators to Pay $65 Million Fine" (1998).

29. Department of Justice, Antitrust Division, press release 1997 WL 784934, December 22, 1997.

30. See plea agreements filed in *United States* v. *HeereMac*, Crim. 97 CR 869 (N.D. Ill.).

31. *United States* v. *Dockwise N.V.*, Crim. 97 CR 870 (N.D. Ill., December 22, 1997); Department of Justice, Antitrust Division, press release, December 22, 1997.

32. "European Union Commission Imposes Record Fines" (1994).

ways prevented the United States from successfully investigating and prosecuting certain international cartels. The most spectacular example is the recent international vitamins cartel grand jury investigation. Through the use of U.S. corporate amnesty programs, the Justice Department obtained extensive help from one of the conspirators in a decade-long conspiracy to inflate the price of vitamins added to a wide variety of prepared foods. The conspiracy involved many of the same companies and individuals involved in the earlier food additives investigation. Some of these companies and individuals affirmatively lied or concealed the existence of this separate conspiracy while ostensibly cooperating with the Justice Department on food additives. The United States ultimately obtained guilty pleas from the corporations and individuals, including breathtakingly large fines totaling more than $1 billion for the foreign corporations and jail terms for the foreign individuals involved.[33] Canada has enjoyed a similar record of success in this matter, presumably in part as a result of its close working relationship, and the Mutual Legal Assistance Treaty, with U.S. antitrust enforcers.[34]

It remains to be seen whether the EU will have similar success in the absence of either an effective corporate leniency program or the ability to obtain confidential information gathered by the U.S. or Canadian competition authorities. Moreover, we will never know whether the EU would have been able to effectively investigate this global cartel had the United States not been in a position to act on its own.

Another example of a case with a good result from an enforcement point of view, but in which more substantial cooperation would have been of great value, is the U.S. graphite electrodes cases. According to the plea agreement, participants fixed prices in the United States and elsewhere, with at least some of the meetings taking place in Europe. Showa Denko Carbon, a U.S. subsidiary of the Japanese firm Showa Financing KK, was charged with participating in a worldwide conspiracy from 1993 to 1997 to fix prices and allocate market shares of graphite electrodes, a product used in steel manufacturing. The company pled guilty to violation of the Sherman Act and agreed to pay a $29 million fine.[35] UCAR International pled guilty in June 1998 and agreed to pay a then record $110 million fine for its participation in the cartel.[36]

33. "Senior DOJ Official Reviews Anticartel Enforcement Program" (1999).

34. "Canadian Court Metes out Record Fines" (1999).

35. Department of Justice, Antitrust Division, press release 1998 WL 74568, February 23, 1998.

36. Department of Justice, Antitrust Division, press release 1998 WL 164982, April 7, 1998. This case has continued with the recent indictment of Mitsubishi for its alleged participation in the same conspiracy. See "Japanese Company Indicted" (2000).

The Federal Trade Commission investigates cartel activity less frequently than the Antitrust Division of the Justice Department, primarily because of its inability to bring criminal charges. Nonetheless, the FTC has been involved in prominent international price-fixing cases and has suffered from the same lack of cooperation from the EU as its sister agency. In 1994, the FTC filed a case against the International Association of Conference Interpreters and its U.S. affiliate, alleging a conspiracy to fix the fees for interpretation services performed in the United States and to restrain competition among interpreters.[37] The association is based in Geneva. It is a voluntary professional association of interpreters from sixty-eight countries who perform interpretation services at multilingual conferences or other high-level meetings. Despite the membership of interpreters from most if not all of the EU member states, there has been no known cooperation between the FTC and the European Commission.[38] Similarly, in the absence of a mechanism for effective cooperation in cartel cases, the FTC and the European Commission have separately investigated alleged price fixing between Boeing and Airbus, presumably duplicating their efforts.[39]

Substantial cooperation has occurred only when the parties have waived confidentiality and allowed the free exchange of information. For example, the initial Microsoft investigation and its settlement was the first informal application of the EU-U.S. cooperation agreement. In the Microsoft investigation, the Antitrust Division worked closely with the European Commission's Directorate General IV in negotiating a settlement and consent decree. Both agencies contributed a unique and critical component to the successful resolution of that case. The cooperation was possible only because Microsoft requested that a single cooperative settlement procedure be employed and waived its rights to confidentiality under both laws.[40] The conduct was simultaneously challenged and settled in the United States and Europe.[41] While "the Microsoft investigation was important from the perspective that it provided the first test of international coordination of antitrust activities between two jurisdictions with different antitrust policies," it also suggests that such waivers are particularly unlikely to occur in the cartel context, in which firms have too much at stake and little incentive to throw themselves on the joint mercy of U.S. and EU antitrust agencies.[42]

37. American Society of Interpreters and the Association of Language Specialists, FTC file 9110022, consent decree accepted for comment February 22, 1994.

38. "Interpreters Groups Face Price Fixing Charges" (1994).

39. "Boeing, Airbus Targets of U.S., European Union Price-Fixing Probe," *Los Angeles Times*, November 27, 1998, C3 (1998 WL 18898110).

40. "Bingaman Briefs Seminar" (1994).

41. "Microsoft Settles Accusations" (1994).

42. Keegan (1996).

The situation in the merger context is different. Firms often need a quick decision on their contemplated transactions and have every incentive to waive confidentiality in order to reach a joint favorable resolution or at least a coordinated remedy. Even in the absence of a party's consent, there is much publicly available information for the agencies to discuss, including vital questions of market definition and remedy, which are not normally as prominent in cartel cases, where the emphasis is on the detection and proof of the illegal conduct itself.

One example of excellent cooperation in the merger area is the WorldCom-MCI telecommunications merger, which involved two U.S. firms and resulted in the divestiture of MCI's $1.75 billion in Internet assets to Cable and Wireless in the summer of 1998—then the largest divestiture in U.S. merger history. In that case, Antitrust Division and EU staffs worked closely to share their independent analyses of the transaction as they evolved; both ultimately reached essentially the same conclusions. The agencies shared confidential information with one another with the parties' consent and held joint meetings with the two U.S. companies to discuss the issues and possible solutions. In addition, before announcing its approval of the transaction in July, the European Commission formally requested, pursuant to the 1991 U.S.-EU antitrust cooperation agreement, the division's cooperation and assistance in evaluating and implementing the proposed divestiture. The commission's press release of July 8, 1998, states that "investigations, and negotiations of remedies, were undertaken in parallel with the examination of the case which is still being conducted by the [Antitrust Division]. The process so far has been marked by considerable . . . cooperation between the two authorities, including exchanges of views on the analytical method to be used, coordination of information gathering and joint meetings and negotiations with the parties."[43] Even in the more controversial Boeing–McDonnell Douglas merger, the FTC and the European Commission engaged in extensive cooperation and exchange of information even though they ultimately reached very different conclusions as to the substantive legality of the transaction.[44]

U.S.-Canadian Cooperation in Antitrust Matters

The U.S.-EU experience is in marked contrast with the recent history between the United States and Canada, which has evolved from one of great

43. Melamed (1998).
44. See Swindle (1998).

suspicion and conflict to one of great cooperation.[45] This evolution has been marked by a growth in institutional arrangements for cooperation and joint enforcement of a kind missing in the U.S.-EU relationship. Following controversy over U.S. use of extraterritorial jurisdiction aimed at Canadian corporations, informal conflict-avoidance mechanisms were put in place in 1959.[46] The 1984 Memorandum of Understanding formalized notification and consultation procedures between the two countries and eliminated as a practical matter the threatened use of blocking legislation by Canada.[47]

The 1995 cooperation agreement between these same two countries emphasized cooperation rather than conflict avoidance.[48] Article 3 of the agreement requires each party to locate and secure evidence and witnesses and provide other information upon request "to the extent compatible with that Party's laws, enforcement policies and other important interests." Article 4 calls for coordinated enforcement activities whenever feasible. Article 5 includes the now familiar positive comity provision.

The 1985 Mutual Legal Assistance Treaty (MLAT) is probably the most valuable weapon in joint cartel investigation and enforcement between the United States and Canada.[49] Parties must provide each other assistance in matters pertaining to investigation, prosecution, and suppression of specified offenses. Antitrust crimes fall within scope of the MLAT as "consumer protection laws." The MLAT commits both parties to the broadest possible range of mutual assistance including

—Examining objects and sites
—Exchanging information and objects
—Locating and identifying persons
—Serving documents
—Taking evidence
—Providing documents and records
—Transferring persons in custody
—Executing requests for searches and seizures

45. See generally Waller (1997).
46. Hunter and Hutton (1994).
47. Memorandum of Understanding between the Government of the United States of America and the Government of Canada as to Notification, Consultation and Cooperation with Respect to the Application of National Antitrust Law, March 9, 1984, reprinted in 23 I.L.M. 275 (1984).
48. Canada–United States: Agreement Regarding the Application of their Competition and Deceptive Marketing Practices Laws, August 1 and 3, 1995, art. 11, para. 1, reprinted in 35 I.L.M. 309 (1996).
49. Treaty on Mutual Legal Assistance in Criminal Matters, March 18, 1985, reprinted in 24 I.L.M. 1092 (1985).

—Locating the proceeds of crimes

—Obtaining forfeitures of proceeds, enforcing restitution orders, and collecting fines

—Providing publicly available documents

—Providing any documents, whether public or not, that it would provide to its own law enforcement or judicial authorities.[50]

The MLAT applies even if the request for assistance applies to a specific matter not illegal under the law of the requested nation. The MLAT was a critical investigatory tool in the *U.S. Plastic Dinnerware* cases. Simultaneous search warrants were executed by the FBI and the Royal Canadian Mounted Police in Montreal, Minneapolis, and Boston. This resulted in such powerful evidence that the defendant corporations immediately entered guilty pleas and paid a total of $9 million in fines.[51]

The investigation depended on crucial assistance from Canadian authorities and culminated in charges against three corporations and seven executives for conspiring to drive up the prices of plastic dinnerware, a $100 million market. The defendants produced 90 percent of the plastic dinnerware used in the United States. The defendants—three U.S. firms and seven executives, including two Canadians—allegedly telephoned and met with each other to further a conspiracy that lasted from December 1991 to December 1992. One meeting took place in Montreal near the headquarters of the parent company of one of the corporate defendants. Two of the corporate defendants pled guilty and paid fines totaling $8.36 million. In March 1995, the president of one of the companies involved in the conspiracy received one of the stiffest penalties ever imposed on an individual defendant for a one-count violation of section 1 of the Sherman Act: a twenty-one-month prison sentence and a fine of $90,000.[52] Each of the six other individual defendants received prison terms of between four and fifteen months and fines exceeding $200,000. Two individual defendants, Canadian nationals, were sentenced to jail in U.S. prisons.[53] The documentary evidence discovered during the simultaneous raids on both sides of the border revealed that the conspiracy did not affect the Canadian market, and no Canadian investigation ensued.[54]

50. Treaty on Mutual Legal Assistance in Criminal Matters, March 18, 1985, reprinted in 24 I.L.M. 1092 (1985), art. 2, para. 2; art. 13, paras. 1, 2; art. 17, paras. 1, 2.

51. See International Competition Policy Advisory Committee, transcript of meeting, February 26, 1998, 63–64.

52. *United States* v. *Izzi, Crim.* CR94-00243 (E.D. Pa. March 16, 1995).

53. U.S. Department of Justice (1996, 4).

54. Klein (1996, 6).

The MLAT also was the critical tool in both the U.S. and Canadian thermal fax paper cases. In that case, the Antitrust Division coordinated a two-year investigation with the Canadian Bureau of Competition and the Canadian Department of Justice. The Antitrust Division and its Canadian counterpart brought criminal charges under their respective laws in 1994 against an international cartel that inflated prices by approximately 10 percent in the $120 million a year thermal fax paper market.[55]

The Canadian authorities first brought the case to the attention of the U.S. Department of Justice, which was not aware of the conspiracy at the time. The authorities of both countries worked closely, exchanging information, sharing documents, and jointly interviewing witnesses.[56] The Antitrust Division ultimately charged Mitsubishi, a Japanese corporation, two U.S. subsidiaries of Japanese firms, and an executive of one of the firms with conspiring to charge higher prices to thermal fax paper customers in North America, primarily small businesses and home fax machine owners. These defendants pled guilty and agreed to pay a total of $6.4 million in fines.

Additional charges in this case were brought in 1995 and 1996, charging Elof Hansson Paper and Board, a wholly owned subsidiary of Elof Hansson of Sweden, and two additional Japanese companies, Mitsubishi Paper Mills and New Oji Paper, with conspiring to fix prices. All of the defendants pled guilty and paid over $3.5 million in fines. The Antitrust Division also brought charges against Appleton Papers of Wisconsin and Jujo Paper of Japan (now Nippon Paper Industries) for fixing prices of the thermal fax paper.[57] The Canadian antitrust enforcement agencies also charged the same defendants and obtained additional guilty pleas.[58]

The thermal fax paper case exemplifies the vital necessity of antitrust cooperation in the fight against international cartels. Without such cooperation, the United States might not have even become aware of the cartel in the first place. Cooperation also was vital to the building of the case against the cartel in the courts of both countries. Much of the necessary evidence was located in Canada and not otherwise obtainable by the Antitrust Divi-

55. "U.S. and Canadian Prosecutors Attack Cartel Behavior" (1994).

56. Klein (1996). There is also evidence that the government of Japan provided some cooperation in the investigation. See Government of Japan, Brief of Amicus Curiae 4, *United States v. Nippon Paper Industries Co. Ltd.*, 96-2001 (1st Cir., November 18, 1996).

57. U.S. Department of Justice (1996). These defendants ultimately were acquitted at trial. See "JUJO/NPI Wins Judgment" (1999).

58. Klein (1996).

sion.[59] Similarly, some evidence from the Antitrust Division proved vital to Canadian authorities.[60]

The Need for New U.S.-EU Cooperation Mechanisms

The United States would like nothing better than to negotiate an international antitrust enforcement agreement with the European Union, to permit the United States and the EU to exchange previously confidential information. However, the implementation of such an agreement would require substantial changes to Regulation 17 of the act if not an amendment to the EU treaties themselves. Even Canada and United States, with their long history of cooperation, have been unable to conclude an international antitrust enforcement agreement because of the required changes in Canadian domestic law necessary to permit exchange of confidential information.

The United States passed the IAEAA with great fanfare and has promoted agreements under the act as the answer to effective antitrust cooperation and as an alternative to the need for international antitrust rules under the auspices of the World Trade Organization. Despite this effort, there has been only one agreement concluded under the IAEAA: between the United States and Australia. So far there is not enough history under the agreement to create an incentive for the EC to push such negotiations as a priority. To the extent that the EU favors the creation of a multilateral competition law regime in the WTO, this makes dramatic progress toward new cooperation regimes with the United States even more unlikely. In light of these factors, perhaps the United States should seek to bypass the EU and negotiate new mutual legal assistance treaties directly with interested EU member states as an alternative, or a supplement, to the cordial but limited cooperation arrangements with the EU.

New investigatory procedures are needed to facilitate meaningful cooperation. If the present procedures are not institutionally suited to extensive cooperation in cartel cases, then antitrust enforcers should consider new and innovative investigative techniques whose results could be shared. One tool that would not run afoul of secrecy requirements is the coordination of the timing and drafting of investigatory instruments, even if the documents

---

59. See "Bingaman Briefs Seminar on International Fronts" (1994).
60. See "Bingaman Briefs Seminar on International Fronts" (1994).

and testimony discovered could not be shared. This could include joint drafting and simultaneous issuance of subpoenas, civil investigative demands,
document requests, and the like. Joint or simultaneous search warrants, dawn
raids, or entry onto premises could be coordinated to minimize the destruction of evidence in far-flung locations.

As the enforcement agencies gain confidence in their working relationships, coordination of amnesty programs and even requiring joint proffers
in appropriate cases could be undertaken. Similarly, enforcers could require
cooperation with their foreign counterparts in plea agreements and consent
decrees. A deeper understanding of the investigatory techniques used in foreign jurisdictions may eventually require formal cross-designation of enforcement personnel on particular investigations and enforcement
proceedings. Each agency should actively support each other's application
for disclosure of waiver of confidentiality. There should be careful study of
cross-border cooperation and enforcement in such areas as securities, tax,
money laundering, and drugs to determine new techniques applicable in
the competition area.[61]

Broader efforts to facilitate such cooperation include

—More aggressive use of positive comity

—Greater participation in the formal proceedings of each other's system

—A substantive agreement prohibiting export cartels, to untie enforcement agencies' hands

—The utilization by the EU of qui tam procedures to share in the recov-
ery of any proceeding brought under the False Claims Act on the basis of
information provided to the United States

—Stronger efforts to include competition law issues in the pending Hague
Convention on the Enforcement of Judgments

—The development of a different role for the OECD and the WTO in
competition matters to promote cooperation on specific matters and perhaps penalize failure to cooperate.

Conclusion

The many institutional arrangements and excellent working relationship
between the European Commission's Directorate General IV and the U.S.
antitrust agencies (the FTC and Justice's Antitrust Division) has not carried

---

61. The unfortunate use of compelled waivers, which created controversy and generated
little usable evidence in other areas of international criminal law enforcement, should be
avoided.

over into the critical fight against cartels. To make further progress toward effective transatlantic cooperation in this area, both sides need to look beyond the status quo and forge innovative investigatory techniques as well as continue to expand cooperation using the current tools of the trade.

References

"Bayer Subsidiary to Plead Guilty to Conspiring to Fix Citric Acid Prices." 1997. *Antitrust and Trade Regulation Report* 72:98.

Beale, Sara Sun, and William C. Bryson. 1998. *Grand Jury Practice and Procedure.* 2d ed. St. Paul: West Group.

"Bingaman Briefs Seminar on International Fronts." 1994. *Antitrust and Trade Regulation Report* 67:543.

"Canadian Court Metes out Record Fines in Vitamin and Food Additive Cartel Cases." 1999. *Antitrust and Trade Regulation Report* 77:353.

"EU Opens Procedure against Air France for Its Alleged Abuse of Dominant Position." 1999. *Antitrust and Trade Regulation Report* 76:276.

"European Union Commission Imposes Record Fines on Companies Engaged in Paper Cartel." 1994. *Antitrust and Trade Regulation Report* 67:78.

Hunter, Lawson A. W., and Susan M. Hutton. 1994. "Where There Is a Will, There Is a Way: Cooperation in Canada-U.S. Antitrust Relations." *Canadian-U.S. Law Journal* 20:101.

"Interpreters Groups Face Price Fixing Charges by FTC." 1994. *Trade Regulation Report* 67:544.

"Japanese Company Indicted in Graphite Electrode Pricing Scheme." 2000. *Antitrust and Trade Regulation Report* 614:1.

"JUJO/NPI Wins Judgment of Acquittal on Charge of Fixing Prices of Fax Paper." 1999. *Antitrust and Trade Regulation Report* 77:149.

Keegan, Laura E. 1996. "The 1991 U.S./EC Competition Agreement: A Glimpse of the Future through the *U.S. v. Microsoft Corp.* Window." *Journal of International Legal Studies* 2:149.

Klein, Joel. 1996. "Address." Royal Institute of International Affairs, November 18 (1996 WL 666205).

———. 1997. "Remarks." Twenty-Fourth Annual Conference on International Antitrust Law and Policy, Fordham Corporate Law Institute, October 16–17.

Melamed, A. Douglas. 1998. "Address." Japan Fair Trade Institute, November 12 (www.usdoj.gov/atr/public/speeches/2092.htm).

"Microsoft Settles Accusations of Monopolistic Selling Practices." 1994. *Antitrust and Trade Regulation Report* 67:106.

"Multinational Conspirators to Pay $65 Million Fine for Rigging Bids." 1998. *Antitrust and Trade Regulation Report* 74:14.

"Senior DOJ Official Reviews Anticartel Enforcement Program." 1999. *Antitrust and Trade Regulation Report* 77:693.

Swindle, Orson. 1998. "Remarks." Sydney Global Commerce Conference, November 10 (1998 WL 801982).

"U.S. and Canadian Prosecutors Attack Cartel Behavior by Fax Paper Distributors." 1994. *Antitrust and Trade Regulation Report* 67:108.

U.S. Department of Justice. 1996. *Opening Markets and Protecting Competition for America's Businesses and Consumers: Goals and Achievements of the Antitrust Division, U.S. Department of Justice, Fiscal Year 1993–1996,* March 27 (1996 WL 149352).

Waller, Spencer Weber. 1988. "An Introduction to Federal Grand Jury Practice." *Wisconsin Bar Journal* 61: 17.

————. 1997. "The Internationalization of Antitrust Enforcement." *Boston University Law Review* 77:343.

6

The Divide on Verticals

PHILIP MARSDEN

This chapter examines some differences in the way vertical arrangements are reviewed on competition policy grounds in Europe and America.[1] These differences may be sufficient to cause bilateral enforcement cooperation between the two jurisdictions to break down, if only in the context of "westward" positive comity requests—that is, from the Commission of the European Union to U.S. antitrust authorities (the Antitrust Division of the Department of Justice and the Federal Trade Commission). If bilateral cooperation cannot bridge the gap between the two regimes, the argument for a multilateral agreement on competition policy standards, particularly at the World Trade Organization (WTO), may gain strength. This would be more likely to be the case if the gap—and any resultant lack of enforcement against suspect vertical arrangements—also resulted in anticompetitive activity going unaddressed. That is not likely to be the case, however. This chapter submits that the gap is based on fundamentally different philosophical approaches to economic freedom. Since these differences are firmly rooted, bridging the gap through an international common approach is not feasible. Nor, far more important, is it desirable.

Attempts to bridge the gap between two well-developed competition policy regimes, while well intentioned, can be successful

---

1. The chapter builds on the analysis and argument in Marsden (1998).

only if one side capitulates to the other. There is no middle way, no common ground, on this particular issue. The European and American approaches may not be as opposite as black and white, but they are sufficiently different in philosophical approach to allow for precious little grey at the margins. Those seeking common ground rely on anecdote and rhetoric to accuse the Americans of having an unduly relaxed or glib enforcement approach to vertical arrangements. The reality is quite different. In fact, if there is any laxity at all, it is in the (explainable but nevertheless) unduly relaxed *analytical* approach prevalent in the European Union. This is not to fault the European approach nor to urge its correction. It is merely to identify where the root of the difference resides and to recognize that review of verticals in Europe is defined by its inability to take a very important analytic step. Given competition policy's role there as an important engine of market integration, European authorities are unable to ask a very important question: Even if a vertical arrangement impedes competitors' abilities to access a particular market, does this act to substantially lessen or prevent competition? The Americans insist on answering this question in its entirety; the Europeans can only rely on the proxy of potential harm to the freedom of competitors to access markets in other member states.

In sum, European competition policy is satisfied that an arrangement should be prohibited upon proof that it may significantly restrict one or more competitors' ability to access or expand its operations in a market; U.S. antitrust law goes a step further, requiring proof that such harm is also likely to lessen competition substantially. The European approach is perfectly defensible in its own jurisdiction on political and even economic grounds. However, it is not the appropriate model for other jurisdictions and should not be used as a model for those seeking an international common approach.

Vertical Arrangements

Vertical arrangements involve a commitment between economic actors at different levels in the channel between supply and demand. They are most commonly entered into between manufacturers and their downstream wholesalers or other distributors. While the agreements themselves are between vertically related parties, their effect on competition, if any, is horizontal. Competition analysis focuses on the impact that such arrangements may have on economic actors competing with one or both of the parties to the agreement.

One of the most common forms of vertical agreement is an exclusive purchasing commitment. Essentially, this is a purchaser's promise to buy all or most of its requirements for a particular product or service from one supplier. The effect on competition obviously depends on the impact that this commitment may have on suppliers competing with the main beneficiary of the purchaser's commitment (that is, the supplier). If the purchaser is large enough, its agreement to purchase exclusively or primarily from one supplier may impede that supplier's competitors' ability to sell to this purchaser (obviously) as well as to sell their products further downstream. A similar effect may result where the purchaser has quite a small share of the market but where a set of similar agreements exists between other purchasers and the supplier in question (or even other incumbent suppliers) that are of enough magnitude to make entry by competing suppliers difficult. Depending on the degree that this impedes other competing suppliers' ability to access this market, competition can be lessened substantially.

Competition Policy Approaches to Vertical Arrangements

According to a review conducted by the Secretariat of the World Trade Organization

> In those countries with modern competition laws, non-price vertical market restraints are subject to case-by-case or "rule of reason" treatment . . . rather than being prohibited per se. This reflects the fact that such restraints can enhance efficiency in various ways, for example, by reducing transaction costs and free-riding, and are unlikely to limit competition when entered into by firms that do not enjoy a dominant position. In most jurisdictions, vertical restraints by a dominant firm that foreclose access to a distribution network would be actionable where no alternative to the foreclosed distribution channel exists; but even here, much will depend on the existence of legitimate efficiency considerations, the definition of the relevant market, and the time, costs and barriers involved in establishing a parallel distribution system.[2]

Given this commonality, one may wonder why it would not be feasible to simply recommend the rule of reason as an appropriate multilateral common approach for the review of vertical arrangements. The answer, of course,

2. World Trade Organization (1997).

is that such a recommendation would not be at all helpful in practice. This reality has been pointed out by both WTO officials and competition law experts. Anwarul Hoda, when he was deputy director of the WTO, stated that "use of a rule of reason approach at the multilateral level would involve considerations quite different from those arising in national jurisdictions, for example, on standards, enforcement and remedies. Thus, if it were decided to employ a rule of reason in any multilateral competition rules, considerable work would be required to adapt this approach to that particular context."[3] The reason for this is simple: there is no *one* agreed upon rule of reason. One commentator identifies several such rules within one jurisdiction.[4] Differences of approach with respect to how one determines whether arrangements are or are not "reasonable" would only appear to lead to interactions among WTO members becoming more divisive, rather than less. Frédéric Jenny, chairman of the WTO Working Group on the Interaction of Trade and Competition Policy, has explained:

> A basic problem in a dialogue between competition and trade is the perception by business that competition policy and law enforcement is not reliable. As a result, because of the rule of reason, there is considerable scepticism about the development of competition policy. . . . Conversely, competition policy practitioners are rather reserved about the use of the dispute settlement mechanism [at the WTO] because it cannot accommodate a rule of reason approach, which is central to economic analysis. I believe you can have rule of reason and predictability.[5]

The question, of course, is how. Jenny contributed to an expert's report to the European Commission on possible WTO competition rules that concludes that the "'rule of reason' approach is desirable" for competition policy reviews of vertical restraints.[6] It suggests that WTO members agree on "minimum standards for national rules of reason" to guide their reviews. The following year, the commission made the following suggestion to flesh out what such agreed minimum standards should address: "[A] common approach to vertical restrictions could be found by concentrating on restrictions which create barriers to market access. The [WTO] . . . could examine to what extent competition authorities could take into account the international dimension and weigh the effects on domestic competition of market access

3. Hoda (1997, 8).
4. Black (1997).
5. "ICC Conference Gets Perspectives" (1998, 222).
6. Commission of the European Union (1995).

restrictions."[7] The recommendation to focus on arrangements that create barriers to market access stems, of course, from European competition policy's longtime (and again, understandable) fixation with removing public and private barriers to the creation of the Common Market—and now Single European Market. Based on its own experience, the commission has recently provided more detail on what it thinks international standards might look like.

> There is a broad consensus that, at the international level, vertical restraints are only a source of concern if such agreements have a foreclosure effect, which significantly raises barriers to entry. The [WTO Working Group on the Interaction between Trade and Competition Policy] may therefore wish to explore the scope for identifying an illustrative list of factors to be considered by competition authorities when assessing whether vertical restraints have such a foreclosure effect. This may include such factors as the presence of market power in upstream or downstream markets, collusion among upstream or downstream firms, cumulative impact of restraints, duration of restraints, role of government barriers to entry and overall structure of the market, including openness to foreign trade and investment. Such an illustrative list of factors could facilitate international co-operation among competition authorities and reduce the scope for disagreements about the trade impact of vertical restraints insofar as the decisions by competition authorities in cases with international dimensions would be based on a detailed analysis of the market.[8]

What is lacking from such an illustrative list is a motivating or guiding ethic, however. It is one thing to offer up a checklist of criteria but quite another to assign these criteria weights and suggest how to tot things up. So far, the commission has not made more detailed public recommendations in this regard. However, its explanations of its own competition policy approach may be expected to have a certain resonance for trade officials or for competitors who want regulatory help in entering new markets. The commission has explained its concerns in this way: "In addition to promoting efficiency and market integration . . . vertical restraints can also give rise to concerns for competition policy. For example, if some manufacturers collectively having significant market power to tie up a large part of the distribution outlets in a country by exclusive contracts, this could result in market

7. Commission of the European Union (1996, 11).
8. European Community (1998, 13–14).

foreclosure negatively affecting competition and access to the market."[9] As a policy matter, the commission is recognizing that vertical arrangements can negatively affect access to a market as well as the level of competition in that market. That is not the approach that has guided—and continues to guide—European competition law enforcement, however. Quite correctly, for a jurisdiction that continually strives for an ever closer economic union, the primary focus remains the removal of barriers to market access, full stop.

The European Competition Policy Approach

The guiding test involves assessing whether business arrangements are inconsistent with the Common Market, as a proxy for deeming them to be anticompetitive. The European Court of Justice has tried to take a more "reasoned" approach to the review of vertical arrangements than that provided by the highly regulatory and formalistic prohibition-exemption system long operated by the commission. The court's increased analysis of the economic effects of such arrangements is still guided, however, by the existence of foreclosure.[10] In Europe, thus

> it is appropriate, according to the case law, to consider whether, taken altogether, all the similar agreements entered into in the relevant market and other features of the economic and legal context of the agreements at issue show that those agreements cumulatively *have the effect of denying access to that market for new domestic and foreign competitors.* If ... this is found not to be the case, the individual agreements making up the bundle of agreements as a whole cannot undermine competition.
>
> If, on the other hand, such an examination reveals that it is difficult to gain access to the market, it is necessary to assess the extent to which the contested agreements contribute to the cumulative effect produced, on the basis that only agreements which make a significant contribution to any partitioning of the market are prohibited.[11]

In other words, European competition policy will not be bothered about individual arrangements unless they make a significant contribution to a

9. European Community (1998, 9).

10. Hawk (1995, 977–78).

11. Case T-7/93, *Langnese Iglo* v. *Commission* (1995), ECR 2-1533, citing *Delimitis* (1991), ECR 1-935, paras 23 and 24. Emphasis added.

situation—to speak plainly—in which competitors are denied access to a particular market.

This approach is also taken up in the most recent commission regulation on vertical agreements.[12] This regulation does move the commission away from requiring approval for practically all vertical arrangements that might potentially affect trade between European member states. However, this respite only holds for certain agreements: those that are not blacklisted; those in which the supplier—or buyer in the case of exclusive supply commitments—has a market share of less than 30 percent; and those that are not part of parallel networks of similar arrangements covering more than 50 percent of a given market. A key aspect of the regulation is that the commission may also withdraw the benefit of the remaining exemption "where *access to the relevant market or competition therein* is significantly restricted by the cumulative effect of parallel networks of similar vertical restraints implemented by competing suppliers or buyers."[13]

This is important. It reveals the commission's continuing concern to prohibit arrangements simply because they may significantly restrict competitors' access to a market along with a new receptivity to a more strictly competition-oriented test. The fact that the regulation uses the disjunctive *or* however, reveals that foreclosure of competitors is itself a sufficient ground for nonexemption—and hence prohibition. Again, this is important because the two grounds for prohibition are quite different. Any substantial lessening of competition necessarily requires that competitors' access to that market be significantly restricted: their absence and lack of constraining effect is what reduces competition to an intolerable degree in the first place. However, this does not work the other way around. A significant restriction of competitors' access to a market does not necessarily lead to substantial lessening of competition. The disciplinary effect that competitors may have exerted may be de minimis, for example; so too, therefore, would be their absence. Alternatively, supposing that their absence is significant, this may be compensated for by existing or potential competition—or even by efficiencies resulting from the arrangement that is supposedly keeping them out.

The commission makes no bones about this and indeed highlights it as the main factor distinguishing its approach from that of the United States. In a pointed reference to the regime across the Atlantic, the commission

12. Commission of the European Union, 2790/1999 (December 22), on the application of article 81 (3) of the treaty to categories of vertical arrangements and concerted practices (L 336/23).

13. Commission of the European Union, 2790/1999. Emphasis added.

notes that "competition law in the European Community and in many Member States provides that even when the different distribution networks on a market are in line with antitrust law, they can be condemned where access to the market is restricted by the cumulative effect of parallel networks or similar agreements."[14] The difference is that European competition law prohibits arrangements that may significantly restrict competitors' access to a market, while U.S. antitrust law requires additional evidence, namely, that competition itself is likely to be substantially lessened. What is more, the U.S. approach requires that the substantiality of any lessening of competition be characterized by either an absence of offsetting efficiency benefits or—what can amount to the same thing—proof of actual harm to efficiency.

The U.S. Antitrust Approach

While a review of the three main evolutions in U.S. antitrust law may not be necessary to help explain this point further, it can help more precisely define where along an antitrust continuum the European approach lies.

According to Robert Pitofsky, chairman of the Federal Trade Commission,

> early American cases, while recognizing the potential efficiencies of exclusive dealing arrangements, nevertheless took a hard line against them. In *Standard Stations*, the Court appeared to suggest that exclusive arrangements were close to per se illegal if a *substantial dollar volume of commerce* was covered by the contracts, even when the particular contracts at issue *foreclosed only a small percentage of a given market.* In that case the seller's contracts covered only 6.7% of all gasoline sales to retailers, though there was a pattern of exclusive contracts, covering many sales in the industry, that concerned the Court.[15]

The issue in *Standard Stations* was whether the statutory standard of a substantial lessening of competition "may be shown 'simply by proof that a substantial portion of commerce is affected or whether it must also be demonstrated that competitive activity has actually diminished or probably will diminish.'"[16] The U.S. Supreme Court took the former view, refusing "to

---

14. European Community (1998, 9).

15. Pitofsky (1997, 1). Emphasis added. *Standard Stations* refers to *Standard Oil* v. *United States,* 337 U.S. 293 (1949).

16. Handler (1957, 34), citing *Standard Oil* v. *United States,* 337 U.S. 293 (1949, 299).

consider the impact of the challenged agreements on 'competitive activity' on the theory that it would implicate the judiciary in the appraisal of economic data for which it is unequipped."[17] The Court held that the requirement of proving that a vertical arrangement lessened competition substantially "is satisfied by proof that competition has been foreclosed in a substantial share of the line of commerce affected."[18] This put a great many vertical arrangements in jeopardy and effectively punished suppliers for succeeding in securing a large dollar amount of orders from their customers, even if this was not a significant amount in the market overall. Under *Standard Station*'s "conception of foreclosure, attention [was] focused entirely on the inability of competitors to obtain the patronage of the stations which have committed themselves to deal exclusively with the seller."[19]

There are at least two problems with this approach. First, it is simply wrong to say that competing suppliers were unable to obtain the patronage of gas stations already being supplied by Standard Oil. Of course they could. All they had to do was make it worth the stations' while, by making a competitive offer. It is incorrect, therefore, to even use the term *foreclosure* in this context. At most, one could just say that Standard Oil was there first; this does not mean that it could not be unseated. Second, "wholly ignored is the ability of the seller's competitors to reach the market through alternative channels which have not . . . been pre-empted."[20] More than 90 percent of the market was not exclusively carrying Standard Oil and therefore was available to competitors. Even if this percentage was considerably less, and Standard Oil had secured a far greater number of stations on exclusive terms, it would not necessarily mean that its competitors—let alone competition itself—had been harmed to any significant degree. "The exclusion of competitors from a substantial number of outlets *may* seriously handicap them in their competition. Conversely, it *may* have no anticompetitive tendency or effect if suitable alternative channels are open to them in adequate number."[21]

The unreality of the approach in *Standard Stations* was soon recognized in the next antitrust development. In contemplating a vertical foreclosure issue in the context of a merger, the Supreme Court stated: "We do not think the dollar volume is in itself of compelling significance; we look rather to

17. Handler (1957, 34), citing *Standard Oil* v. *United States,* 337 U.S. 293 (1949, 299).
18. Handler (1957, 34), citing *Standard Oil* v. *United States,* 337 U.S. 293 (1949, 314).
19. Handler (1957, 35), citing *Standard Oil* v. *United States,* 337 U.S. 293 (1949, 314).
20. Handler (1957, 35), citing *Standard Oil* v. *United States,* 337 U.S. 293 (1949, 314).
21. Handler (1957, 36), citing *Standard Oil* v. *United States,* 337 U.S. 293 (1949, 314). Emphasis added.

the percentage of business controlled, the strength of the remaining competition, whether the action springs from business requirements or purpose to
monopolize, the probable development of the industry, consumer demands,
and other characteristics of the market."[22] It took a few more years, however,
before the Supreme Court expressly applied this more comprehensive analysis
to exclusive dealing arrangements themselves. Once it did so, however, it has
never looked back. Pitofsky explains:

> In *Tampa Electric*, decided twelve years after *Standard Stations*, the Court
> outlined the analysis that lower courts have looked to since. The Court first
> defined the product and geographic markets and then sought to deter-
> mine whether the contract at issue foreclosed competition in a "substantial
> share of the relevant market." The Court explained that "opportunities for
> other traders to enter into or remain in that market must be significantly
> limited" before the contracts would be declared invalid. Factors the Court
> thought relevant to the determination of "substantiality" were: the strength
> of the parties, the percentage of commerce involved, and the present and
> future effects of foreclosure on effective competition in the market. Finally,
> the Court seemed implicitly to measure these effects against the efficien-
> cies that exclusive contracts generate."[23]

This implicit recognition of the offsetting power of efficiencies has become explicit in the third and final iteration of competition policy analysis
in the United States.

> In the 1960s, U.S. law was construed to prohibit restraints that foreclosed
> less well situated firms from a significant share of the market, even if the
> exclusion resulted from strong preferences for dealing with one's friends
> (reciprocity). The United States has abandoned this construction of law in
> favor of permissive legal principles that value freedom of firms to impose
> vertical restraints unilaterally. Plaintiffs challenging vertical restraints un-
> der U.S. law today must normally prove that the restraint will limit output
> and harm consumers; it is not enough to show that the restraint merely
> blocks competitors "unreasonably."[24]

Under American antitrust law, vertical arrangements are reviewed for their
effect on competition and on the efficient operation of the market as a whole,
as measured by output. However, it would be a mistake to think that Ameri-

---

22. Handler (1957, 55), citing *U.S.* v. *Columbia Steel Co.*, 334 U.S. 495 (1948, 527).

23. Pitofsky (1977, 3). He refers to *Tampa Electric Co.* v. *Nashville Coal Co.*, 365 U.S. 320
(1961).

24. Fox (1997, 22).

can competition authorities do not consider the effects that such arrangements have on competitors. This is a key step in their analysis.

A promise of exclusivity is a promise not to deal with others. This promise *may* act to exclude competitors. Antitrust analysis does not presume this effect, however, but evaluates whether the exclusivity commitment is in fact acting to exclude competitors. It then asks whether this exclusion is in turn harming the competitive process and the efficiency of the market. Recent policy guidance from the Justice Department makes this clear. As Douglas Melamed, principal deputy assistant attorney general for antitrust, explains:

> We need to evaluate the exclusionary agreements ourselves, without relying on the market to tell us whether they are on balance pro competitive or anti-competitive. Thus, where (i) exclusion, (ii) market power, and (iii) efficiency are inextricably intertwined, the proper resolution is a more comprehensive rule of reason analysis—one that weighs the anti-competitive consequences of the agreements against their pro competitive or efficiency-enhancing implications. . . .
>
> It is important to be careful about what the term "rule of reason" means in this context. Often—perhaps usually—the term "rule of reason" is used to connote the evaluation of a collaboration among competitors, such as a joint venture, an information exchange, a joint buying arrangement, and the like. In those cases, the issue is whether the arrangement reduces or increases output of the parties to the arrangement. In the case of exclusionary vertical agreements, such as exclusive dealing arrangements between a manufacturer and its distributors, the question is very different. In such a case, *the question is whether overall output is increased or decreased in the market in which the manufacturer is likely to gain market power, taking into account both the exclusion of rival manufacturers—which reduces their output—and the efficiencies—which could increase the output of the manufacturer that is a party to and benefits from the agreements.*
>
> Therefore, in applying the rule of reason to exclusionary vertical agreements, we should undertake an analysis much like that which the agencies use in considering efficiencies in merger cases. We should first estimate the impact of the exclusionary agreements on rivals or, to be more precise, on their output in the market. We should then ask, assuming that impact, whether the efficiencies created by the agreements will increase the beneficiary's output enough so that, on balance, marketwide output will be higher, in the market in which the agreements will create or preserve market power, than if the exclusionary agreements were prohibited. If not, the agreements are illegal.[25]

25. Melamed (1998, 12–13). Emphasis added.

Transatlantic Differences in Competition Law Standards: The Effect on Bilateral Cooperation

Recall that the potential exclusion of competitors from a significant share of the market is the prevailing concern in the EU. This represents little more than the U.S. stage of analysis in *Tampa Electric*, without the subsequent evolution to consider the offsetting effect of intrabrand efficiencies and how these can enhance interbrand competition by providing increased output in the market overall.

One should not be blinded by references to efficiencies, however. The difference in approach is defined by something far deeper: their difference in philosophical approach to the concept of economic freedom, which is essentially about whom—and what—competition policy should protect. Should it protect vertically related companies' freedom to choose with whom they contract, subject to there being no downstream harm to consumer welfare? Or should it protect the freedom of competitors to access new markets, thereby guaranteeing (one hopes) an ever expanding set of choices for consumers in the process? Barry Hawk puts it this way:

> The . . . explanation for the inadequate economic analysis [in Europe] . . . lies in [an] adherence to the definition of restriction on competition as a restriction on the "economic freedom" of operators in the marketplace. The principal weaknesses of the Freiberg School notion of restriction of economic freedom are (1) its failure to generate precise operable legal rules (i.e., its failure to provide an analytical framework); (2) its distance from and tension with (micro) economics, which does provide an analytical framework; (3) its tendency to favour traders/competitors over consumers and consumer welfare (efficiency); and (4) its capture of totally innocuous contract provisions having no anti-competitive effects in an economic sense.[26]

In contrast, the U.S. conception is, according to the U.S. government, "that not all practices that restrict *business choices* represent a net loss to *consumer welfare*."[27] The underlying philosophically different approaches to economic freedom and choice, being so subjective and perhaps by definition unquantifiable, are represented by the difference in focus: What does one protect, competitors or competition? It is this difference in approach that

26. Hawk (1995, 977–78).
27. Communication from the United States, WT/WGTCP/W/66 at 15 (emphasis added).

would most likely result in U.S. authorities rebuffing positive comity requests by the European Commission to act against certain vertical arrangements in the United States. If the arrangements do not substantially lessen competition in a U.S. market through a decrease in overall output, the United States would be hard pressed to act against them (under its most recent approach) even if they significantly impede the ability of a European competitor to enter the U.S. market.

Suppose AGFA complained to the European Commission that it was being significantly restricted from accessing the U.S. market because Kodak had signed exclusivity agreements with the lion's share of film wholesalers? Would the U.S. authorities necessarily crack down on such arrangements upon receipt of a positive comity request from the commission? There is room for doubt. Despite the Justice Department's best efforts, Kodak's current market coverage and its network of exclusivity arrangements has recently been approved by the U.S. courts.[28]

An even more real-life example of the divergence in approaches is available however. Pitofsky explains how the transatlantic differences in approach to vertical arrangements have already impacted merger analysis by reference to the conflicting decisions the two governments reached on Boeing's acquisition of McDonnell Douglas:

> Given the somewhat different approaches to exclusives that the United States and EC have historically taken, it is perhaps not surprising that we viewed the issue of the exclusive contracts in the Boeing case differently. As you will recall, prior to consummating the merger, Boeing had entered into contracts with three major U.S.-based airlines in which the airlines agreed to buy substantially all of their aircraft requirements exclusively from Boeing for twenty years. The exclusives accounted for about 11% of the commercial aircraft market. . . . Without more, our courts likely would not have recognized the exclusives as an anticompetitive problem. While it is true that Boeing has an approximately 60% market share in commercial aircraft, U.S. courts have not typically analyzed exclusives by looking primarily at the market share of the seller. That is one factor, but only one of many, in determining how the exclusive dealing arrangements actually affect competition. In the Boeing case, the market foreclosure was not substantial in U.S. antitrust terms. . . . Recent United States cases seem to have created a safe harbor for exclusive dealing arrangements that foreclose under 30% of the market, and certainly under 20%. The FTC's majority state-

28. *United States* v. *Eastman Kodak Co.*, 63 F. 3D 95, 102 (2d Cir. 1995).

ment did note that the exclusives were "troubling" and that the FTC would monitor the effects of them and any future agreements. Because Community law appears more willing to characterize exclusives as a way that a dominant firm may increase its influence, the EC may have looked at Boeing's exclusives differently.[29]

It certainly did. The European Commission focused on the fact that a European competitor to Boeing and McDonnell Douglas—Airbus Industrie—had been "foreclosed from a significant part [11 percent] of the market for commercial aircraft for two decades." Karel Van Miert, then competition commissioner, addressed the issue directly:

> Regarding the exclusivity arrangements I would like to stress that we have long had in Europe a rigorous approach to vertical restraints. It is said that under U.S. law exclusivity deals of a cumulative order of 13% market share would fall into a safe harbour. However, if it is true that there was no chance to challenge such agreements successfully in court, even in cases like Boeing, I would be tempted—with all due respect—to find this worrisome. Particularly since exclusivity deals can, under certain circumstances present in Boeing (such as the long duration of the agreements), snowball into something very hard to stop. This is of course an internal U.S. problem. *Nevertheless, such agreements can exercise a direct foreclosure effect on foreign companies.*[30]

As it turned out, the clash between the competing policies was resolved by capitulation, not of either government on this occasion but by Boeing, which agreed to sacrifice its vertical arrangements to get its deal past both authorities.

Are such verticals really a problem in the first place, however? Is the U.S. approach to vertical arrangements too lax? Should it be tightened up to European standards?

Proposals for Reform, and a Critique

Trade experts from the Organization for Economic Cooperation and Development (OECD) find that where "incumbent manufacturers have tied up all retailers, for instance through exclusive dealing arrangements or through full vertical integration, a foreign entrant will have to overcome barriers cre-

---

29. Pitofsky (1997, 3–4).
30. Van Miert (1997). Emphasis added.

ated by the larger amount of capital necessary to set up its own distribution network as well as by 'learning effects,' owing to the likely greater efficiency of established retailers over new ones."[31]

> Although there may be some efficiency gains from exclusive dealing arrangements which provide customer services and information (largely non-appropriable and, therefore, subject to free riding by competing distributors), such gains are outweighed by the very significant exclusionary impact on imports. Some experts argue that it is essential to compare the efficiency gains from enhanced intra-brand co-ordination with those from greater inter-brand competition and expanded foreign trade and that vertical restraints can retard the entry of foreign manufacturers. In that respect, *the relaxed policies towards these restraints in . . . the United States may have artificially raised entry barriers.*[32]

William Comanor and Patrick Rey explain that

> potential entrants into many markets are often foreign producers. Where imports are concerned, a foreign manufacturer is a non-integrated supplier who seeks to use the distribution system of the host country. When he is impeded from doing so, and when this result occurs because of vertical restraints . . . then the failure of competition policy authorities to move against these restraints can have protectionist effects. . . .
>
> A tolerant attitude towards these restraints can therefore discriminate against foreign producers and in favour of domestic ones. On the other hand, a vigorous policy against these restraints can promote international trade.[33]

To support this argument, they submit that

> a particular historic example where the vigorous enforcement of competition policy towards vertical restraints not only promoted competition but also stimulated the flow of international trade concerns the United States automobile industry in the years immediately following the Second World War. In this era, the leading manufacturers used exclusive dealing arrangements such that dealers were effectively limited to selling the cars of a single manufacturer.[34]

---

31. Zampetti and Sauvé (1995, 20).
32. Zampetti and Sauvé (1995, 254). Emphasis added.
33. Comanor and Rey (1995, 468).
34. Comanor and Rey (1995, 466).

They also find that

> in many small cities and rural areas, demand was not sufficient to support
> a number of independent dealers. It was thereby difficult for single brand
> dealers to achieve full distribution economies so that dealerships were not
> common. As a result, smaller manufacturers and new entrants were placed
> at a substantial disadvantage since prospective buyers had to travel longer
> distances to find full-service dealers. . . . This disadvantage would not exist
> if dealers could sell more than a single brand of automobile. The culprit
> was a system that limited dealers to a single brand of automobile.
>
> While this distribution system persisted into the 1960's, it incurred vari-
> ous attacks before it was finally dissolved. An important blow to the disso-
> lution of exclusive distribution was the *Standard Stations* case of 1949, where
> exclusive contracts by sellers with large market shares were deemed in vio-
> lation of the antitrust laws. That decision directly called into question the
> legality of the exclusive dealing arrangements employed in the automobile
> industry.
>
> Eventually, exclusive dealing in automobiles dissolved, although the pro-
> cess did not occur until the 1970s, some 20 years after the original court
> decision. Various foreign manufacturers entered the U.S. market through
> distributors who often sold American cars as well as other foreign makes.
> By the 1990s, the U.S. market had become much more competitive.[35]

These findings and conclusions appear quite plausible. However, it is difficult to reconcile them with a more detailed study of the same sector that
takes into consideration the subsequent evolution in antitrust analysis in
the United States.

Mike Scherer finds that increased antitrust scrutiny of vertical restraints
in the U.S. automobile industry has had little or no effect on the ability of
foreign manufacturers to access the U.S. market.[36] He agrees that the more
stern approach to vertical restraints that was introduced with the *Standard
Stations* case made it more difficult for large American auto manufacturers
to require their dealers to carry only their cars.[37] He notes, however, that

---

35. Comanor and Rey (1995, 467).

36. Scherer (1999, 77).

37. Scherer (1999, 89): "Under the somewhat unclear legal precedents existing during the
1980s, it is unlikely that the Big Three, with their large market shares, could have successfully
defended themselves against antitrust charges in the United States if they cancelled a dealer's
franchise for diffusing sales efforts by taking on a competing auto line, but smaller auto manufacturers were able to do so."

auto manufacturers . . . had means more subtle than explicit contractual restrictions for maintaining the exclusivity of their dealers. The dealer who strayed too far from the fold was likely to have difficulty securing timely delivery of the models it sought. . . . Despite the passage of so-called "dealer day in court" laws . . . unfaithful dealers were also susceptible to various other forms of harassment by their manufacturer-suppliers. As a result . . . most of the showrooms handling the leading American producers' cars have remained effectively exclusive to a single manufacturer's offerings.[38]

Since American suppliers were able to maintain de facto exclusivity at the dealer level, the more stern antitrust approach to vertical restraints would not appear to have helped foreign suppliers to access the U.S. market. Indeed, Scherer finds that "for importers, the easiest, if not the most effective, access to the U.S. market was through a dealer marketing other foreign cars. . . . Most of the foreign cars that sought U.S. sales during the period following World War II were in fact sold through multi-manufacturer foreign car specialists."[39]

Volkswagen, Porsche, and Mercedes-Benz used each other's toeholds—just as did Toyota, Honda, and Nissan—to gain their first real presence in the U.S. market. This kind of cooperation was not enough to allow them to expand their operations, however. To do that, Nissan and Volkswagen in particular created their own independent dealer networks, which required a great deal of investment in training, promotion, and after-sales service.[40] Loyalty bonuses and other vertical arrangements were needed to win and maintain a dealer's customers. The small market share of these new entrants allowed them to maintain such vertical arrangements even under the strict antitrust regime of the 1950s. Although Volkswagen was prevented from stipulating resale prices, it was allowed to terminate its agreement with a dealer who sold a competing brand.[41] "As events ensued, VW's retail channels remained substantially exclusive."[42]

38. Scherer (1999, 89–90): "In 1960, for example, although 33 percent of all General Motors car dealers in the United States carried more than one GM nameplate (e.g., Pontiac and Cadillac), a mere 0.5 percent of 'Big Four' dealers stocked the cars of competing manufacturers. . . . By January 1998 . . . among the 17,580 dealers holding franchises to sell new U.S. Big Three cars and light trucks, 1.6 percent carried competing companies' vehicles."

39. Scherer (1999, 90).

40. Scherer (1999, 90–93).

41. Scherer (1999, 91), citing *U.S.* v. *Volkswagen of America, Inc. et al.*, CCH 1960 Trade Cases, para. 69, 643, District Court of New Jersey (February 1960); and *Reliable Volkswagen Sales and Service Co.* v. *Volkswagen of America, Inc. et al.*, CCH 1960 Trade Cases, para. 69, 644, District Court of New Jersey (February 1960).

42. Scherer (1999, 92).

It would have been reasonable to assume that as foreign suppliers' market share grew, their vertical restraints would be challenged by U.S. competition authorities. This did not happen, however, for one important reason: the further evolution in antitrust analysis that occurred with the *Tampa Electric* decision. In effect this removed from suspicion many of the exclusivity arrangements of U.S. suppliers and also allowed foreign entrants to make more use of such arrangements, thereby ensuring that their own dealers focused only on selling and servicing their cars. Foreign suppliers could further consolidate their operations without fear of antitrust challenge, which allowed them to attain their own economies of scale and better satisfy the enormous demand that the oil shocks of the early 1970s produced for their more fuel-efficient cars. In 1960, only 20 percent of U.S. dealers selling foreign cars were bound by vertical restraints that required them to carry only one manufacturer's products. By 1998, this figure had reached 80 percent.[43] Foreign suppliers now compete directly with the Big Three automakers for dominance of the U.S. market.

From these facts, two preliminary conclusions may be drawn. First, a stern approach to vertical restraints did not help foreign auto suppliers enter the U.S. market. In fact, it would likely have hindered their ability to expand their U.S. operations. Foreign suppliers were able to expand in the United States only because the prohibition of vertical restraints was relaxed through more rigorous antitrust analysis. Second, foreign suppliers were able to gain effective access to the U.S. market only because they were willing and able to build their own independent distribution channels.

Conclusion: A More Appropriate Focus for International Rule Making

Vertical arrangements can exclude interbrand competitors. Some of these competitors may be foreign firms. It is therefore unlikely that they or their trade representatives will stop trying to tighten up enforcement against such arrangements. Even Scherer accepted that it might be beneficial if the WTO was able to "receive complaints about complex practices [such as vertical restraints] upon which a general international consensus would be difficult or impossible to achieve."[44] Making this facility available could "reduce the

43. Scherer (1999, 90).
44. Scherer (1994, 95).

risk that unilateral action will evoke retaliation, mutual recrimination, and a breakdown of harmonious trading relationships."[45]

Scherer's suggestion may miss a crucial aspect of his own findings, however. Obtaining effective access to a market dominated by vertical restraints depends on the willingness and ability of foreign entrants to build their own independent distribution channels. Their willingness may differ in accordance with their resources and plans. Their ability will depend on a range of factors that pertain to the new market itself. An incumbent's presence will affect only the degree to which demand for the product is already satisfied. There is not much that a foreign entrant can do about this other than to offer a better or cheaper product. An incumbent's vertical arrangements will not affect the entrant's ability to build a new distribution channel, however. More important, the incumbent's vertical arrangements will not affect the possibility that such a channel could be built. That would depend on regulatory matters such as laws on incorporation, distribution, importation, and investment.

It is not the role of trade or competition policy to allow new entrants to free ride on the efforts of their competitors. Breaking up or mandating access to existing distribution channels would amount to regulatory intervention that would be likely to harm efficient business arrangements. Why should any supplier, domestic or foreign, expand its distribution network to meet demand if at any moment part of it might be ordered to be handed over to a foreign rival? If such a risk existed, economies of scale that might be realized through such expansion—and concomitant improvements in interbrand competition—would be forgone.

Preventing significant barriers to market entry is the proper role of trade policy—and the proper focus of European competition policy. Competition rules in jurisdictions that are not part of a grand project of economic union should prohibit only those vertical restraints that lessen competition substantially. As the American Bar Association points out, "The idea of challenging access-restricting private conduct without an antitrust rationale raises the risk of prohibiting efficiency-enhancing conduct."[46] In Europe, this risk is not only politically acceptable but also economically justifiable. The European approach to vertical arrangements is truly endemic, however. Efforts to bridge the international divide that this approach creates should pay more heed to the legitimacy of the antitrust focus on competition and rely less on

45. Scherer (1994, 95).
46. American Bar Association (1995, 956).

the rhetoric of calls for global common approaches to increase market access opportunities for individual competitors.

References

American Bar Association. 1995. International Law and Practice Section, Report to the House of Delegates. "Using Antitrust Laws to Enhance Access of U.S. Firms to Foreign Markets." *International Lawyer* 29:945.

Black, Oliver. 1997. "Per Se Rules and Rules of Reason: What Are They?" *European Competition Law Review* 18 (April): 145.

Comanor, William, and Patrick Rey. 1995. "Competition Policy toward Vertical Foreclosure in a Global Economy." *International Business Lawyer* 23 (November).

Commission of the European Union. 1995. "Competition Policy in the New Trade Order: Strengthening International Co-operation and Rules." July. Luxemburg: OOPEC.

———. 1996. "Towards an International Framework of Competition Rules." June 18. COM (96) 296 final.

European Community. 1998. "Impact of Anti-Competitive Practices on Trade." February 23. WT/WGTCP/W/62.

Fox, Eleanor. 1997. "Toward World Antitrust and Market Access." *American Journal of International Law* 93:1.

Handler, Milton. 1957. *Antitrust in Perspective*. Columbia University Press.

Hawk, Barry. 1995. "System Failure: Vertical Restraints and EC Competition Law." *Common Market Law Review* 32 (973): 32.

Hoda, Anwarul. 1997. "Trade, Competition Policy and the World Trade Organisation." Global Forum on Competition and Trade Policy Conference, New Delhi, March 17–19, 8 (on file with the author).

"ICC Conference Gets Perspectives on Report from Business Executives." 1998. *Antitrust and Trade Regulation Report*.

Marsden, Philip. 1998. "The Impropriety of WTO 'Market Access' Rules on Vertical Restraints." *World Competition* 21 (16): 5–24.

Melamed, Douglas. 1998. "Remarks." American Bar Association, Antitrust Section, April 2.

Pitofsky, Robert. 1977. "Vertical Restraints and Vertical Aspects of Mergers: A U.S. Perspective." Twenty-Fourth Annual Conference on International Antitrust Law and Policy, October 16–17.

Scherer, Frederic M. 1994. *Competition Policies for an Integrated Economy*. Brookings.

———. 1999. "Retail Distribution Channel Barriers to International Trade." *Antitrust Law Journal* 67:1

Van Miert, Karel. 1997. "International Cooperation in the Field of Competition: A View from the EC." October 16.

World Trade Organization. 1997. *WTO Annual Report, 1997: Special Topic—Trade and Competition Policy*.

Zampetti, Americo, and Pierre Sauvé. 1995. "Overview" and "Summary of Discussions." In *New Dimensions of Market Access in a Globalising World Economy*. Paris: OECD.

Case Studies

The Boeing–McDonnell Douglas Merger

THOMAS L. BOEDER

A ntitrust clearance reviews of the Boeing–McDonnell Douglas merger in the United States and Europe present sharp contrasts in approach, highlighting great difficulties in transatlantic merger review cooperation in the context of a case involving significant political and international trade considerations. Aggressive assertion by the European Commission of extraterritorial application of European merger control law to the proposed combination of two U.S. companies with virtually no manufacturing facilities in Europe led to a political controversy so heated that the possibility of a major trade war was being discussed on a regular basis in the press on both sides of the Atlantic.

Ultimately the risk of such a clash was avoided by a negotiated agreement resulting in clearance by the European Commission, albeit on a very different basis than the earlier clearance without condition by the U.S. Federal Trade Commission.

It may be that this particular industry and the principal protagonists in the merger review drama in Europe (Boeing, McDonnell Douglas, and Airbus) are sufficiently unique that experience from this transaction has little general application to questions of how effectively future merger reviews can be conducted and coordinated simultaneously in Europe and the United States. However, to the extent that this situation presents lessons to be learned, it suggests that the existence of two fundamentally different antitrust merger review regimes in the United States and Europe is likely to create additional conflicts in the future and substantial difficulties to companies required to seek merger clearance in both jurisdictions.

Background of the Transaction

In December 1996, the Boeing Company and the McDonnell Douglas Corporation announced their agreement to merge, thus forming the world's largest aerospace company and second-largest defense supplier. The deal was estimated at the time of announcement to be a $13.3 billion transaction. The new company would employ 200,000 people, with operations in twenty-seven states, and estimated combined 1997 revenues of $48 billion. Although the two firms had no significant overlap with respect to defense programs, they were direct competitors with respect to the sale of large, commercial jet transport aircraft, in which market they constituted two of the only three remaining manufacturers worldwide. The fact that the only other remaining competitor, the second-largest manufacturer in this market, was Europe's Airbus Consortium—perhaps the most successful example of postwar European economic cooperation—gave rise to the political issues that dominated European Commission merger clearance review virtually from the time of announcement of the proposed transaction.

Since both companies had a sufficient level of sales to Europe to meet the merger control filing thresholds of the European Commission, it was understood from the outset that the proposed transaction would be subject to antitrust merger review in both the United States and Europe, despite significant questions raised by the parties as to the jurisdiction of the European Commission or the appropriateness of commission review in light of the principles of international comity.

Review in the United States

Antitrust review in the United States proceeded in the standard manner in connection with notification under the Hart-Scott-Rodino Act (HSR) and was completed by the FTC in slightly over six months—a significant accomplishment for a transaction of this magnitude. The Boeing–McDonnell Douglas HSR forms were filed on January 29, 1997, shortly after announcement of the proposed merger; the anticipated second request was issued by the FTC on February 28, 1997; substantial compliance with the second request was certified and then confirmed by the FTC on June 11, 1997; and antitrust clearance was confirmed, without condition, in a written decision issued by the FTC on July 1, 1997, with a dissenting statement by Commissioner Azcuenaga. This clearance came to stand in sharp contrast to the ultimate result of the review by the European Commission.

The review process, although relatively swift, was not without a substantial element of pain to the merging parties, since by the time of clearance they had gathered, processed, coded, indexed, and produced millions of documents in a production described by the FTC at the time as the most extensive in the history of merger review.

As is generally the case in merger review by U.S. antitrust agencies, the FTC conducted its investigation in private, with no substantive comments on the matter until the investigation had been concluded and the FTC's written statement had been issued. Despite some public challenges to the appropriateness of this merger between two of the three remaining manufacturers of large commercial jet aircraft, the FTC's clearance of the merger (as described in the FTC statement) was based on conventional antitrust principles—specifically, the diminished competitor doctrine.[1] The FTC's focus in reaching this result was to determine whether the merger would have any substantial adverse effects on consumers, that is, airlines that purchase airplanes manufactured by the merging companies.

Review in Europe

The European merger review process is governed by a firm timetable. In the instance of this transaction, review was formally commenced by Boeing's filing of a form CO on February 18, 1997.[2] On March 19, 1997, the European Commission announced its decision to proceed with an in-depth, phase 2 investigation of the merger, thereby triggering the four-month deadline for completion of final review as prescribed by European Union merger control law. On June 12–13, 1997, the commission held nonpublic hearings on the proposed merger, leading to a July 4, 1997, recommendation to the European Commission's Competition Advisory Committee to oppose the merger and, after a period of intensive negotiations, a final decision by the

1. See *United States* v. *General Dynamics Corp,* 415 U.S. 486 (1974).

2. In Europe, only Boeing was required to make a merger review filing. In the United States, both Boeing and McDonnell Douglas were required to make an HSR filing.

commission on July 30, 1997, to clear the merger, based on certain under-takings agreed to by Boeing.[3]

Three aspects of the commission's review process were striking from the perspective of a U.S. antitrust practitioner. First, while millions of pages of party and third-party documents were produced as part of the HSR review by the FTC, form CO filing and subsequent document requests by the commission's merger task force resulted in production of a relatively small volume of documents, numbering in the thousands, rather than millions, of pages. One of the consequences of this difference from the approach taken by the FTC is that discussion of issues in the European context tended to be based more on general industry assumptions than on specific evidence of a sort that would be admissible in a legal proceeding in the United States.

Second, the merger review process by European authorities was highly political and very public. From the time the merger was announced until the time the review was concluded, interviews, press releases, and speeches by the European Commission's top competition official, Commissioner Karel Van Miert, on the merits of the transaction became frequent. Indeed, he at one time declared that the transaction would be disapproved without major concessions and further described the specific concessions that would be demanded. The political nature of the process also was highlighted by specu-lation that the merger would not be cleared absent a renegotiation of the bilateral treaty between the EU and the United States on aircraft manufac-turing subsidies.

Third, from the perspective of the parties seeking clearance, the role of Boeing's principal competitor, the Airbus Consortium, was dominant in the review in a way inconsistent with U.S. practice. While U.S. antitrust agencies are generally cautious and somewhat skeptical of submissions by a com-petitor seeking to derail a proposed merger, the European Commission fo-cused primarily on potential adverse effects on Airbus or advantages to Boeing over Airbus that might result from the merger. On the other hand, expressions of support and lack of concern by airline customers (a major factor in the FTC's decision not to act against the merger) appeared to have no effect on the commission's position in opposition to the merger. This factor highlights a primary difference in approach to antitrust analysis be-tween the United States and Europe: the focus in the United States is on the

---

3. The actual time between notification of the institution of a phase 2 investigation and announcement of the result on July 30, 1997, is slightly more than four months by virtue of the fact that intervening holidays during that time period are not counted in calculating the deadline. Art. 8, Commission Regulation (EC) 3384/94.

process of competition and consumer impact; the focus in Europe is on the interests of both competitors and consumers.

Conflicting Approaches

Public pronouncements by the European Commission with respect to a potential European challenge to the merger, regardless of the outcome of the FTC review, had political repercussions in the United States. The stakes by this point in the merger review battle were perhaps best summarized by a Boeing spokeswoman, who was quoted by *Agence France Presse* and other media as saying that, "if the Federal Trade Commission says yes and the European Commission says no or fines Boeing, it will no longer be a Boeing-EC issue. I think that would elevate it to a trade issue between the United States and Europe."[4] The credibility of this view was supported by a quote the next day from U.S. vice president Al Gore stating that the administration would take "whatever action is appropriate" to prevent the EU from "impeding the merger."[5]

When the European Commission continued to challenge the merger after the FTC statement had been issued, clearing the transaction without condition, the level of political controversy heated almost to the boiling point. The Clinton administration at this point began to take an active role in the political battle with Europe over merger approval. Thus for example the administration was described as "considering how to retaliate against Europe if it makes good on its threat to try and undermine the merger of U.S. aerospace giants, the Boeing Company and the McDonnell Douglas Corporation."[6] The article went on to describe the controversy as a "looming trans-Atlantic dispute" and as being the subject of White House meetings attended by a number of key government agency representatives. Administration officials were described as considering a number of possible actions against the Europeans, including limiting flights between the United States and France, imposing tariffs on European airplanes, and filing an official protest with the World Trade Organization.[7]

The extent to which international political considerations were involved in the review of the transaction at this stage also is shown by the involve-

4. *Agence France Presse,* May 13, 1997.
5. *The Financial Times,* May 14, 1997.
6. *Washington Post,* July 17, 1997.
7. *Washington Post,* July 17, 1997.

ment of officials from the U.S. Department of Justice's Antitrust Division
and the U.S. Department of Defense, rather than the FTC, in discussions of
the merger with EC competition officials.

Conclusion

Fortunately, the danger of a transatlantic trade war over this merger was
averted when Boeing and the European Commission negotiated an agreement whereby the merger was cleared on the condition of Boeing's compliance with certain undertakings, including agreement by Boeing not to enforce
the exclusivity provisions in its airplane sales agreements with three U.S.
airlines.

In my view, the Boeing–McDonnell Douglas experience does suggest the
potential for serious conflicts between U.S. and European merger control
regimes in the future, particularly when the differing practices and legal standards involved are applied to companies with few assets in the jurisdiction
seeking to block or modify a proposed merger.[8]

8. For an interesting contemporaneous discussion of such issues, see the article on this
merger in the *Christian Science Monitor,* June 11, 1997.

The American Airlines and British Airways Alliance

GARY R. DOERNHOEFER

On June 11, 1996, American Airlines and British Airways announced their agreement to form an alliance, an increasingly common form of joint venture in the airline industry. Following the examples of KLM-Northwest, United-Lufthansa-SAS, and Delta-Sabena-Swissair-Austrian, American and British Airways intended to link their respective networks and "code share" by marketing seats on their partner airline under their own two-letter identifier (AA for American and BA for British Airways). American Airlines and British Airways also agreed to integrate their operations in other ways, hoping eventually to operate their combined transatlantic networks as though merged.[1] The parties subsequently filed their application for code sharing and seeking antitrust immunity with the U.S. Department of Transportation under its statutory authority.[2]

The proposed transaction was expressly contingent on the negotiation of a new bilateral aviation agreement between the United States and the United Kingdom. The existing bilateral agreement contains a number of limitations to new entry, which the parties

1. Outright merger of a domestic and foreign airline is prohibited by statute in most countries, including the United States. 49 U.S.C., sec. 40102 (a) (15), defining "U.S. citizen" for purposes of ownership and control of a U.S. airline.
2. 49 U.S.C., secs. 41308, 41309.

acknowledged would have to be removed if the proposed agreement were to go forward with an acceptable impact on competition. For example, the number of airlines that may serve London's Heathrow Airport from the United States is limited to just four, and Heathrow may be served only from designated U.S. cities. In addition to the elimination of regulatory barriers to entry, the public debate fostered by competitors of the two airlines quickly focused on another potential barrier, the availability of landing rights, known as slots, at London's airports.

Because of the structure of the transaction, no notification was required under the Hart-Scott-Rodino Act in the United States. Likewise, the transaction did not fall within the definition of a merger under European regulations.

Initially, the parties believed that no notification to the European Commission was necessary at all. Although the transaction could have been considered a concentrative joint venture subject to review by the Directorate General IV (DGIV), the European Commission had never been granted competence by the member states to apply articles 85 and 86 of the Treaty of Rome to international air transportation. Moreover, this was the fourth international alliance formed by European and U.S. airlines, and none had been reviewed previously by the commission. Accordingly, the parties had no reason to anticipate regulatory scrutiny by the DGIV.

Jurisdiction

Among the early challenges in the administration of the regulatory review of the American–British Airways alliance was the determination of jurisdiction between the various agencies claiming primary competence. In Europe, the Office of Fair Trading began its review of the proposed alliance pursuant to article 88, while in parallel the commission pursued its review under article 89. Where no implementing regulation had been adopted pursuant to article 87 of the Treaty of Rome, as was the case for international air transportation, precedence should be granted to the member state's regulatory body, which has primary responsibility for the application of European Union competition rules and the authority to grant exemptions under article 85 (3).[3] Although the member state's competition authority and the DGIV have a reciprocal obligation under the Treaty of Rome to cooperate in these cir-

---

3. The parties relied on the advocate general's opinion in *Asjes* as the authority establishing precedence between member states and the commission in parallel investigations.

cumstances, that cooperation was hindered in the early stages by political considerations on both sides and the lack of established procedures between the Office of Fair Trading and the DGIV.

The U.S. side had its own complications. The parties' joint application for code sharing and antitrust immunity was filed with the Department of Transportation, with a copy to the Department of Justice, Antitrust Division. The two agencies were expected to cooperate in their review, although they applied different standards. The Antitrust Division's standards are well known due to the publication of the merger guidelines, decisional history, and scholarly critique. On the other hand, the Transportation Department's standards for antitrust immunity grant that agency greater discretion and draw on more ephemeral considerations, such as international comity and foreign relations.

The U.S. process was further complicated by vastly different procedures employed by the two U.S. governmental agencies that review international airline alliances. The Justice Department used its authority to engage in highly confidential civil investigations to request documents and specific data. The parties met with Justice Department attorneys and economists and engaged in spirited debate about the proper conclusions to be drawn from the assembled information. Although the bargaining power is held mostly by the Justice Department, there is some ability to negotiate remedies that respond to the competition concerns in a way that best fits the business objectives. On the other hand, the Transportation Department process was conducted in an open docket, that is, the documents and data that the parties were compelled to produce were made available to other participants, including, in a limited way, the parties' competitors. Further, Transportation Department attorneys, economists, and decisional authorities are bound by rules proscribing ex parte communications, thus chilling any meaningful discussion of analytical methods or negotiation of remedies.

Analytical Differences

All regulatory authorities defined the relevant market similarly, as nonstop air transportation in a single city pair and focused on the time-sensitive passenger on such routes. According to the regulatory authorities, certain time-sensitive passengers (typically business travelers) generally do not perceive one-stop connecting service as a viable alternative to nonstop service. Each regulatory authority seemed willing to concede that purely leisure passengers would not suffer a loss of competition by the proposed transaction because of the number of alternative routes and alternative London airports available to passengers who are less time sensitive. Nevertheless, there were significant differences in the perceived level of competition within the defined markets among those involved.

At one extreme, the U.S. Transportation Department has generally accepted that one-stop service disciplines pricing for nonstop passengers. The parties believe that the department's view is correct. Although there may be passengers who will not substitute one-stop service for nonstop in the face of a material price differential, there are customers at the margin who will, and airlines are not able to price discriminate between these marginal passengers and the more inelastic customers. Thus the inelastic customers benefit from the pricing driven by the more elastic, marginal passenger.

The DGIV contended that the parties' argument might be true but would not apply to the American–British Airways transaction because of London's unique geographical position. The DGIV concluded that one-stop service via London would constrain pricing for nonstop services between the United States and the Continent but that no European hub offered such competitive connecting opportunities to discipline prices between London and the United States. Unfortunately, the DGIV's analysis failed to consider the competitive discipline by other U.S. hubs on the nonstop routes that would be operated by American Airlines and British Airways. For example, pricing for nonstop Dallas–Fort Worth–London service would clearly be competitive with connecting service that would be offered under an open bilateral agreement via Cincinnati by Delta Air Lines or Cleveland by Continental.[4]

The Justice Department never accepted more than very limited crosselasticity between nonstop and one-stop service in the narrowly defined relevant market of time-sensitive business passengers. The Justice Department also remained convinced that airlines possess the ability to price discriminate among relatively inelastic full-fare passengers for these purposes.

Each of the regulatory authorities was interested in the efficiencies the parties expected to achieve by the integration of their route networks. However, both the Justice Department and the DGIV were reluctant to allow the acknowledged efficiencies to offset perceived harm to competition. In both venues, regulatory officials wanted to accept the efficiencies and mitigate all perceived harms by a series of remedies.

---

4. The analysis performed by the U.S. authorities assumed the elimination of bilateral constraints to new entry. Because the European Commission believed the negotiation of individual bilateral aviation agreements between member states and the United States to be unlawful, its analysis was never fully consistent with reasonable expectations of new entry resulting from a new bilateral agreement.

Despite the precise variations in the application of the relevant market definitions, the Office of Fair Trading and the DGIV each concluded that without remedies relating to the availability of slots, the proposed transaction would harm competition in violation of article 85. These conclusions were roughly consistent with the analytical outcome at the Department of Justice but varied in the precise city-pair markets in which they should be applied. However, the DGIV went even further, also contending that the proposed alliance constituted an abuse of a dominant position, in violation of article 86. There was no finding by U.S. or U.K. officials that correlated with this conclusion.

The DGIV determined that American Airlines and British Airways were "dominant" in each city pair in which they enjoyed a combined market share in excess of 50 percent. They determined that dominance existed, within the meaning of article 86, in large part because of higher nonstop fares to London than to Frankfurt or Paris. This analytical error seemed to have been based on the DGIV's refusal to attempt a forecast of the marketplace in the absence of a restrictive bilateral agreement between the United States and the United Kingdom. The parties contended that current prices and market share statistics reflected the restrictive impact of the current bilateral agreement and that in a market that was open to entry, which was a recognized prerequisite to the proposed transaction, these factors would change dramatically, precluding dominance. Regulatory authorities in the United States seemed to agree with the parties' contentions on this point, as long as new entry was facilitated by the availability of slots as well as the elimination of the bilateral constraints.

Remedies

The most dramatic difference between the United States and the United Kingdom on the one hand and the European Commission on the other occurred in the nature of the proposed remedies necessary to approve the proposed transaction. In each jurisdiction, regulatory authorities identified open entry as the most important goal to be achieved by the remedies. Clearly, after the elimination of the bilateral restrictions, slots became the most important factor. Each agency believed that without a means of making slots available, the elimination of bilateral restrictions would not be sufficient. However, the DGIV insisted on a divestiture, without compensation, of all necessary slots to meet the level of new entry it deemed necessary to offset the dominance of the alliance. Transportation Department authorities never reached a stage of declaring their view in full detail but seemed to believe that the parties would have to divest themselves of slots. The U.S. authorities also believed that American Airlines and British Airways should receive remuneration for the slots they divested. The Justice Department, taking the most liberal view, conceded that some slots might be available in the marketplace and that, as long as the total prescribed level of new entry occurred, the source of the slots was irrelevant. If slots had to be divested to meet their prescribed entry targets, American Airlines and British Airways would be entitled to compensation for the divestiture.

On the surface, the different outcomes of this debate related not to disparate application of antitrust principles but to varying interpretations of the legal status of slots. The DGIV strongly believed that slots were not the assets of the airlines but government rights that were granted without cost and should be divested without compensation. Digging a little deeper, the parties quickly discovered the competition factors influencing this issue. The DGIV felt that a completely free "buy-sell" market in slots would lead to adverse concentration in the hands of a few large airlines. In contrast, U.S. and U.K. authorities recognized the utility and efficiency advantages incumbent in allowing a free market to determine the distribution of slots. They were willing to permit some concentration of slot holdings, recognizing that in a network industry any one slot can be utilized more efficiently by a larger hub carrier than a carrier that serves a smaller number of destinations. Thus the large carrier is more likely to pay more for it.

Aside from some basic similarities in remedies relating to slots, very serious differences developed among the other proposed remedies. In addition to the divestiture of slots, the DGIV insisted on capacity decreases and freezes in specified markets, ostensibly to ensure that incumbent airlines could not respond to new entry by adding capacity in competition with the new entrant. U.S. and U.K. officials strongly disagreed with this approach, contending that holding capacity out of the market was more likely to injure consumers in both the short run and long term than to help competition.

Another unique facet of the DGIV's concerns focused on the disparate impact on competition among EU member states that would arise from a bilateral agreement between a single member state and the United States. The DGIV contended that such agreements must, in order to mitigate the unequal effect, allow not only member states' national airlines—in this case British Airways and Virgin—but also all other member states' airlines to fly between the United Kingdom and the Unites States. This issue overlapped with the jurisdiction of other directorates general and has not yet been resolved.

The DGIV also proposed a market basket of other remedies relating to computer reservation systems, travel agencies' compensation schemes, and interline cooperation between incumbent carriers and other airlines. These remedies were perceived by U.S. officials as unnecessary and unduly regulatory in nature, highlighting one clear distinction in approach between the DGIV and the Justice Department. European competition authorities are far more willing to engage in regulatory remedial efforts than their U.S. counterparts.

Analytical Input

Among the factors that seriously complicated the decisional process were the input data. The airline industry is awash in data about every aspect of its operations. However, unless care is exercised in their use, they can be meaningless at best, misleading at worst. Most important, in parallel proceedings such as these, it would have been tremendously helpful to the parties and government participants to have agreed on a single set of data requests and application of the data.

Some airline data sources are available publicly, some are not. Other sources are available to carriers within one country but withheld from distribution to foreign airlines and, presumably, foreign governments. Moreover, the terms used by regulatory officials in requesting data must be very precise. In the case of American Airlines and British Airways, different regulatory authorities asked for different data both in terms of time periods and markets. While it was never clear whether the differences in the data requested were intentional and understood by the government staffs, the parties believe that these differences must have complicated discussions between the regulatory officials. The parties offered to waive the Justice Department's civil investigatory demand confidentiality protections with respect to the European competition officials, but the DGIV never acted upon that offer, preferring to work with data responsive to its own requests.

Conclusion

Joint procedural aspects must be improved between international regulatory agencies if we are to avoid inconsistent remedies, in particular regarding analytical data. The current situation is like the parable of the three blind men describing an elephant as each is touching only one small part; each has a very different perception of the whole. Each agency views the situation very differently depending on its precise focus and the nature of the input data it requested. Even where the analytical approach is similar, such as the experience with the DGIV's application of article 85 and the analysis by the Justice and Transportation Departments under the Sherman Act, if the input data are very different, the outcomes will not coincide.

Another important recommendation for future proceedings is to recognize the role of noncompetition regulatory authorities. Here, the Transportation Department had statutory authority for granting the parties' request for immunity. The Justice Department had a consulting role only. However, Justice had experience and established protocols for communications with the DGIV; Transportation had not. A process that incorporates all regulatory participants and establishes common data resources would eliminate much of the distraction and wasted effort that precludes concentration on the more important and fundamental differences in theoretical approach.

Although the DGIV appears to apply article 85 in a manner roughly equivalent to the standards developed by the Justice Department under section 1 of the Sherman Act, it does not appear that section 2 of the Sherman Act is as close a counterpart for article 86. The DGIV did not find dominance through a process that determines the parties have market power. Instead, the test for dominance was not well defined but seemed more related to market share in a defined relevant market. Greater focus by the agencies on the determination of similarities between monopolization or attempted monopolization and the abuse of a dominant power might be fruitful.

Last, the most difficult difference to overcome is likely to be in the area of remedies. The Europeans are much more tolerant of regulatory solutions than their U.S. colleagues. Without a great deal more effort at harmonization, this divide is likely to remain.

PricewaterhouseCoopers

WILLIAM J. KOLASKY

B efore their merger in July 1998, Price Waterhouse and
Coopers and Lybrand were two of the smaller Big Six professional services organizations.[1] From their roots in England in the
mid-nineteenth century, both organizations had grown into worldwide networks providing a broad range of professional services
on a global basis. These included, in addition to the traditional
function of auditing and reporting on financial statements, professional services in such diverse areas as tax, litigation support,
corporate finance, information technology, management consulting, human resources, and business process outsourcing. Their
merger created the largest professional service network in the
world, with estimated worldwide revenues of over $15 billion
in 1998.

Price Waterhouse and Coopers announced a full merger of their
international networks on September 17, 1997. Since both entities were organized as networks of individual member firms in
different regions of the world, the proposed merger required the
approval of the member firms worldwide. This approval was obtained in late November 1997.

---

1. This case study is based on the response of PricewaterhouseCoopers to the
request of the International Competition Policy Advisory Committee of the U.S.
Justice Department for information on multijurisdictional merger review policy.

Although the ultimate objective was to merge the entire global networks of both organizations, practicalities dictated that implementation of the merger proceed in a more stepwise fashion. The initial step was to merge the two networks, and their individual member firms, in the United States, Europe, Canada, Australia, New Zealand, Africa, and the Middle East. This was followed with mergers of the member firms in the rest of the world.

The Merger Clearance Process

Price Waterhouse and Coopers each had member firms in more than a hundred countries worldwide. The span of their operations, therefore, presented a uniquely difficult challenge in terms of navigating the premerger clearance process.

As indicated above, the two organizations decided from the outset to implement the merger in a stepwise fashion. This enabled them to seek antitrust clearance first in those jurisdictions with the most well-established merger clearance regimes. These jurisdictions included the United States, the European Commission, Canada, Australia, New Zealand, and Switzerland. The two organizations also surveyed the merger clearance requirements in all other countries of the world in which there were operations to ensure that they made whatever mandatory filings were required in a timely fashion. As detailed below, each jurisdiction presented somewhat different procedural issues, although the substantive analysis applied in each jurisdiction was nearly identical.

The United States

In the United States, the merger was structured as a merger of two partnerships and, as such, was not subject to the usual Hart-Scott-Rodino premerger notification requirements. As soon as the merger was announced on September 17, 1997, representatives of both firms promptly met with the assistant attorney general for antitrust. At this initial meeting, the parties described the proposed merger and the reasons for it and offered voluntarily to provide the Antitrust Division any information it needed to satisfy itself that the merger would not substantially lessen competition in any relevant market. The parties also told the division that they would adhere voluntarily to the schedule provided under the HSR Act for premerger review but that they hoped to complete the antitrust review in all jurisdictions by the end of the first quarter of 1998.

During the initial thirty-day review period, two other Big Six networks, Ernst and Young and KPMG Peat Marwick, announced a similar merger of their worldwide operations. This immediately raised an issue as to whether the Antitrust Division would review the two mergers together or would take them in the order in which they had been announced, under a first-in, first-out approach. After initially indicating that its general policy was to adopt this approach, the division decided that because the two mergers had been proposed so closely together it needed to review the two mergers together. It indicated, however, that in the event it concluded that only one merger could go forward, it would take into account the order in which they were announced, but only as one of a number of factors in evaluating the likely effect of each merger on competition.

During the initial thirty-day period, Price Waterhouse and Coopers both provided substantial information and documents to the Antitrust Division describing their operations and showing that the only possible area of competitive concern related to auditing the financial statements of large, publicly traded companies. The division issued civil investigative demands to both firms on October 15, 1997, limited to this one area of overlap. The parties made representatives of the clients knowledgeable about the sectors of the auditing business at issue available for interviews by the division staff, and they subsequently responded through white papers, letters, and economic data to address specific concerns voiced by the staff or in response to additional questions. This process was facilitated by the staff's focused analysis of the issues and their accessibility and frankness. Both firms responded to the civil investigative demands within twenty days, completing their responses on November 4.

In mid-November 1997, the Antitrust Division staff reviewing the proposed merger decided it needed additional information to complete its review. On December 4 it issued a second round of civil investigative demands not only to Price Waterhouse and Coopers but also to the other four Big Six firms. This subsequent request was limited to data and did not seek additional documentation. Price Waterhouse and Coopers both completed their responses within eight days, on December 12. At this time, the parties and the division staff entered into an informal agreement under which the staff undertook to attempt to complete its review by the end of January, and the parties agreed not to close before then.

In January, the staff asked for additional time to complete its review, indicating that, although the parties had responded promptly to the division's request, the other parties had taken longer to do so and that it needed more time to analyze the data. The two firms agreed to delay the closing until the

end of March 1998 in return for a commitment from the Antitrust Division
to complete its review by March 13. The division represented that Ernst and
Young and KPMG had done likewise.

In early February 1998, the division issued a third round of civil investigative demands, seeking information from the parties on the efficiencies
they claimed from the merger in order to determine whether they met the
criteria contained in the revised merger guidelines. The investigative demands
were again narrowly tailored, and the parties were able to complete their
responses within thirteen days, having to produce very few documents.

On February 13, 1998, Ernst and Young and KPMG announced that they
were abandoning their proposed merger, citing among other factors the regulatory obstacles they were encountering, particularly in Europe. This cleared
the way for the Antitrust Division to complete its review of the Price
Waterhouse–Coopers merger expeditiously, which it did, informing the parties on March 13 that it would not challenge the merger.

Europe

In Europe, the initial issue was whether the transaction satisfied the filing
thresholds for a notification at the European Commission level, thereby allowing the parties to take advantage of the "one-stop shopping" offered by
Brussels. This issue arose because of the structure of both Price Waterhouse
and Coopers as networks of member firms separately organized in each country in order to comply with national rules governing the public accounting
profession. After meeting with the Merger Task Force in early October 1997,
the parties made an initial submission describing the structure of the two
networks and the degree of integration among the member firms of each
network. Based on the information in this submission, the Merger Task Force
determined that the merger satisfied the thresholds for notification at the
commission level.

The second issue in Europe related to the timing of the filing. Under the
EC merger regulation, a filing is required within seven days of the signing of
a definitive purchase agreement. In this instance, the parties signed a merger
agreement in principle on September 17, 1997. The Merger Task Force took
the position that because this merger agreement was subject to approval by
individual member firms, it would not be ripe for notification until such
approval was obtained. The task force agreed, however, to accept a draft filing in advance, to ensure that once the official filing was made, it would be
deemed complete and would start the clock running on the review periods
under the merger regulation.

The parties submitted a draft form CO to the Merger Task Force on November 11, 1997. The partners in the member firms of the two organizations approved the merger on November 27, and the parties were then able to file their official form CO notification on December 12, making minor changes from the earlier draft to correct deficiencies identified by the task force.

On January 21, 1998, having completed its phase 1 review, the commission issued a decision to initiate proceedings, thereby commencing a phase 2 review. The decision indicated that after preliminary examination of the notification, and especially in light of the pendency of another proposed merger between two other Big Six networks, the commission had concluded that the proposed concentration could create or strengthen a dominant position. As in the United States, the European concern was largely limited to what the commission identified as a market for auditing and accounting services for large, publicly traded companies, which it found were provided principally by the Big Six. The commission did, however, also seek information as to one other line of business: providing tax advisory and compliance services to large companies.

The commission promptly issued an article 11 request for additional information. This request, as is the usual case, principally sought data and other information and did not require the production of any significant number of documents. Responding to the request was nevertheless extraordinarily difficult because it sought information as to the parties' operations in each individual member country, as necessitated by the commission's preliminary conclusion that each country constituted a separate geographic market for Big Six auditing services. The parties responded to these requests in a timely fashion, completing their responses by the end of February 1998.

Based on the information supplied, the Merger Task Force identified particular economic sectors, such as banking and insurance, in which the four firms that were proposing to merge had particularly strong positions in several member states. The task force accordingly sought additional information from the parties to determine what effect the merger would have on competition in each of these sectors.

On March 13, 1998, after having received and reviewed this information and having met with the parties to discuss it, the Merger Task Force advised the parties that, like the U.S. Department of Justice, it had concluded that the merger would not lessen competition and should, therefore, be cleared. The final decision of the commission, released on May 20 and adopting the task force's recommendation, made it clear that the withdrawal of the parallel Ernst and Young–KPMG notification played an important role in this decision and that the commission would have been very concerned about joint dominance had both mergers proceeded.

Canada

Canadian merger review generally involves less sweeping document and information reviews than either the U.S. or European review. The Canadian process tends to be more interactive, involving a series of detailed and issue-specific information requests. Price Waterhouse and Coopers made their initial submission to the Competition Bureau on November 10, 1997. The bureau submitted a lengthy information request, to which the parties responded with a supplementary submission on November 25. Each submission consisted of a position paper analyzing the issues of inquiry, with attached documentary exhibits and data compilations. The authorities continued to raise new specific issues in response to each submission, frequently the same issues that had arisen in the context of the merger review in the United States or Europe. Canadian counsel prepared more position papers than counsel in any other jurisdiction. In all, the Canadian parties made approximately one dozen separate submissions in addition to the prenotification filing and the numerous responses to lengthy requests for information and documentation.

Toward the end of the review process, Competition Bureau staff indicated that it did not expect that the director would close his file in Canada until it was clear what the United States and Europe were going to do. Even though all substantive issues had been addressed to the satisfaction of bureau staff, the parties were unable to obtain a clearance from the bureau until after the U.S. decision was announced and the direction of the European Commission's thinking was clarified. (Official Canadian clearance was issued the day after the U.S. Justice Department announced its investigation closed.) Thus collaboration between agencies appeared to have the effect of somewhat delaying decisionmaking in Canada. While the Canadian component of the transaction would not have closed before other key international jurisdictions, the Canadian merging parties were nonetheless legitimately concerned about receiving a prompt decision in order to reduce marketplace uncertainty (particularly since competitors were using the regulatory uncertainty to raid clients and professional staff) and to proceed with legitimate transition planning.

New Zealand and Australia

Price Waterhouse and Coopers informally notified the authorities in Australia and New Zealand of the pending merger in early October 1997. Early indications were that the issues in these jurisdictions would be resolved before Christmas. New Zealand commissioners initially indicated to the parties that they approved of the merger but, upon receiving word of the proposed merger between KPMG and Ernst and Young, held off on issuing a "no action" letter until they had been notified of both deals. Australian counsel prepared information submissions to the Australian Competition and Consumer Commission (ACCC) on a private and voluntary basis and were told they could expect a decision within two to six weeks of their formal submission.

In November 1997, after several meetings between merger authorities and counsel, the New Zealand Commission issued its "no action" letter, thus becoming the first country to close a substantive investigation into the merger. At the same time, Australian counsel suffered a setback when the Australian filing had to be indefinitely postponed because of outstanding uncertainties regarding the ultimate structure of the merger that made it technically impossible to submit a filing, as this choice of structure would determine what section of Australia's anticompetition law governed.[2]

In Australia, the ACCC staff launched into a full-scale independent investigation of the market competition among the Big Six, issuing information requests and interviewing firm members. Counsel for the parties arranged a conference with the staff to present their own analysis of market structure in late November 1997. The investigation continued into 1998, with numerous members of all the Big Six firms being interviewed by the ACCC, which promised to issue its final report by the end of January. That deadline, however, elapsed without comment. As in Canada, the authorities apparently resolved all of their substantive concerns but remained hesitant to act without guidance from the United States and Europe. Consequently, the ACCC study approving the merger was not issued until the U.S. Justice Department announced in March that it was closing its investigation.

---

2. If § 45 (regarding anticompetitive agreements) governed, both parties would be prohibited from cooperating on tender requests or price until the merger is final; to do so would be a per se boycott or exclusionary offense. To facilitate joint operations, the parties would have preferred to have the merger analyzed under § 50 (governing acquisitions), but to do so the merger would have to be structured so as to centrally feature an acquisition of some kind and could not be a simple agreement between partnerships.

Switzerland

The competition authority in Switzerland, a non-EU nation, conducted a full-scale review of the merger after the parties notified the merger on November 3, 1997. The Swiss commission, like its EU counterpart, was particularly concerned about the combined effects of the proposed merger and the proposed KPMG–Ernst and Young merger on auditing choices available to banks and insurance companies. The Swiss commission's concern was heightened by its perception that the two other Big Six networks, Deloitte Touche and Arthur Andersen, were relatively weak in Switzerland.

The commission issued a preliminary analysis that took a critical view of the merger and made requests for extensive statistical data and other information, to which the parties provided lengthy, detailed responses. The parties also filed a copious legal and factual submission, arguing that the merger did not present significant competitive concerns and incorporating economic analyses from U.S. and British economists as well as an industrial organization expert from a Swiss university.

The investigation continued at full pace into 1998. The commission was one of the last competition authorities to approve the merger. It did not do so until April 20, several weeks after the U.S. Justice Department announced it was closing its investigation and the European Commissions Merger Task Force recommended approving the merger.

Eastern Europe

The rapidly emerging merger notification regimes in Eastern Europe were a source of some concern and confusion at the outset. It was generally very difficult to determine whether formal notification would be required in any Eastern European nation, because of both the unusual nature of the transaction (which was a network of member firms) and the lack of any applicable precedents to determine the scope of the government's premerger authority under comparatively new regulatory regimes. Even local counsel were generally uncertain as to how to interpret filing regulations. Further, determining the parties' national revenues or market shares required access to local information that was often not readily available. As it turned out, local counsel contacted the competition authorities in just three jurisdictions: the Czech Republic, Slovakia, and Poland.

In the Czech Republic, Price Waterhouse and Coopers determined that formal notification was not required, even under the most restrictive market definitions. The authorities met with the parties informally on several occasions and requested some information but refrained from any further involvement in light of the uncertainties regarding the merger's legal structure. Once the United States and the EC announced clearance in March 1998, Czech authorities accepted a formal notification letter and informally agreed not to review the merger further.

In Slovakia the parties contacted authorities anonymously through their counsel and obtained a general preliminary opinion that a merger such as the proposed one would not be subject to review. Counsel then prepared a draft letter for the Slovakian authorities requesting a formal ruling that the merger would not be subject to their jurisdiction, in confirmation of this telephone advice. In March 1998 the authorities decided to assert their jurisdiction to review the merger but took no action after being formally notified.

In Poland, Price Waterhouse and Coopers prepared a notification for filing by November 14, 1997, which triggered a two-month review period. The difficulty in Poland, as elsewhere, was the regulatory requirement that the filing set forth a complete and detailed description of the structure of the merger. Shortly after the EC accepted notification, on December 16, 1997, Polish authorities finally allowed a filing to take place despite the remaining uncertainties as to the merger's ultimate structure. Eventually they approved the merger.

For the remaining Eastern European countries with premerger regulations, Price Waterhouse and Coopers determined that the merger did not meet the local reporting thresholds.[3] In Bulgaria, Lithuania, and Romania the parties were never able to determine filing requirements with any certainty due to lack of revenue data on a national level and lack of clarity in the regulations. The parties planned to brief the local authorities in each of these jurisdictions and request a ruling that the merger was not reportable. Local counsel advised that this briefing be postponed until after the U.S. and EC authorities had acted—for two reasons. First, the structure of the merger on a local level was still too uncertain to describe.[4] Second, the inclination of local authorities to intervene regarding the merger might be lessened once clearances were obtained from the leading jurisdictions. In the event, this advice proved sound, and once the U.S. and EC decisions

3. In Hungary, branch offices of the client were able to confirm their national revenues fell below the reporting threshold. In Latvia, parties initially planned to notify the authorities, but the merger process dragged on past January 1, 1998, when Latvia's new and more lenient reporting regulations took effect, eliminating this need.

4. In Lithuania, the structural uncertainty actually prevented official review of the merger under local regulations.

were made public, the authorities in these countries waived the merger through.

Other Jurisdictions

Sweden and South Africa followed the pattern described for other jurisdictions: relatively quick approval of the merger announcement in November 1997, succeeded by mounting concerns and belated imposition of local filing requirements as the U.S. and EC review intensified, giving way at last to relaxed review and approval once the KPMG–Ernst and Young merger had been abandoned and the major competition authorities decided to allow the merger to proceed.

Throughout much of the rest of the world, and particularly in Latin America and Asia, confidentiality concerns and factual uncertainties prevented cooperation by local member firms, rendering notification impossible. Because the parties were international networks of national member firms, a large number of professional, legal, and economic questions needed to be resolved. Partnership votes, merger implementation issues, and premerger notification in these countries were therefore postponed until after the European and U.S. mergers were completed. By the time the parties made local filings in Venezuela, Mexico, and Brazil, there was no longer a need to coordinate with all international counsel on a global basis.

Substantive Issues

In all of the major jurisdictions, the merger review was conducted in an extremely professional, collegial manner, despite some initial expressions of possible concerns about other issues, which rather quickly proved to be unfounded. In each jurisdiction, Price Waterhouse and Coopers maintained an ongoing dialogue with the agencies at both the staff and the senior policymaking levels. This enabled the parties to identify the agency's substantive concerns at an early stage and to address them effectively.

All of the major jurisdictions applied essentially the same analytical framework in evaluating the proposed merger, although the application of the analysis varied somewhat from jurisdiction to jurisdiction because of differences in the structure of the market in each jurisdiction.

All of the jurisdictions applied the same basic approach to market definition. In each case, they concluded that the principal product market of concern was a market for providing services in auditing and reporting on the financial statements of large, publicly traded companies. They all concluded that the Big Six were the only firms that could compete effectively in this market. Each jurisdiction also concluded that the geographic market for these services was national, even though many of the companies using the services operated multinationally. The principal reason was that each country, in regulating the accounting profession, required that accountants be licensed in that country; as a result, a company needed a public accounting firm licensed in the country in which it was incorporated.

Each jurisdiction also looked closely at the possibility that there might be narrower markets for auditing the financial statements of companies in particular sectors of the economy. The sectors most of concern were banking and financial services, which were thought to have somewhat specialized auditing requirements. In Europe, this issue was treated primarily as part of the commission's market definition analysis. In the United States, it was treated more as a part of the competitive effects analysis in determining whether the merger would enable the merged firm to raise prices unilaterally or in coordination with other firms in any of these individual sectors. All the reviewing jurisdictions ultimately concluded that the auditing needs of these sectors were not so unique as to create any serious risk that the merger would lead to an increase in audit fees. Among other things, the agencies all found that all of the Big Six firms were able to provide auditing services in all sectors.

The other major issue of concern, particularly in Europe, was whether the Price Waterhouse–Coopers merger, in combination with the KPMG–Ernst and Young merger, would create a position of joint dominance in the provision of audit services in some individual countries or economic sectors. The abandonment of the KPMG–Ernst and Young merger largely resolved this issue.

International Agency Cooperation

U.S., Canadian, Australian, and European competition authorities requested waivers of confidentiality quite early in the process, for the purpose of sharing information gleaned in their respective investigations. The parties believed there was no real alternative to granting these requests in the interest of furthering a rapid, efficient, and friendly review process. They felt that the various authorities would be communicating thoughts and theories on some level and that withholding the requested waivers would antagonize reviewing officials without insulating them from each other's knowledge except as to specific facts and arguments raised by the parties' counsel in various jurisdictions, which might in themselves be rather helpful.

The likelihood of interagency communication had in any case been foreseen. From the beginning, filings in each nation were reviewed by counsel in multiple jurisdictions. Representatives of the parties in the United States and Europe read and approved every submission before it was filed, and copies of white papers, studies, and other materials prepared by counsel in the United States and Europe were distributed to counsel worldwide. This effort was necessary to maintain close coordination between filings in various countries. It was essential that everyone should have the facts straight but even more so that no argument should be raised in one jurisdiction that would undermine arguments in another.

The close communication between the authorities seeking information waivers apparently accounted for much of the coincidence in timing. In Canada and Australia, the firms and their counsel realized that they had addressed all of the concerns of their respective merger officials weeks before clearance was announced in the United States and Europe. In the end, with the United States leading the way, all four jurisdictions cleared the merger within a short span of days in March 1998.

Politicization

The antitrust and competition authorities in all the major jurisdictions appeared to conduct their reviews in a professional manner, free from any undue political influence. This is a testament to the integrity and professionalism of the agencies in dealing with a merger that attracted a high level of attention in the financial press, particularly in Europe, and that was the subject of an intensive effort by certain of the other Big Six firms to generate opposition. These efforts included soliciting the Antitrust Subcommittee of the Judiciary Committee of the U.S. Senate to hold hearings on the proposed mergers, which the subcommittee declined to do. They also included commissioning a survey of chief executive officers and chief financial officers of large companies about their attitudes toward the mergers. The results of this survey, which appeared designed to bias the results against the mergers, were released to coincide with the World Economic Forum in Davos. Copies were distributed to all attendees, who included Karel Van Miert and Joel Klein.

In addition to the competition authorities, securities regulators from a number of countries expressed some concern about the combined effect of the two mergers on the regulation of the financial markets. This concern focused primarily on whether the merged firms would be less independent due to the wider breadth of the nonauditing consulting and other professional services they would be providing to their audit clients. An international organization of securities regulators, IOSCO, announced that it would initiate a study of these issues. Again, the abandonment of the parallel KMPG–Ernst and Young merger substantially mitigated these concerns.

The Treatment of
Transatlantic Liner Shipping
under EU and U.S. Law

MATTHEW LEVITT

It may be a fair assumption that the objectives of EU and U.S. competition law are broadly similar: that while terminology and concepts may differ, EU and U.S. law would arrive at roughly similar results in the assessment of similar situations. Indeed, even though the EU and the United States have not yet sought to harmonize their substantive competition laws, cooperation in the *enforcement* of EU and U.S. competition law presupposes that the basic principles of those respective regimes are at least consistent.

The case of the Trans-Atlantic Conference Agreement illustrates the difficulties that arise when the substantive appraisals of EU and U.S. law differ radically. These difficulties are exacerbated in the context of that case by the fact that the very nature of the service in question (transportation between EU member states and the United States) necessarily involved the concurrent application of two different legal regimes to that service.

The Framework of U.S. and EU Regulation

At the time of the events described in this case study, the U.S. foreign ocean liner industry was regulated by the Shipping Act of 1984. Consistent with the Shipping Act of 1916 (which first regulated the industry), the Shipping Act of 1984 retained antitrust immunity for liner conference agreements and the requirement that liner operators publish their tariffs establishing rates and services. The Shipping Act of 1984 was modified by the Ocean Shipping Reform Act of 1998, with effect from May 1, 1999. The 1998 act continues to provide general antitrust immunity for liner conferences, including through intermodal rate making and service contracts, described in further detail below.

The EU's Council Regulation 4056/86/EEC confers a block exemption on liner conferences, in view of their stabilizing role.

While both the EU and United States confer antitrust immunity on liner conferences, and while the authorities in both jurisdictions exercise close and active regulatory control over shipping activities falling within their jurisdictions, the policy considerations applied and the results achieved differ considerably. The difficulties resulting from these differences in approach are most apparent in the case of liner operators present in the transatlantic trade since they are simultaneously subject to both legal regimes.

The differences in approach are best illustrated by the European Commission's decision of September 16, 1998, concerning the Trans-Atlantic Conference Agreement (TACA). Following a lengthy investigation by the European Commission and, it is understood, some contact with the U.S. Federal Maritime Commission, the European Commission adopted the decision, which found various infringements of articles 81 and 82 EC (ex articles 85 and 86) and imposed fines of 273 million ECU (roughly US$300 million) on the parties to the TACA. This decision represented the first occasion on which any authority of the EU had made any assessment of the compatibility of certain long-standing liner conference practices with EU competition law.

Summary of the Differences of Approach

The differences in approach between the European Commission and the United States may be illustrated by a number of examples.

Authority to Agree on Rates for the Inland Portions of Through-Intermodal Moves

Under U.S. law, the agreement of the rates for the inland portions of through-intermodal transport moves is lawful. The Shipping Act provided that ocean common carriers may "discuss, fix, or regulate transportation rates, including through rates, cargo space accommodations, and other conditions of service" (section 4 (a) (i)). The 1998 act maintains this right. The European Commission, by contrast, found that the agreement by the members of a liner conference of rates for the inland portions of through-intermodal transport within the European Economic Area (EEA) fell outside the scope of Regulation 4056 (decision, paragraphs 400–08). It also found that such agreement does not satisfy the conditions of individual exemption of article 81 (3) EC (ex article 85 (3)) and Regulation 1017 (TACA decision, paragraphs 409-41).

Conference Service Contract Authority

The Shipping Act allowed conference members to enter into service contracts. Section 3 (21) defined the term *service contract* as "a contract between a shipper and an ocean common carrier or conference in which the shipper makes a commitment to provide a certain minimum quantity of cargo over a fixed time period, and the ocean common carrier or conference commits to a certain rate or rate schedule as well as a defined service level—such as, assured space, transit time, port rotation, or similar service features; the contract may also specify provisions in the event of non-performance on the part of either party."

The 1998 act maintains this right. The European Commission, by contrast, found that the TACA parties' conference service contract authority was an infringement of article 81 (1) EC (ex article 85 (1)), which did not benefit from the block exemption of Regulation 4056 (TACA decision, paragraphs 442–71).

The Regulation and Prohibition of Service Contracts

The Shipping Act permitted ocean common carriers to regulate and prohibit their use of service contracts. The 1998 act continues to provide that ocean common carriers may regulate the use of service contracts; there are, however, limitations on the extent to which such regulation is permitted.

In addition to the general authority to include such service contract rules conferred by section 4 (a) (7) of the Shipping Act, sections 3 (21) and 8 (c) (7) specifically envisaged the agreement of liquidated damages clauses. The Federal Maritime Commission or the Department of Justice has taken positions supporting the agreement of liquidated damages clauses, the prohibition of contingency clauses, and the prohibition of "independent action" on service contracts.

The European Commission, by contrast, found that the conference's service contract rules did not fall within the scope of the block exemption of Regulation 4056 (decision, paragraph 464) and were not eligible for individual exemption under article 81 (3) EC (ex article 85 (3)) (TACA decision, paragraphs 487–502). This assessment also constituted an important part of the European Commission's first finding of abuse of article 82 EC (ex article 86) (TACA decision, paragraphs 551–58).

The Prohibition of Individual Service Contracts

Under the Shipping Act, the prohibition of individual service contracts was also lawful. While the Federal Maritime Commission required the parties to the TACA to permit individual service contracts in 1996, it also required them to make such contracts subject to the service contract rules of the conference. The European Commission, by contrast, found that the prohibition of individual service contracts, and the subjecting of such contracts where they were available to the service contract rules of the conference, was an infringement of both articles 81 and 82 EC (ex articles 85 and 86) (TACA decision, paragraphs 477–86 and 551–58).

Further, U.S. law requires the publication of the "essential terms" of service contracts. The European Commission, by contrast, found that the disclosure by the parties to each other of the terms of all service contracts to which they were a party constituted an infringement of both articles 81 and 82 EC (ex articles 85 and 86), notwithstanding that the "essential terms" of all contracts were publicly available (TACA decision, paragraphs 496, 551–58).

The Admission of New Lines to the Conference

Section 5 (b) (2) of the Shipping Act provided that each conference agreement must "provide reasonable and equal terms and conditions for admission and re-admission to conference membership for any ocean common carrier willing to serve the particular trade or route." This requires all conferences serving the United States to be "open" and to allow any line wishing to join a conference to have access to information necessary for its effective operation as a conference member, including access to existing service contracts.

The European Commission, by contrast, claimed that the steps taken by the parties to comply with the "open" conference obligations of U.S. law had constituted an abuse of their (allegedly) dominant position. It found that the request by one non-TACA line for certain information at the time of its application to join the conference and another line's participation in service contracts existing at the time of its accession to the conference constituted "inducements" offered by the TACA parties to these lines to persuade them to enter the transatlantic trade as parties to the conference rather than as independents (TACA decision, paragraphs 563–64). This finding was a key part of the European Commission's case that the TACA parties took steps to alter the competitive structure of the market contrary to article 82 EC (ex article 86).

Consequences of the Differences of Approach

It is apparent from the above that there are real risks of contradictory assessments being made by the competition authorities of the EU and the United States. Short of a formal commitment to align the substantive competition laws of the EU and the United States, there is some scope within the existing rules and principles of EU law for the avoidance of differences in the assessment of practices that are concurrently subject to EU and U.S. law such as those described above.

Substantive Appraisal

The concurrent application of U.S. law to a set of practices may be relevant to the assessment of those activities under articles 81 and 82 EC (ex articles 85 and 86).

In the TACA case, conduct relied on by the European Commission in finding an abuse of article 82 EC (ex article 86) was permitted or required by U.S. law. However, the assessment of that conduct under article 82 EC (ex article 86) depends on its objective justifiability. Where a practice has already been examined by the relevant U.S. institutions and found to be compatible with U.S. law, that assessment must be relevant to a consideration of the objective justifiability of the conduct in question under article 82 EC (ex article 86). Similarly, in weighing the benefits or disbenefits of a practice pursuant to a rule of reason approach under article 81 (1) EC (ex article 85 (1)) or for the purposes of applying article 81 (3) EC (ex article 85 (3)), it would be relevant to have regard to the assessment of that practice under U.S. law.

Article 253 EC (ex Article 190) and the Avoidance of Conflict

It has been held that where the facts and issues under review by the European Commission have already been assessed and found to be compatible with the laws of a foreign jurisdiction, the commission is required to take due account of such an assessment and, if it wishes to make a different assessment, it should provide an adequate explanation as to why the assessment of the foreign jurisdiction is not relevant (case C-360/92, *Publishers Association* v. *Commission* [1995] ECR I-23).

In my view, it follows that when the European Commission is considering practices that have already been assessed under U.S. antitrust law, it should take account of the U.S. legal position on the lawfulness of the practices in question and if, following that consideration, it maintains an assessment different from that of the United States, it should explain why the appraisal of those practices under U.S. law is not relevant. This principle should apply a fortiori where the commission addresses issues for the first time and where it does so in a way opposed to the legal assessment, adopted for many years in another major legal system, which is concurrently applicable to the practices and issues concerned.

A number of further points are relevant. First, in case T-65/98R, *Van den Bergh Foods Limited* v. *Commission*, the president of the court noted the need, in the interests of the general principle of legal certainty, to avoid conflict in the application of articles 81 and 82 to the same practice by national competition authorities and the commission, respectively (order of July 7, 1998, at paragraphs 70–74). It is submitted that there is a similar interest in the avoidance of the contradictory application of EU and U.S. competition law where both apply to the same agreement or practice.

Second, the commission's failure to address the differences between its assessment and that of U.S. law is at odds with its commitment to the principles of cooperation and positive comity in the application of EU and U.S. competition law by their respective authorities. On September 23, 1991, the European Community and the government of the United States signed an agreement regarding the application of their competition laws and exchanged interpretative letters dated May 31 and July 31, 1995, in relation to that agreement. On May 29, 1998, the EU Council and the European Commission adopted a decision concerning the conclusion of the agreement between the European Community and the government of the United States on the application of positive comity principles in the enforcement of their competition laws, which recognizes that the 1991 agreement "has contributed to coordination, cooperation and avoidance of conflicts in competition law enforcement" (recital 1 of the decision; see also the second sentence of the preamble to the 1998 agreement).

The 1998 agreement is intended to "enhance the. . . effectiveness" of the 1991 agreement (recital 3 of the decision of the council and commission). In the context of a discussion of the application of competition law at the international level, the commissioner for competition observed:

> Dans le domaine de la politique de concurrence, nous sommes tenus de coopérer à l'échelle internationale et de parvenir—du moins à long terme— à un consensus sur les principes de base. Dans un contexte où, dans de nombreuses parties du monde, il n'existe pas encore de règles de concurrence, ou du moins des règles très différentes, la coopération internationale doit avoir deux objectifs clairs:
>   —l'extension géographique du concept de base de la politique de concurrence, notamment afin de garantir une égalité des chances pour les enterprises,
>   —et la réduction du risque que l'application de ces règles différentes n'aboutisse à des décisions contradictoires.
>   . . . Actuellement, les accords de coopération bilatéraux, comme celui qui existe par exemple avec les États-Unis, sont pour nous beaucoup plus importants, ne serait-ce qu'en raison du nombre de plus en plus important d'affaires à traiter.

[Unofficial translation: In the area of competition policy, we are obliged to cooperate on the international sphere and to reach—at least in the long run—a consensus on the basic principles. In a context in which, in many parts of the world, there are still no competition rules, or at least rules that are very different, international cooperation should have two clear objectives: the geographical extension of the basic concepts of competition, to guarantee, in particular, equal opportunities for companies, and the reduction of the risk that the application of these different rules does not lead to contradictory decisions. . . . Currently, these bilateral cooperation agreements, like the one existing with the United States, are much more important to us, not only because of the number of increasingly important matters to deal with.]

While the 1991 and 1998 agreements are not intended to harmonize the substantive competition laws of the United States and the EU, the existence of the agreements, having as one of their stated aims "the avoidance of conflicts in competition law enforcement" in the United States and the EU, may provide scope for the institutions of both the EU and United States to minimize the differences in the application of their respective competition laws. Such an approach may provide the basis for the development of a principle of "solidarity," or mutual respect, by the institutions of each jurisdiction for the laws of the other.

The First Microsoft Case

ROBERT E. LITAN

The joint 1993–94 investigation of Microsoft by the U.S. Department of Justice and the European Union's Directorate General IV relating to certain unlawful licensing practices in connection with the marketing of DOS and Windows 3.1 was a model in cooperative behavior between the two authorities. To my knowledge, it was the first such joint investigation and the first one that resulted in a jointly negotiated (identical) consent decree.

The Justice Department began its investigation of Microsoft in July 1993, after the Federal Trade Commission had deadlocked in a two-to-two vote over whether to bring a complaint. The DGIV initiated its investigation (just before the Justice Department did) in response to a complaint filed by Novell claiming that certain of Microsoft's licensing practices, notably its per processor license, violated EU antitrust laws.

The per processor license was one that Microsoft entered into with manufacturers of personal computers under which such manufacturers (or OEMs) agreed to pay royalties for Microsoft's operating systems based on the number of computers it shipped, whether or not the PC had a Microsoft operating system preinstalled. Novell in particular complained that this type of license effectively charged OEMs twice if they decided to ship their computers with another operating system, such as the DR-DOS, then one of the two principal competing operating systems (the other being the OS-2, made by IBM).

During the course of the investigation, which was pursued in parallel by the Justice Department and the DGIV, other licensing practices also attracted attention, including the length of the license term (often as long as three years) and what were perceived to be large "minimum commitments." In combination, both Justice and the DGIV concluded that these two other features of the license together with the per processor charge amounted to exclusive dealing by a monopolist. At no point during the investigation did the authorities from either side of the Atlantic disagree about this finding.

Novell's complaint to the DGIV also alleged that Microsoft unlawfully tied Windows to DOS. The Justice Department investigated this complaint, too, as well as other complaints about Microsoft's behavior: that Microsoft was unlawfully leveraging its monopoly power in the operating systems market by providing its applications programmers with unfair lead time, notifying them first about the design of the operating system and the way in which it would interface with applications programs; that Microsoft was hiding some interfaces (called APIs) from third-party applications software companies; and that Microsoft was intentionally sending "error messages" to users of other software when users tried to use it in conjunction with Microsoft's operating system.

After roughly one year of investigation, in June 1994, the Justice Department notified Microsoft that it intended to bring a complaint about the licensing practices only, but not the other matters. At the same time, the department said it was prepared to enter into negotiation of a consent decree to resolve these issues. Shortly thereafter, the DGIV filed a formal notice of objections (the equivalent of a Justice Department "complaint") making the same allegations but also including an allegation concerning the tying of Windows to DOS. From that point forward, Microsoft engaged in negotiations with Justice and the DGIV simultaneously, until a settlement was reached in mid-July 1994. Microsoft consented to such an arrangement and indeed, in my view, affirmatively desired a joint negotiation so that all outstanding complaints against it would be resolved at one time.

In the end, Microsoft signed identical consent decrees, ending the investigations on both sides of the Atlantic. The decrees also addressed the tying issue and prohibited Microsoft from pricing its products in a way that could result in exclusive arrangements with its OEMs. The U.S. decree was initially rejected, however, by Judge Stanley Sporkin, who was later overruled by the District of Columbia Court of Appeals.

One procedural note: the two antitrust authorities issued discovery requests separately. To the best of my recollection, the two authorities also negotiated with Microsoft a response-sharing mechanism so that the same documents provided in response to these requests were provided to both authorities.

This initial investigation of Microsoft was followed by two further investigations and ultimate court actions, pursued by the United States alone without the EU. In 1994 the Justice Department challenged Microsoft's purchase of Intuit. The two firms were the only real competitors in the personal finance software market, with Intuit having roughly a 90 percent share of that market. Accordingly, the proposed merger would have taken the market structure from a duopoly to a monopoly. Microsoft abandoned plans for the merger several weeks after the suit was brought.

The other well-known court action was filed by the Justice Department in the fall of 1998, following three years of investigation into various other Microsoft practices. This action, too, was brought by the Justice Department alone (although twenty states initially joined the Justice Department in the litigation). To oversimplify, the department's case had three basic claims: that Microsoft had engaged in exclusive dealing, penalizing its only other real competitor in the browser market (Netscape); that Microsoft attempted to divide markets with various competitors; and that Microsoft tied the sale of its operating system (in which the Justice Department claimed the company had a monopoly) to the sale of its browser. In the spring of 2000, Judge Thomas Jackson sided with the government and ordered the breakup of the company into two parts: one engaged in operating systems and the other in applications software. At this writing, Judge Jackson's opinion is on appeal.

In sum, the 1993–94 investigation of Microsoft was a model in joint activity. The complaints investigated on both sides were similar, discovery was pursued in parallel and with significant cooperation, and the final consent decree was negotiated jointly.

Two Joint Ventures in International Telecommunications

JANET L. McDAVID

International joint ventures involving U.S. and foreign firms are becoming increasingly common. Two examples from the telecommunications industry are the 1993 joint venture between British Telecommunications (BT) and MCI Communications Corporation (MCI) and the Sprint–France Telecom–Deutsche Telekom joint venture of 1995.[1]

British Telecommunications–MCI

In late 1993, MCI and British Telecommunications entered into agreements by which BT acquired a 20 percent equity stake in MCI for approximately $4.3 billion, becoming the largest single shareholder in MCI. Under the investment agreement, BT received a number of special shareholder rights, including the need for BT's consent to various MCI actions, access to internal MCI informa-

Lynda Marshall and Greg Parisi participated in preparing this chapter.

1. *United States* v. *MCI Communications Corp.*, 59 Fed. Reg. 33009 (June 27, 1994); *United States* v. *Sprint Corp.*, 60 Fed. Reg. 44049 (August 24, 1995).

tion, and proportionate board representation. MCI gained certain special rights with respect to BT as well, including a seat on BT's board of directors. In addition, both companies agreed that if either party competed with the other in its core business in its assigned territory, the Americas for MCI and the rest of the world for BT, it would lose all special rights, including board membership.

In addition to the investment agreement, BT and MCI also committed to the formation of a joint venture, Concert, to be owned 75 percent by BT and 25 percent by MCI. The purpose of Concert was to provide to large international users, primarily multinational corporations, international enhanced telecommunications services: data services, messaging and video conferencing, global calling card services, intelligent network services, and certain global outsourcing. These services were to be available from a single source and consistent in quality, features, and capabilities wherever purchased. Both parent companies contributed international telecommunications facilities to the venture. MCI was the exclusive distributor of Concert services in the Americas and BT was Concert's exclusive distributor in the rest of the world. Furthermore, BT and MCI agreed not to compete with Concert anywhere in the world. Consequently, BT and MCI realized all gains from the areas of business in which Concert was engaged through their ownership interests in Concert and the sale of its services. After the formation of Concert, BT participated in the U.S. market only through Concert and its investment in MCI. Both the European Union's Directorate General IV and the U.S. Department of Justice conducted thorough investigations of this transaction.[2]

BT was privatized in 1991. At the time of the transaction it faced competition at home but still was the largest telecommunications carrier in the United Kingdom, providing most local services and possessing a high market share in long-distance domestic and international services. Unlike most providers of local telecommunications service, BT faced several competitors in the United Kingdom and all of its lines were open to competition.

---

2. The EU and the United States closely coordinated their investigations, although they focused on somewhat different issues. The EU limited the duration of MCI's agreement not to compete with BT outside the Americas to a period of five years, which was also the initial term of the joint venture. *BT-MCI*, 1994 OJ 94/C, notice re case 4-34,857 (March 30, 1994). In the United States, the Federal Communications Commission conducted a separate proceeding to determine whether the transactions were in the public interest and entered an order generally consistent with the consent decree. In re *Request of MCI Communications Corp.*, 9 F.C.C.R. 3960 (declaratory ruling and order) (1994).

MCI was the second-largest long-distance telecommunications carrier in the United States and, in terms of traffic, the fifth-largest telecommunications carrier in the world. Consequently, according to the Justice Department, BT's investment in MCI and the formation of Concert resulted in a vertical affiliation between the dominant telecommunications carrier in the United Kingdom and the second-largest long-distance provider in the United States. This was particularly important because the Justice Department claimed that BT's market power in the provision of telecommunications services in the United Kingdom gave it the potential to control access into the United Kingdom. Indeed, at the time of the transaction, although BT had several local and long distance competitors, approximately 97 percent of all telecommunications traffic in the United Kingdom terminated through BT's local network, and the great majority of it originated on BT's network. BT also controlled the largest and most comprehensive long-distance domestic and international telecommunications network in the United Kingdom, carrying approximately 84 percent of domestic switched long-distance traffic in the United Kingdom.

In this context, the Justice Department had concerns about possible preferential treatment by BT of both MCI and Concert at the expense of other U.S. telecommunications providers. The Justice Department's concerns were resolved through a consent decree to which MCI and Concert were parties. The complaint alleged that BT's acquisition of 20 percent of MCI's stock could substantially lessen competition in the provision of international telecommunications services between the United States and the United Kingdom. BT could increase incentives and its ability to use its dominant gatekeeper position in the United Kingdom to favor MCI at the expense of its U.S. competitors by making competitors' offerings less attractive in quality and price than those of MCI and by impairing the ability of MCI's rivals to compete effectively in those services.[3] BT could favor MCI with respect to prices, terms, and conditions on which international services were provided as well as quality of provisioning of those services. It could also provide MCI with advance information about planned changes to the BT network. In addition, BT's ownership interest in MCI could increase BT's incentive to provide MCI confidential competitively sensitive information that BT obtained from other U.S. carriers through their correspondent relationship

3. This incentive to discriminate was alleged to increase by the provision in the investment agreement that subjected BT to the loss of its special rights if it competed in the Americas in the provision of telecommunications service.

with BT. Finally, the complaint alleged that the investment agreement would give BT the motivation and ability to send its international switched traffic to the United States exclusively or largely to MCI, creating an increased incentive to keep international accounting rates above cost.

The Concert joint venture was evaluated in the context of the market for seamless global telecommunications services provided in the United States. By their nature, seamless global telecommunications services must be offered on a consistent basis in all the major countries where customers are located. Consequently, nondiscriminatory access to the telecommunications networks in these countries is essential for any provider of these services. Access to the United Kingdom and the United States is particularly important, as 10 percent of the world's largest multinational corporations are headquartered in the United Kingdom and most potential large business customers need access to both the United Kingdom and the United States. According to the complaint, by virtue of its involvement in Concert and MCI and the associated non-compete agreements, BT would have increased incentive and ability to use its dominant position in the United Kingdom to favor Concert and MCI and to disfavor their U.S. competitors in the provision of global seamless telecommunications services.

The consent decree recognized that BT faced greater competition than most local exchange service providers. It also recognized that telecommunications services in the United States are regulated by the Federal Communications Commission, that these services in the United Kingdom are regulated by OFTEL, and that these two agencies provide effective, independent regulation of telecommunications services, including prohibitions on discrimination against competitors. The consent decree designed to remedy the alleged antitrust issues contained three categories of substantive restrictions and obligations.

The first requirement was transparency: the decree required MCI and Concert to disclose certain information regarding the telecommunications services they received from BT or provided together with BT, particularly prices, terms, and discounts provided by BT to MCI or Concert pursuant to interconnection and correspondent agreements, as well as information on equipment purchases and servicing. The theory of the decree was that if competitors had this information they could determine whether they were victims of discrimination and seek relief in the first instance from the FCC or OFTEL.

Second, the decree imposed certain confidentiality requirements. It also prohibited MCI and Concert from receiving certain nonpublic and confidential information provided to BT by other U.S. telecommunications service providers in connection with the arrangements between these providers and BT to provide both international correspondent relationships and interconnection with BT in the United Kingdom.

Third, the decree established requirements relating to international simple resale, which involves bypassing existing correspondent relationships to send traffic into the United States. Under the decree, neither MCI nor Concert could provide facilities to BT to engage in this practice until all qualified U.S. telecommunications services providers that had applied for licenses in the United Kingdom to engage in international simple resale on or before December 1, 1993, were granted such licenses and afforded an opportunity to interconnect with BT on standard nondiscriminatory rates.

All of these requirements were designed to diminish the risk of BT using its market power to discriminate against MCI's U.S. competitors by making discrimination easier to detect; by precluding the misuse of confidential information obtained by BT from MCI's competitors; and by increasing the likelihood that U.S. competitors of MCI and Concert, if licensed, would be able to interconnect with BT in the United Kingdom so they could respond effectively to any international discrimination and diversion of BT's traffic to MCI. Of particular note, however, is the fact that the consent decree did not impose substantive nondiscrimination requirements on either BT or MCI. Instead, in recognition of the fact that the FCC and OFTEL were effective, independent regulators and that both agencies already prohibited discrimination, the decree relied on those agencies to enforce their regulatory schemes.

The United States considered including in the final judgment specific nondiscrimination conditions, enforceable through contempt sanctions, to deter discrimination by BT in favor of MCI (and Concert). It concluded that the other provisions of the final judgment, existing regulatory requirements and enforcement practices in the United States and the United Kingdom, and the ability of the United States to seek modifications of the final judgment were sufficient to protect competition.

The United States was not prepared to rely on existing regulation alone to prevent harm to competition and consumers in the United States. While U.K. regulatory authorities share with those in the United States a generally procompetitive approach to telecommunications policy, protection of competition and consumers in the United States is not the primary goal of U.K. regulators. A number of important telecommunications regulatory issues remain unsettled in the United Kingdom, and some policies specifically limiting competition remained in effect at the time of the decree, such as the duopoly on international facilities-based competition. Historic experience and the present state of competition in the United States and the United Kingdom were also taken into account in determining that this relief was needed.

Because, however, the telecommunications regulatory regime in the United Kingdom now embodies or is developing important competitive policies and safeguards, the United States concluded that it was possible to protect competition adequately in these circumstances without placing specific antidiscrimination prohibitions in the proposed final judgment or prohibiting the BT-MCI transaction altogether, as would likely have been necessary otherwise.

In sum, the U.K. telecommunications regulatory regime has taken steps to promote and foster competition, steps that have not yet been taken in most of the world, and it was appropriate for the United States to take these developments into account in not requiring more extensive relief to be included in the proposed final judgment.

The United States also considered issues of international comity in shaping the proposed final judgment. Consistent with its long-standing enforcement policy, the United States sought in the substantive provisions of the final judgment to avoid situations that could give rise to international conflicts between sovereign governments and their agencies. The substantive requirements imposed on MCI (and Concert) have been tailored to avoid direct U.S. involvement in BT's operation of its telecommunications network in the United Kingdom on an ongoing basis, minimizing the potential for conflict with U.K. authorities.[4]

Sprint–France Telecom–Deutsche Telekom

In 1995 Sprint, France Telecom, and Deutsche Telekom entered into a joint venture, GlobalOne, aimed at providing services similar to those of the BT-MCI alliance:

—International data, voice, and video business services for multinational corporations and business customers

—International consumer-based services

—A carrier's carrier services, including transport services for other carriers.

Each party contributed international resources and capital. The international backbone formed by these contributions was held 50 percent by Sprint and 50 percent by France Telecom and Deutsche Telekom, the latter two

---

4. Competitive impact statement, *United States* v. *MCI Communications Corp.* (www.usdoj.gov/atr/cases/f1100/1177.htm).

holding their share of GlobalOne through their own joint venture, Atlas. Under the agreement, Sprint had the exclusive right to provide GlobalOne services in the United States. France Telecom and Deutsche Telekom refrained from competing with Sprint in the United States in these and similar services, while Sprint refrained from competing with France Telecom and Deutsche Telekom in their home countries. Moreover, none of the parties would compete with GlobalOne.

In addition to the joint venture agreement, the parties entered into an investment agreement under which France Telecom and Deutsche Telekom were entitled to acquire up to 20 percent of Sprint stock for a price that could rise as high as $4.2 billion. As a result of the investment, France Telecom and Deutsche Telekom also would acquire special shareholder rights, much as British Telecommunications did in MCI, including the right to appoint directors to a number of seats on Sprint's board of directors in proportion to ownership interest.

Many of the same concerns that arose in the Justice Department review of the BT-MCI transaction also arose in the antitrust review of the Sprint-FT-DT alliance, but those concerns were even greater in the GlobalOne joint venture.[5] This transaction was a strategic alliance between three of the largest telecommunications carriers in the world, creating a vertical affiliation between a major U.S. long-distance carrier and two of the largest foreign telecommunications carriers. Moreover, these foreign telecommunications carriers were government-owned monopolies representing more than 75 percent of all telecommunications revenues and market power in other key services such as public data networks. These monopolies were purportedly regulated by the same government agencies that owned and operated both firms and profited from their monopolies, whereas British Telecommunications was subject to both existing and developing competition in its home market and had an effective, independent regulator. Virtually all interna-

---

5. As in the BT-MCI case, the DGIV conducted a separate but closely coordinated investigation. The DGIV expressed substantial concerns about possible abuses by France Telecom and Deutsche Telekom of their dominant positions in France and Germany and the loss of potential competition in data services that might otherwise have existed among Sprint, France Telecom, and Deutsche Telekom. Like the Department of Justice, the DGIV recognized that both France Telecom and Deutsche Telekom were still monopolists and prohibited discrimination in favor of the joint venture or Sprint, which was deemed particularly important until competitors were licensed in both France and Germany. It also prohibited cross-subsidization and tying, established audit and accounting requirements to ensure compliance with nondiscrimination requirements, and required liberalization of the telecommunications infrastructures of France Telecom and Deutsche Telekom. *Atlas-Phoenix-GlobalOne*, OJ 47, 15.2 (1997)(1996).

tional telecommunications traffic between the United States and France and between the United States and Germany originated or terminated over France Telecom's or Deutsche Telekom's public switched networks, their transmission infrastructure, or both. Indeed, of the costs of potential competitors of France Telecom and Deutsche Telekom for domestic, international, and enhanced telecommunications services, a very large portion was the costs of obtaining transmission infrastructure from France Telecom and Deutsche Telekom. In addition, there was substantial evidence in both France and Germany of discrimination against potential competitors, misuse of competitively sensitive information, and abuse of monopoly positions.

The Justice Department evaluated this transaction in terms of the market for telecommunications between the United States and France and between the United States and Germany—as well as the market for seamless international telecommunications services. To compete effectively in all of these markets, international telecommunications providers must have nondiscriminatory access to the United States, France, and Germany. Consequently, as in the BT-MCI case, the department focused on the incentives of France Telecom and Deutsche Telekom to discriminate in favor of Sprint in regard to access, price, and information.

In this case, however, these concerns were exacerbated by the government-owned monopoly status of France Telecom and Deutsche Telekom and by the complete absence of independent, effective regulation. Additionally, the transaction between Sprint, France Telecom, and Deutsche Telekom took place within a context of significant regulatory changes in Europe. Regulation of telecommunications in Europe is carried out by a combination of EU and national law. During the time the transaction was under investigation, the EU set January 1, 1998, as the target date by which most of its member states, including France and Germany, were expected fully to liberalize the existing monopolies on public voice telecommunications services and transmission infrastructure. These circumstances made it more likely that the French and German telecommunications markets would shortly open to competition.

The complaint alleged that after the consummation of the transaction, France Telecom and Deutsche Telekom would benefit through their ownership interests and in the competitive success of the services offered by GlobalOne and Sprint. Consequently, France Telecom and Deutsche Telekom would have increased incentives and ability to use their monopoly positions to favor GlobalOne and Sprint by

—Diverting traffic to GlobalOne and Sprint

—Offering GlobalOne and Sprint advantageous prices, terms, and discounts

—Denying operating agreements, or offering operating agreements on discriminatory terms, to other competitors, particularly new entrants

—Sharing confidential information that France Telecom and Deutsche Telekom obtained from other U.S. carriers and competitors through their correspondent relationships

—Providing revenues from the monopoly services or by shifting costs of GlobalOne and Sprint to the monopoly services.

The resulting remedy took into account the possibility of liberalizing the telecommunications markets in France and Germany but addressed the antitrust concerns of discrimination on the assumption that the monopoly status would continue. The decree is in two phases.

Restrictions under phase 1 of the decree remained in effect until all prohibitions on competition had been removed and actual competitors were licensed in France and Germany. During this period, the decree imposed substantive requirements on Sprint, France Telecom, and Deutsche Telekom. These restrictions included limitations on facility ownership, nonexclusive distribution requirements, prohibitions against Sprint's acceptance of disproportionate traffic, preclusion of cross-subsidization, and access to public networks.

Phase 2 began when the national government of each country removed legal prohibitions on construction, ownership, or control of domestic and international telecommunications facilities or use of such facilities; and when the national government issued one or more licenses to entities other than or unaffiliated with France Telecom, Deutsche Telekom, Sprint, or GlobalOne. Once phase 2 was entered, the restrictions in phase 1 were lifted, and transparency and confidentiality requirements similar to those in the BT-MCI case were to be in effect throughout the life of the decree.

The shift from phase 1 to phase 2 was assessed separately for France and Germany, so that development of a competitive market in one country was taken into account notwithstanding delays in the other. Because Germany allowed competition at an earlier date than France, phase 1 ended earlier in Germany than in France.

The competitive impact statement issued by the Justice Department explains the differences between the decrees in the BT-MCI case and in the Sprint-FT-DT case:

> There are . . . crucial differences between this transaction and the BT-MCI alliance. Although BT continued to have some market power in basic telecommunications services and facilities and control over local bottlenecks in the United Kingdom at the time it formed its alliance with MCI, all of its lines of business were already open to competition and BT actually faced

facilities-based competition to some extent at all levels, from independent carriers and cable television companies. Moreover, since 1993 BT has ceased to be government-owned, so that it is independent from its government regulator in the United Kingdom. Here, in contrast, FT and DT retain legal monopolies over three-quarters of all telecommunications business in France and Germany, as measured by revenues, and have market power over additional types of services such as public data networks that have already become competitive in the United Kingdom. FT and DT do not have the same degree of independent regulatory oversight of their conduct by national authorities as BT, because of their continuing government ownership. Accordingly, in this transaction it was necessary to impose more stringent conditions governing the relationship between FT and DT on the one hand, and Sprint and the joint venture on the other, particularly in the period before France and Germany fully liberalize their telecommunications markets pursuant to EU requirements, in order adequately to protect competition.[6]

Conclusion

International transactions, particularly when activities of foreign governments and their enterprises are at issue, give rise to special considerations that are not present in the domestic context. One unique issue involves international comity, which has both substantive and procedural implications. It is worthwhile to note that the United States considered issues of international comity in both the BT-MCI transaction and the Sprint-FT-DT transaction. The decrees in both cases show that the Justice Department is sensitive to comity issues but also that it will not ignore major competitive concerns to take comity considerations into account.

In the BT-MCI consent decree, British Telecommunications was not a party to the decree and was not named as a defendant in the complaint. In addition, the substantive obligations on MCI and Concert were tailored to avoid direct U.S. involvement in British Telecommunications's operation of its telecommunications network in the United Kingdom, to avoid imposing substantive requirements on BT, and to defer to the independent regulation by the FCC and the OFTEL.

6. Competitive impact statement, *United States* v. *Sprint Corp.* (1995) (www.usdoj.gov/atr/cases/f0400/0452.htm).

In an attempt to avoid imposing direct obligations on foreign government-owned entities, neither France Telecom nor Deutsche Telekom was made a defendant in the Sprint-FT-DT complaint and decree. Additionally, an effort was made to apply the substantive obligations—to the extent that they could indirectly affect the conduct of France Telecom and Deutsche Telekom—to practices over which either foreign regulation was insubstantial or nonexistent or, to the extent regulation existed, it was consistent with the decree.

Because both France and Germany are members of the European Union and, because the European Commission was simultaneously undertaking a liberalization of European telecommunications policy, the commission had fewer concerns about imposing substantive obligations on France Telecom and Deutsche Telekom. As a result, comity issues arose mainly in the United States, rather than in Europe.

There was extensive cooperation between the Department of Justice and the DGIV in both investigations. In the BT-MCI case, antitrust authorities identified different areas of concern, but it appears that their cooperation was both smooth and extensive. In the Sprint-FT-DT case, U.S. and European authorities identified similar concerns and agreed on the steps necessary to remedy those concerns. Again, their cooperation was both smooth and extensive.

The WorldCom-MCI Case

ALEX NOURRY

At the time of its announcement, the plan to effect a $37 bil-
lion merger between two U.S. telecom companies—
WorldCom and MCI—was the largest merger plan in corporate
history. The case was notified to the competition authorities of
the European Union and the United States. After an initial assessment of the notification, the European Commission declared the
notification incomplete on the basis of insufficient information
about possible product and service markets in the Internet sector.
The information requested was received in the early part of 1998
but was not sufficient to resolve the commission's concerns about
the impact of the merger in this area, and phase 2 proceedings
were opened. After a full investigation, and after the receipt of undertakings jointly offered to the U.S. Department of Justice and
the European Commission (involving the divestment of MCI's
Internet activities, the largest divestment in antitrust history at
the time), the case was cleared on July 8, 1999, subject to the carrying out of commitments by the parties.

This was the first major investigation by the European Commission of a merger of significant players in the Internet sector.
The main issue for consideration was whether the merger would
give the parties concerned a dominant position in the market for
the supply of universal connectivity, that is, the ability to offer
access to anywhere and everywhere on the Internet, without hav-

ing to pay others to complete the connections. Although the parties initially argued that the Internet was a "free-for-all" in which any player, no matter how large or small, could set itself up to offer such service, it became clear on closer examination that the Internet is a hierarchical structure, with only a few comparatively large players capable of offering such service, of which the merging parties were two of the biggest.

Assessment of the case was hampered by the lack of publicly available, reliable information. The European Commission thus had to rely on information from market players. This information confirmed that the parties enjoyed a relatively large market share. The commission formed the view that, as a result of network effects—the phenomenon whereby the attractiveness to subscribers of one network relative to a competing network relates to the size of the network—the size of the combined entity's network would have been such that it would have been in a position to dictate terms to all other competitors who needed interconnection.

The Internet by nature is a cross-border phenomenon and international in scale. The case was marked by particularly close cooperation between the European Commission and the U.S. Department of Justice. This cooperation extended to coordination of information requests, the presence of Justice Department observers at the oral hearings in Brussels, joint negotiations with the parties on remedies, and coordination of market testing.

The remedy offered by the merging parties to the competition problem was the removal of the overlap—in a way designed to maintain existing conditions of competition by ensuring that the divestment was to a new entrant rather than to an existing player in the same market. The parties offered the same undertaking jointly to the European Commission and the Justice Department. The means of enforcing the remedies had to reflect the different procedures of the two authorities, and although the commission took powers to appoint independent trustees to oversee and if necessary to carry out the divestment, these powers were held in reserve while the parties were given the opportunity to complete the divestment, under the supervision of the Justice Department, before closing the merger.

There was no overlap in the Internet sector between WorldCom and MCI in Europe—MCI had no Internet operations or assets in Europe. All the principal competitors were American (GTE, Sprint-GlobalOne, AT&T), with emerging competition from European telecom operators. There was an effect on the EU market only because a significant part of Internet traffic originating in or destined for Europe goes to or comes from the United States. The sector was subject to low barriers to entry (with a number of recent new entrants such as Qwest, IXC, and Level 3), explosive growth and rapid technological change, and customer insistence on adherence to open Internet standards.

The European Commission took a rather static view of the market, focusing on so-called top-level Internet service providers (all of which were American and based in the United States) and taking a global approach to the geographic market in contrast to the Justice Department's national (U.S.) approach. This led the commission to adopt a rather artificial and inevitably narrow market definition, namely, the market for the supply of top level or "universal" connectivity (that is, the ability to offer access to anywhere and everywhere on the Internet without having to pay others to complete connections). On this basis, the commission concluded that the combined WorldCom-MCI entity would have more than 50 percent of the market and an Internet backbone network of such a size that it could behave to an appreciable extent independently of competitors and customers.

Given that the commission's principal concern seemed to arise from the overlap between the parties in the provision of backbone network services, the parties offered to divest MCI's Internet backbone business by way of a settlement proposal. This was rejected by the commission as being insufficient, because as a result of network externalities the merged entity would still be able to behave independently of competitors. The parties argued that network externalities in fact acted as a strong procompetitive force on the Internet by creating strong incentives for all networks to interconnect so that consumers on all networks reap the full benefits of the whole network. However, the commission's view was supported by the Justice Department as well as by interested third parties. This led the two parties to offer a second settlement proposal, which in addition to MCI's Internet backbone business also included the divestiture (to Cable and Wireless) of MCI's Internet retail business, a proposal acceptable to both the European Commission and the Justice Department.

The European Commission was the dominant authority in the proceedings, probably because of the stricter time limits under its merger regulation, although the merger concerned two U.S. companies and principally affected the U.S. market. The stricter time limits under the commission's procedure inevitably led to greater pressure being placed on the merging parties to reach a settlement with both the commission and the Justice Department.

The merging parties' need to obtain clearance from both antitrust authorities made it difficult or impossible for them to withhold their consent to the exchange of information and cooperation between the two authorities. Such exchange of information and cooperation inevitably gave rise to increased concerns about disclosure of information to third parties, especially against the background of intense and persistent representations from such parties.

As the commission has recognized, assessment of the case was hampered by the lack of publicly available, reliable information. In such a situation, the commission should as a matter of course appoint independent experts at an early stage rather than relying entirely on information provided by interested third parties. The commission did eventually consider the appointment of an independent expert, but this came far too late in the proceedings to play any useful role.

An interesting postscript to the WorldCom-MCI case is the European Commission's recent prohibition of the proposed merger between MCI-WorldCom and Sprint, especially since this is the first merger that the commission has prohibited between two non-EU companies. The merger was prohibited on the grounds that it would have resulted in the creation of a dominant market position for top-level universal Internet connectivity. The companies proposed divesting Sprint's Internet business, but the commission considered this insufficient to resolve its competition concerns.

The A. C. Nielsen Case

JAMES F. RILL AND
CHRISTINE C. WILSON

The effects of anticompetitive conduct have no regard for national boundaries. Consequently, the efficient and effective enforcement of competition laws requires cross-border cooperation among antitrust enforcement authorities. Numerous mechanisms can be employed by these authorities to enhance cooperation across national boundaries, but perhaps the most common is informal cooperation within the framework of a bilateral antitrust accord. The A. C. Nielsen–Information Resources Incorporated matter provides an excellent example of how this type of informal cooperation can lead to deference to the enforcement interests of another jurisdiction, the efficient use of scarce prosecutorial resources, and consistency in enforcement outcomes.

Nielsen and Information Resources (IRI) compete on an international scale in the sale of retail tracking services: the gathering of information on product sales, prices, promotions, advertisements, and other market data over time. Historically, this information was obtained through manual audits; now, much of this information is obtained by scanning the bar codes of products purchased by consumers. The collected data are analyzed to determine the performance of specific products during a given period of time. This processed information is then sold to manufacturers and retailers in the form of market reports, which can be used to design promotional and marketing plans.

A U.S.-based company, Nielsen is the largest provider of retail tracking services in the world. Arthur Nielsen, the company's founder, was the first to provide manual audit retail tracking services. Nielsen is the dominant provider of retail tracking services in the United States, Canada, and the European Union and now offers these services in more than ninety countries. IRI, also a U.S.-based retail tracking services company, derived the majority of its 1994 revenues from sales in the United States but had entered several European countries through joint ventures with local partners.

Both the European Commission and the Antitrust Division of the U.S. Department of Justice opened investigations to determine whether practices employed by Nielsen in Europe were designed to inhibit IRI's ability to compete effectively in the European market. As disclosed later by the Department of Justice, the Antitrust Division was investigating whether Nielsen, in contracting with multinational customers, illegally bundled or tied the terms of contracts in one country with those in other countries.[1] Specifically, the Antitrust Division sought to determine whether Nielsen offered customers more favorable terms in countries where Nielsen had market power only if those customers agreed to use Nielsen in countries where Nielsen faced significant competition.

Similarly, following a complaint filed by IRI in September 1994, the European Commission launched an investigation into the contracting practices of Nielsen in various European countries. On May 7, 1996, the European Commission issued a statement of objections against Nielsen that indicated that Nielsen had implemented various exclusionary practices designed to impede IRI from further entering the European market.[2] Specifically, the European Commission found that Nielsen had engaged in contracting practices that raised IRI's costs of obtaining data from retailers. In addition, the statement of objections indicated that Nielsen had offered substantial price reductions and large discounts (without cost justification) in return for its customers' commitments to purchase Nielsen's services in a wide range of countries. According to the statement of objections, this practice encouraged customers to purchase from Nielsen a bundle of services covering both countries in which Nielsen had a near monopoly on retail tracking services and countries in which Nielsen faced competition from other retail tracking service providers.

1. U.S. Department of Justice, press release, December 3, 1996.
2. Statement of objections, addressed to A. C. Nielsen Company and Nielsen International S.A., relating to proceedings pursuant to article 86 of the EC Treaty and article 54 of the EEA Agreement (4-35.239, IRI-Nielsen), May 7, 1996.

In early December, both the Department of Justice and the European Commission indicated that Nielsen had signed undertakings with the European Commission that addressed the concerns raised in the statement of objections.[3] According to the European Commission, Nielsen agreed to refrain from concluding contracts with retailers that contained exclusivity provisions or restrictions on retailers' freedom to supply data to other retail tracking services providers. In addition, Nielsen agreed to forgo linking the terms of its contracts with multinational customers in one country to the terms of contracts for similar services in other countries.

The two antitrust enforcement agencies indicated that the Department of Justice and the European Commission cooperated extensively during their investigations into Nielsen's conduct. This cooperation took the form of discussing legal and economic theories and exchanging confidential information with the consent of the parties. Indeed, recognizing that "most of the conduct occurred in Europe and had its greatest impact there," Joel Klein, acting assistant attorney general, indicated that the Department of Justice decided to let the European Commission take the lead in the investigation when it became clear that "the European Commission had a firm intention to act." In this way, the Department of Justice deferred to the enforcement agency with the greater interest in addressing the challenged conduct, while at the same time providing input and support to that agency.

The cooperative approach employed by the two agencies created benefits for Nielsen and for antitrust enforcement generally. After ensuring that the undertakings into which Nielsen had entered would address the anticompetitive conduct about which the Department of Justice was concerned, the Department of Justice closed its own investigation into Nielsen's conduct. In choosing to rely on the relief implemented by the European Commission, the Department of Justice created benefits for Nielsen by ensuring that Nielsen was not subjected to multiple and perhaps inconsistent remedies. In addition, reliance on the undertakings negotiated by the European Commission permitted the Department of Justice to minimize the expenditure of scarce prosecutorial resources.

3. European Commission, press release, December 4, 1996; U.S. Department of Justice, press release, December 3, 1996.

The Amadeus Global
Travel Distribution Case

JAMES F. RILL
CHRISTINE C. WILSON
AND SARAH E. BAUERS

Through the signing of an antitrust accord on September 23, 1991, the United States and the European Union Commission sought to promote greater coordination of their antitrust enforcement efforts.[1] Although the 1991 agreement was not the first antitrust accord into which the U.S. had entered, it differed from the others in at least one important respect. This difference is contained in the positive comity provisions of article 5, which are premised upon the recognition that anticompetitive activities occurring in the territory of one party to the agreement (and that violate the laws of that party) may adversely affect the interests of the other party to the agreement. Based on this recognition, article 5 permits a party whose interests are being affected adversely to request the party in whose territory the challenged conduct is occurring to initiate appropriate enforcement activities.

Following the signing of the 1991 agreement, the level of cooperation between antitrust enforcement authorities in the United

1. Agreement between the Government of the United States of America and the Commission of the European Communities Regarding the Application of Their Competition Laws, September 23, 1991, reprinted in 4 *Trade Reg. Rep.* (CCH), and 13,504 (April 23, 1997).

States and the European Union increased significantly. Despite this increased cooperation, however, it was not until 1997 that the first formal referral was made under the positive comity provisions of article 5. On April 28, 1997, the U.S. Department of Justice announced that, in January 1997, it had formally requested the Directorate General IV (DGIV) of the European Commission to investigate activities within the European computer reservation system market that allegedly were preventing U.S.-based computer reservation systems from competing effectively in certain European countries.[2]

A computer reservation system is composed of a central computer database and processor that contain information on a variety of travel products. Travel providers such as airlines and railroads, known as associates, pay the system to distribute information about their products and services. Travel agents and others who pay for access to this travel information are known as subscribers. In addition to providing its subscribers with access to flight, fare, and seat availability information, a computer reservation system also enables its subscribers to perform electronically many tasks that, in the absence of such a system, would have to be performed manually. The ability of the system to facilitate the electronic completion of these tasks depends upon its associates' providing these capabilities, known as functionalities, to the system. The effectiveness with which a computer reservation system is able to market its products and services depends upon its ability to offer potential subscribers comprehensive and accurate travel information in conjunction with a broad array of functionalities.

SABRE, the leading computer reservation system in the United States, had lodged complaints with the Antitrust Division of the Justice Department regarding the allegedly anticompetitive practices of the three large European airline owners of Amadeus Global Travel Distribution, the dominant system in Europe. Specifically, SABRE told the Antitrust Division that these airline owners refused to give SABRE timely access to complete and accurate fare data and denied SABRE certain functionalities that had been made available to Amadeus. In announcing its referral, the Antitrust Division observed that "accurate and up-to-date fare data and functionality . . . are critical for a computer reservation to compete effectively." The data and functionality of the airline owners of Amadeus would appear to be particularly critical to the viability of a computer reservation system attempting to compete in the home markets of these carriers because each of the airline owners is the national flag carrier, and the dominant air carrier, in its home market.

2. U.S. Department of Justice, press release, April 28, 1997.

In announcing the formal referral, Joel Klein, acting assistant attorney general for antitrust, stated that the Department of Justice "believe[s] there are indications that exclusionary conduct may be preventing U.S. companies from vigorously competing in computer reservation system markets in Europe." He explained the Antitrust Division's decision to invoke the positive comity provisions of the 1991 agreement by noting that the "European Commission is in the best position to investigate this conduct because it occurred in its home territory and consumers there are the ones who are principally harmed if competition has been diminished."

In September 1997, Alexander Schaub, director general of the DGIV, acknowledged the importance of the Amadeus referral to the development of the positive comity mechanism. In this regard, Schaub stated that the DGIV had instructed its staff "to consider [the Amadeus referral] as a priority case," because the way they handled positive comity requests from the United States would "certainly determine largely how the U.S. authorities will handle our future requests."[3] Schaub also noted that "following this request we have had very close cooperation with the parties concerned and with the American authorities."

In October 1998, the U.S. Senate Judiciary's Subcommittee on Antitrust held hearings on international antitrust issues. One of the witnesses at the hearings was Andrew Steinberg, senior vice president, general counsel, and corporate secretary of the SABRE Group. During his testimony, Steinberg described what he characterized as "obstacles" that SABRE had encountered during the positive comity referral process. Among other things, he expressed concern about the delay posed by the formal referral process and the differences in investigatory techniques and evidentiary standards employed by the United States and the European Union.

Based on his company's experience with the Amadeus referral, Steinberg also offered the Subcommittee on Antitrust his views regarding changes that could be made to improve the positive comity mechanism. Specifically, he recommended a candid assessment at the outset of whether the party receiving the referral could devote adequate resources to the investigation; "more intensive and more frequent" communications between the parties; status updates by the referring party to the private party whose complaint has been referred; convergence of investigative procedures between the parties; and the establishment of a timetable for the processing of each referral.

3. Amelia Torres, "EU Gives Priority to U.S. Airline Reservation Case," Reuters, September 9, 1997 (biz.yahoo.com/finance/97/09/09/amr_tsg_y_1.html).

On March 15, 1999, the European Commission announced that it had issued a statement of objections against Air France for potential abuse of a dominant position in the computer reservations system market. Its press release states that "the Commission considers that the French airline has discriminated against SABRE . . . owned by American Airlines, to favour a CRS which it partly owns, Amadeus." The statement further asserts that Air France denied SABRE the same full and timely access to fare and flight information that it provided to Amadeus. The DGIV noted that, throughout the investigation that followed the positive comity referral, it maintained close contact with the Department of Justice.

At a second round of hearings covering positive comity held by the U.S. Senate Subcommittee on Antitrust in May 1999, Assistant Attorney General Klein expressed optimism with the announcement by the European Commission regarding the initial positive comity referral but urged that experiences gained through this process be used to enhance the prospect of future referrals between the two jurisdictions.[4] Based on the issuance of the statement of objections by the DGIV, the Department of Justice announced that its own investigation of the matter was officially closed. On July 25, 2000, the European Commission issued its own statement, announcing that it had officially closed its investigation of Air France following a private settlement agreement entered between SABRE and Air France. This "code of good behavior" addresses the commission's original concerns regarding alleged discrimination by Air France against SABRE. Previously, SABRE had entered into similar settlement agreements with SAS and Lufthansa.

It is hoped that the obstacles described by Steinberg in his testimony resulted not from fatal flaws in the positive comity process but from the fact that this referral constituted the inaugural invocation of the formal referral process. The parties to the 1991 agreement have already strengthened the positive comity mechanism through the adoption in June 1998 of a supplemental agreement on positive comity. It is hoped that the Amadeus referral has provided an opportunity for the United States and the European Union to explore additional improvements that can be made to enhance the use of the positive comity mechanism in the future.

---

4. Joel I. Klein, "Statement," U.S. Senate Judiciary Committee, Subcommittee on Antitrust, Business Rights, and Competition, May 4, 1999.

Index

ABB Group, 6
A.C. Nielsen Corporation, 38, 103, 192–94
Aérospatiale Alenia, 65n19
Agrawal, Anup, 74
Airbus Industrie, 65n19, 108, 130, 139, 140, 142
Air France, 39, 103, 198
Ajinomoto Company, Inc., 105
Amadeus Global Travel Distribution, 19n35, 39–40, 103, 195–98
American Airlines, 5, 145–52, 198
American Telephone and Telegraph Company (AT&T), 9, 58, 93n16, 189
Amoco Corporation, 29, 64n17
Antitrust analysis: data impact, 151–52; and efficiency criteria, 15–16, 17, 18, 21–22, 58, 84, 85–86, 126–27, 128, 148; of merger effects, 15–16, 141; of network-based industries, 9–10, 15–16, 154–65; of vertical arrangements, 117–36. *See also* Merger reviews, U.S.-EU
Antitrust Division, U.S.: American Airlines–British Airways alliance, 147–52; anticartel activity, 18, 108, 112, 114–15; Boeing–McDonnell Douglas merger, 144; foreign antitrust investigations, 15, 104–06, 117, 193, 196–97; interactions with DGIV, 39, 43, 108, 109, 114–15; international guidelines *(1995)*, 32, 147; PricewaterhouseCoopers merger, 154–56, 157, 158, 159, 160. *See also* Justice, U.S. Department of
Antitrust enforcement: and bilateral agreements, 18–19, 53–54, 192, 195–96; cross-border effects, 1, 17–18; and globalization, 13–17, 53; implications of business strategy changes, 2, 3–11; industries exempt, 16; investigatory techniques, 99–102, 113–14; and trade liberalization, 14–15, 24, 54–55; transatlantic policy issues, 2, 17–18; U.S.-Canada cooperation, 99, 109–13; U.S.-EU cooperation, 2, 18, 25, 30–55, 99, 102–04, 113–15, 117, 166, 172–73, 192–98; and vertical disintegration, 8–9. *See also* Cartels; Merger reviews, U.S.-EU; Mergers and acquisitions; Positive comity; Vertical arrangements

199